BIG BIBLE GUIDE

KIDS' BIBLE DICTIONARY & HANDBOOK

Fun and Fascinating Bible Reference for Kids Ages 8 to 12

JEAN FISCHER
TRACY M. SUMNER

KiDS' Bible Dictionary starts on page 3!

KiDS' Bible Handbook

BARBOUR
PUBLISHING

ISBN 978-1-62416-216-9

Published by Barbour Publishing, Inc., P.O. Box 719, Uhrichsville, Ohio 44683 www.barbourbooks.com

Our mission is to publish and distribute inspirational products offering exceptional value and biblical encouragement to the masses.

 Member of the
Evangelical Christian
Publishers Association

Printed in the United States of America.
Versa Press, Inc. East Peoria, IL 61611; June 2013; D10003977

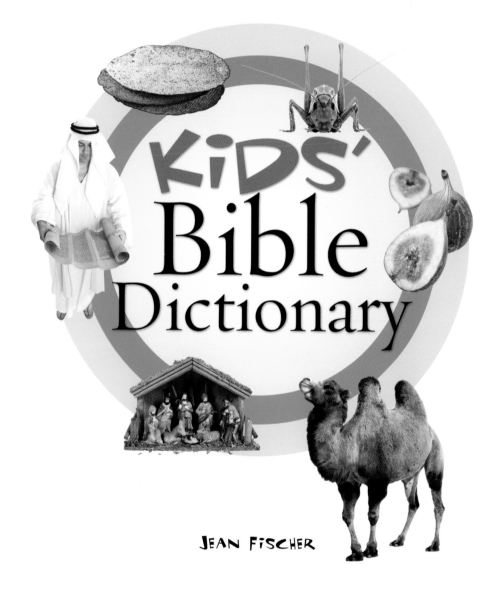

Kids' Bible Dictionary

JEAN FISCHER

Entries in the *Kids' Bible Dictionary* are based on verses from the Bible—but for ease of reading, the chapter-and-verse references have been listed separately, after each entry. The order of the references follows the order of the verses in the entry, not necessarily the biblical order.

Where no translation information is noted, the word or phrase of scripture quoted is common to multiple translations.

AARON.

Moses' big brother. Moses wasn't a good speaker. So God told Aaron to speak for him. Aaron did the talking. Moses was the leader. Aaron helped Moses lead the Hebrew slaves out of Egypt. God chose Aaron to be Israel's first high priest. But Aaron wasn't perfect. The people asked him to make a statue of a god they could worship. Aaron agreed and made a golden calf. God forgave Aaron after Moses prayed for him. Neither Aaron nor Moses made it to the Promised Land because they disobeyed God one time at a place called Meribah. They were supposed to speak to a rock to create miracle water in the desert —but Moses was angry with the people and hit the rock with a stick instead.

Exodus 7–12
Exodus 32:1–4
Numbers 20:6–12

This model of a Jewish high priest shows the kind of clothes Aaron wore—including the shield-like "breastplate" with 12 colorful stones. Each stone stood for a tribe of Israel.

ABBA.

An Aramaic word meaning "daddy." (Aramaic is the language that Jesus and His disciples spoke.) Before He was crucified, Jesus prayed in the Garden of Gethsemane. When He prayed, He cried out to God: "Abba, Father." The apostle Paul used the word *Abba*, too. He said when we're saved, God adopts us and we can call him "Daddy."

Mark 14:36
Romans 8:15

ABBADON.

A Hebrew word that means "destruction." Abbadon was also the name given to the angel in charge of the "bottomless pit".

Revelation 9:11 KJV

ABEDNEGO.

A Hebrew man thrown into a fiery furnace. Abednego and his friends, Shadrach and Meshach, would not worship a golden statue that King Nebuchadnezzar made. They refused to bow down to the false god. As punishment, the king had them thrown into a fiery furnace. God protected them. They came out of the fire unhurt. (Read all about it in Daniel 3.)

ABEL.

The second son of Adam and Eve. The New Testament says that Abel was "righteous." He was faithful and good. Abel always gave his best to God, including his offering. That made his older brother, Cain, very jealous. Cain was unfaithful. He did not give God the offering He desired. Instead of trying to be more like Abel, Cain did an awful thing. In a fit of anger, he murdered his younger brother. Afterward, God sent Cain away from his family. Cain settled in the land of Nod, east of Eden.

1 John 3:12
Genesis 4:1–10

ABIGAIL.

Wife of a mean man named Nabal. Nabal was rude to David's servants. That made David angry. Abigail was sorry about her husband's attitude. She packed up a tasty feast for David and his servants. Then she hurried off to find them (1 Samuel 25:14–35). David was kind to Abigail, and he forgave Nabal. Later, after Nabal died, Abigail and David got married.

1 Samuel 25:2–3

b
c
d
e
f
g
h
i
j
k
l
m
n
o
p
q
r
s
t
u
v
w
x
y
z

5

A
b
c
d
e
f
g
h
i
j
k
l
m
n
o
p
q
r
s
t
u
v
w
x
y
z

ABIMELECH.

A king during Abraham's time. Abimelech was king of an ancient town called Gerar. Gerar was in the southern part of Israel. Abimelech is known for taking Abraham's wife, Sarah, and making her part of his collection of women. After he had a dream in which God told him Sarah was Abraham's wife, Abimelech gave her back to Abraham.

Genesis 20:1–18

ABNER.

Commander of King Saul's army. Abner introduced David to Saul. After Saul died, Abner was loyal to David. He convinced the tribes of Israel to follow David's leadership.

2 Samuel 3:17–21

ABOMINATION.

A nasty, terrible, disgusting, or wicked act, person, or thing. In Bible times, the Hebrews had a long list of abominations. Back then, it was common for people to kill animals and offer them as a gift to God. If someone offered God an animal that wasn't perfect, that was an abomination. Worshipping statues of gods is an abomination, too. So are witchcraft, magic, and the belief that dead people can communicate with people who are alive. If you want an easier word that means "abomination," try *sin*. Anything that is a sin is an abomination.

Deuteronomy 7:25–26 KJV
Deuteronomy 17:1 KJV
Deuteronomy 18:9–12 KJV

ABRAHAM.

A man of great faith. Abraham and his wife, Sarah, had a son named Isaac. They loved him very much. One day, God decided to test Abraham's faith. He asked Abraham to offer Isaac as a sacrifice to Him. That means God wanted Abraham to kill his own son to prove that God was the most important thing in Abraham's life. Abraham was about to do what God asked. Then the angel of the LORD appeared. "Don't hurt the boy!" the angel said. God was totally sure that Abraham would do anything for Him. Because Abraham was so faithful, he was called "the father of us all."

Genesis 22:1–13
Genesis 22:12 CEV
Romans 4:16

ABRAHAM'S BOSOM.

A term that refers to the life after this life. The Jews believed that when they died and went to heaven, they joined their ancestors, especially Abraham. (The phrase "Abraham's bosom" is found in Luke 16:22 KJV.)

ABSALOM.

King David's badly behaved son. Absalom and his brother, Amnon, had a fight about their sister. Absalom was so mad at Amnon that he had him killed. Afterward, Absalom ran away. King David was angry. He wanted nothing to do with his son. So Absalom got even. He went to war against his dad. At first, it looked like Absalom's army would win. But God helped David win, because he was a godly king. Absalom lost most of his troops. Then he tried to get away riding on a mule. His

An angel stops Abraham from sacrificing his son Isaac in this painting from the 1500s. God sent a ram for the sacrifice instead.

head got caught in some tree branches. While Absalom was hanging from the tree, a soldier named Joab speared him in the heart and killed him. (Check it out in 2 Samuel 18:1–18.)

2 Samuel 13:27–29
2 Samuel 15:10

ABSTINENCE.

Not doing something. The Bible talks about avoiding food and drinks that are harmful to our bodies. In the New Testament, the apostle Paul tells us that we should abstain from doing anything that will cause other people to sin. "It is better not to eat meat or drink wine or to do anything else that will cause your brother [or sister] to fall."

Romans 14:21 NIV

ABYSS.

The dark, ugly place where demons live. The word *abyss* means "bottomless pit."

Revelation 9:1–2, 11 NASB

ACELDAMA.

A field near the city of Jerusalem. Jesus' disciple Judas was given money to betray Jesus. He used his reward money to buy a field. Afterward, Judas killed himself there. The field was later named Aceldama. This word means "field of blood." (Find out more in Acts 1:15–19 KJV.)

ACHAN.

A thief. Joshua's army invaded Jericho. His warriors were not supposed to steal from the city. Everything there belonged to God. But Achan stole gold, silver, and a beautiful robe. He hid them in his tent. Later, Joshua lost a battle in a place called Ai. He thought it was because God was punishing his army. Then he found out what Achan had done. People threw stones at Achan and killed him. Then he and all his things were burned. His ashes were covered up with stones. (Read more about it in Joshua 7:19–26.)

ACTS OF THE APOSTLES.

Another name for the New Testament book called Acts. Acts of the Apostles comes after the four books called the Gospels: Matthew, Mark, Luke, and John. Luke wrote the book of Acts. He was the same man who wrote the Gospel of Luke. Acts starts where the Gospels leave off. It begins with the ascension of Christ (Jesus going up into heaven). It tells about the early days of the Christian church. You'll also learn about the apostle Paul and his ministry. Acts shows Christianity spreading from Jerusalem throughout the world.

Acts 12:25–28:31
Acts 13–28

ADAM.

The first person on earth. Adam was awesome! He was good and smart, but he wasn't perfect—because he disobeyed God's one rule and ate the fruit of a tree God had said to stay away from. Adam was the first worker and the first husband. God made a woman named Eve to be Adam's wife. Their home was the Garden of Eden, but when Adam and Eve sinned, God sent them away from their perfect home forever.

Genesis 2:8, 15
Genesis 2:18–25
Genesis 3:22–24

ADONAI.

A Hebrew word for God. *Adonai* is another way of saying "LORD."

Ezekiel 11:8 NIV

ADOPTION.

To take someone into your family and make them your own. Sometimes children are not born into a family. Instead, they are adopted by someone who loves them. The apostle Paul talked about a different kind of adoption. It is called *spiritual adoption*. Paul said that all of us can be adopted as God's children. You can be a child of God if you are sorry for your sins and have faith in Jesus Christ.

Romans 11:1–32;
Galatians 4:4–7
Galatians 3:24–26

A
b
c
d
e
f
g
h
i
j
k
l
m
n
o
p
q
r
s
t
u
v
w
x
y
z

A
b
c
d
e
f
g
h
i
j
k
l
m
n
o
p
q
r
s
t
u
v
w
x
y
z

ADVENT OF CHRIST.

Another way of saying "the birth of Christ." Jesus' birth was the beginning of a wonderful thing. He was God's only Son. And he was God's special gift to all humans—then and forever. God sent His Baby to earth to save us from our sins. In Bible times, people gave their best animals to God. They killed them and put them on an altar. It was a sacrifice—a way of telling God that He was more important than anything they owned. When Jesus was born, He was already chosen by God as His sacrifice for us. When Jesus grew up, God allowed Him to be crucified on the cross. God gave us His precious Son to show that He loves us more than anything else! In all of time, there will never be a sacrifice as great as that.

Matthew 1:21
John 3:16
Hebrews 10:10

ADVERSARY.

An opponent. Some are enemies. They are out to get you. The Bible says to watch out for the worst adversary—Satan. "Your adversary, the devil, prowls around like a roaring lion, seeking someone to devour."

1 Peter 5:8 NASB

Rough shepherds are the first people to visit the baby Jesus, in this painting from the 1600s.

ADVERSITY.

Bad times. Adversity is when things go wrong. Adversity can happen when God tests our faith. It might also happen because God punishes sin. The first time a human was punished was when Adam broke God's rules. God told Adam: "You listened to your wife. You ate the fruit of the tree that I commanded you about. I said, 'You must not eat its fruit.' So I am putting a curse on the ground because of what you did. All the days of your life you will have to work hard to get food from the ground.'"

1 Peter 1:6–7 NIrV
Genesis 3:17 NIrV

ADVOCATE.

A person who supports someone or something. Is there a cause that you really believe in? If you speak up or do something about it, then you are an advocate. An *advocate* is a helper. The Bible says that Jesus is our Advocate: "If you. . .sin, Jesus Christ always does the right thing, and he will speak to the Father for us."

1 John 2:1 CEV

AFFLICTION.

Anything that causes pain or suffering. An affliction can affect your body and make you feel hurt or sick. It can also affect your spirit and make you feel sad. People with afflictions came to Jesus. They knew He understood and had power to help.

Jesus healed a man who was born blind. He also got rid of demons that made men act crazy. Affliction might happen because God is judging sin. We grow stronger in faith as we trust God to help us with our afflictions.

John 9:1–41
Matthew 8:28–33
Romans 2:9
Romans 5:3–5

AGAPE.

To love someone without thinking about yourself. A great example is God's love for us. He loves us so much that He allowed His only Son, Jesus, to die on the cross for our sins. To understand agape love, remember this Bible verse: "God loved the people of this world so much that he gave his only Son, so that everyone who has faith in him will have eternal life and never really die."

John 3:16 CEV

AHAB.

A wicked king of Israel. Ahab was a really bad man. He was married to Jezebel. She was wicked, too. Together they got the people of Israel to worship a false god named Baal.

1 Kings 21:25
1 Kings 16:30–33

AIJALON.

A town west of Jerusalem. Joshua fought a battle with five kings in Aijalon. During this battle, the sun and moon stood still until Joshua defeated his enemies.

Joshua 10:12–13

ALEXANDRIA.

The capital city of Egypt in New Testament times. Seventy-two wise Jewish men came to this city to translate the Old Testament from Hebrew to Greek. That ancient version of the Bible is called the Septuagint.

ALIEN.

A stranger from a land other than Israel. This kind of alien wasn't from outer space! In Bible times, he or she was a foreigner who did not have the same rights as citizens of Israel.

Deuteronomy 14:21
Job 19:15

ALLEGORY.

A story that tells an important truth. Allegories often use symbols —one thing stands for something else. The apostle Paul used the births of Ishmael and Isaac as an allegory to explain the difference between God's law and grace.

Galatians 4:22–31

ALLELUIA.

"Praise the Lord!" *Alleluia* is a Greek word used to praise God.

Revelation 19:1–6

ALLIANCE.

An agreement between specific people or nations. Old Testament prophets warned against forming an alliance that would cause people to turn from God.

Jeremiah 2:17–19

ALMIGHTY.

The one with the greatest power. "Almighty" is a title used for God. It shows that He has endless power to do all things. God used "Almighty" to describe Himself. "When Abram was ninety-nine years old, the LORD appeared to Abram and said to him, 'I am Almighty God; walk before Me and be blameless.' "

Genesis 17:1 NKJV

ALMOND.

A kind of nut tree. If you go to Israel, you might see orchards of almond trees. They bloom in January. Then they produce lots of flavorful nuts. In Bible times, almonds were among the best products of the land.

An almond on the tree branch.

Genesis 43:11

A b c d e f g h i j k l m n o p q r s t u v w x y z

ALPHA AND OMEGA.

A term that means the beginning and the ending. In the Greek alphabet, *alpha* is the first letter and *omega* is the last. These words are sometimes used to describe God. Alpha and omega remind us that God the Father, His Son Jesus, and the Holy Spirit are here forever and ever. Jesus promised that it was so when He said, "I am the Alpha and the Omega, the Beginning and the End. . .who is and who was and who is to come, the Almighty."

Revelation 1:8 NKJV

ALTAR.

A place where sacrifices are made. An altar might be a table, a platform, or another raised surface. In early Bible times, altars were made of rocks or earth. Noah was the first one to build an altar: "Then Noah built an altar to the LORD and, taking some of all the clean animals and clean birds, he sacrificed burnt offerings on it."

Exodus 20:24–25
Genesis 8:20 NIV

AMALEKITES.

A tribe that was an enemy of the Israelites. For a neat story about how Moses and his friends defeated the Amalekites, read Exodus 17:8–16.

AMBASSADOR.

A messenger for a ruler, king, or queen. Paul thought of himself as an ambassador for Christ. He said that all believers could be ambassadors for Jesus.

Ephesians 6:20
2 Corinthians 5:20

AMEN.

A word that many people use to end a prayer. *Amen* is also used to show approval and to agree with a promise. Jesus is sometimes called "the Amen" because He is good and dependable right to the end.

Psalm 89:52
Nehemiah 5:13
Revelation 3:14

AMMONITES.

The relatives of Lot's grandson, Ammon. The Ammonites became enemies of the Israelites during the Exodus (a time when the Israelites traveled from Egypt to their homeland). When the Ammonites' country was ruled by an Amorite king, he did not allow the Israelites to cross their land, and the Ammonites did not offer the Israelites food and water when they came out of Egypt.

Numbers 21:21–24
Deuteronomy 23:3–4

AMNON.

King David's oldest son. Amnon behaved badly with his half sister, Tamar. When King David found out, he was very upset. But he did not punish Amnon. Amnon's brother Absalom was angry with Amnon, too. He was so angry

This altar was built in Beersheba, Israel, to show what an old-time Bible altar looked like.

that he decided to take matters into his own hands. Absalom told his servants to kill Amnon, which they did. Then Absalom ran away. (Read more about it in 2 Samuel 13.)

2 Samuel 3:2

AMOS. ———————

A herdsman, farmer, and prophet. He criticized the rich for not helping the poor. He also encouraged people to worship the one true God. Amos thought of himself more as a farmer than a prophet. He said, "I was neither a prophet nor a prophet's son, but I was a shepherd, and I also took care of sycamore-fig trees but the LORD took me from tending the flock and said to me, 'Go, prophesy to my people Israel.'" A prophet is someone who speaks for God.

Amos 8:4–6
Amos 7:14–15 NIV

ANANIAS. ———————

A man who lied, fell down, and died! Ananias and his wife, Sapphira, belonged to the Christian church in Jerusalem. Many church members were selling their things for money they could give to the poor. Ananias and Sapphira agreed and sold their land. But they kept part of their money for themselves and then lied about it. The apostle Peter scolded Ananias for what he had done. Just then, Ananias dropped dead! Even spookier, the same thing happened to Sapphira a few hours later.

Acts 4:34–35
Acts 5:1–10

ANCIENT OF DAYS. ———

An Old Testament name for God. The prophet Daniel was the first to use "Ancient of Days." He wrote this awesome description of God in Daniel 7:9: "As I looked, thrones were set in place, and the Ancient of Days took his seat. His clothing was as white as snow; the hair of his head was white like wool. His throne was flaming with fire, and its wheels were all ablaze" (NIV).

ANDREW. ———————

One of Jesus' disciples; also Peter's brother. Andrew was a fisherman from the town of Bethsaida. He was a follower of John the Baptist, and he introduced Peter to Jesus. Andrew was the disciple who brought to Jesus a boy with five loaves of bread and two fishes. Jesus used that small lunch to feed more than five thousand people. (Read all about it in John 6:1–14.)

John 1:44
John 1:35–42

ANGEL. ———————

A heavenly being. Angels are sent from heaven to help humans on earth. They are God's special messengers. Angels are not equal to God, because they are made by God. He tells angels what to do. Some of their jobs are delivering messages for God, protecting God's people, helping the thirsty, and praising God's name. Before the earth was created, some bad angels turned against God. Their leader was Satan. Another one of these bad angels was Abaddon, "the angel of the bottomless pit." These guys were so awful that God kicked them out of heaven.

Psalm 148:2, 5
Psalm 103:20
Luke 1:13
Daniel 3:28
Genesis 21:17–19
Psalm 103:20–21
Revelation 12:7–9
Revelation 9:11 KJV

ANGEL OF THE LORD. ———

A special angel who serves as God's spokesman. This angel stands out from all the rest. He was around a lot in Old Testament times. He was with the Israelites during the Exodus. He was with Hagar in the wilderness and with Moses in the burning bush. The Angel of the LORD appeared to Abraham when he was about to sacrifice his son Isaac. He also appeared to Gideon, Balaam, Elijah, David, and others.

Genesis 16:7–12
Exodus 3:2–3
Genesis 22:11–12
Judges 6:11–12
Numbers 22:21–35
2 Kings 1:3
1 Chronicles 21:16

A
b
c
d
e
f
g
h
i
j
k
l
m
n
o
p
q
r
s
t
u
v
w
x
y
z

A
b
c
d
e
f
g
h
i
j
k
l
m
n
o
p
q
r
s
t
u
v
w
x
y
z

ANGER.

A strong unhappy feeling. God gets angry sometimes, but He is slow to anger. You should be slow to anger, too. When you feel angry, take time to listen. Think before you speak. The Bible says, "A gentle answer turns away wrath, but a harsh word stirs up anger." Jesus said not to be angry with our brothers or sisters. We shouldn't let the sun go down while we're still angry. That means don't go to sleep feeling angry with someone. Try hard to work out your differences.

Nahum 1:3
James 1:19
Proverbs 15:1 NIV
Matthew 5:22
Ephesians 4:26

ANGUISH.

Terrible sadness and pain. Sometimes anguish is caused by a pain in your body. It can also happen when you feel worried, unsettled, or discouraged.

Exodus 6:9
2 Samuel 1:9
Job 7:11

ANNA.

An old prophetess. Anna was eighty-four years old. She never left the temple. She worshipped there night and day. It was the law, in Bible times, that all boy babies be brought to Jerusalem and blessed in the temple. When Mary and Joseph brought Jesus to the temple, Anna was there. She praised God and spoke about Jesus.

Luke 2:22–24
Luke 2:36–38

ANNAS.

Father-in-law of the high priest who ruled at Jesus' trial. Annas asked Jesus about His disciples and His beliefs. Afterward, he had Jesus tied up and sent away for sentencing.

John 18:19–24

ANOINT.

To set someone apart as holy or special. In Old Testament times, people were anointed with oil. The oil was poured on their heads. This honored them as God's special helpers. In New Testament times, people were anointed with oil for healing. You might know the word *anoint* from Psalm 23:5: "You prepare a table before me in the presence of my enemies; You anoint my head with oil; my cup runs over" (NKJV).

Exodus 29:7
Mark 6:13

ANTICHRIST.

Someone who is against Jesus. Many believe an antichrist will appear at the end of time as the enemy of Christ and all Christians. He will be powerful and bad. Another name for this antichrist is the *beast*. He will say that Jesus is not the Christ. He will brag and go against everything holy. He will even sit on God's throne and pretend to be God. In the end, the antichrist will die. "The Lord Jesus will kill him simply by breathing on him."

Revelation 13
1 John 2:22–23
2 Thessalonians 2:3–4
2 Thessalonians 2:8 CEV

ANTIOCH.

A major city in Syria, north of Israel. Other places were named Antioch, too, so this one was called Antioch of Syria. This is where believers were first called Christians. The apostle Paul used Antioch as his home base for missionary travels.

Acts 11:26
Acts 13:1–4
Acts 15:35–41

APOCALYPSE.

The unveiling of hidden things known only to God. The last book of the Bible, Revelation, is all about apocalypse. The apostle John wrote the book. It tells about the end of the world as we know it. God's true message about the end-times is hidden. The book of Revelation uses symbols, visions, and numbers to give us hints about what will happen. The truth about it can only come from God. The Holy Spirit helps us to understand some of the apocalypse. God gave John hints about the end-times through a messenger angel. Then John shared what he learned by writing his book.

Galatians 1:12
1 Corinthians 2:11–14
Revelation 1:1–2

APOCRYPHA.

Books included in the Bibles of some religious groups. These books were written between 150 BC and AD 70. Their names are: Baruch; Bel and the Dragon; the Wisdom of Jesus; the Son of Sirach; the First and Second Books of Esdras; Additions to the Book of Esther; the Epistle of Jeremiah; Judith; First and Second Maccabees; the Prayer of Azariah and the Song of the Three Young Men; the Prayer of Manasseh; Susanna; Tobit; and the Wisdom of Solomon.

1 Corinthians 3:4–7

APOLLOS.

A disciple of John the Baptist. Apollos was a Jew who became a Christian. Like the apostle Paul, he was a servant of God. He came from Alexandria to Ephesus to teach about Jesus. Apollos was very smart, but his knowledge of Christ was limited. So Priscilla and her husband, Aquila, invited him to their home. They taught him more about the Lord. (Check out Acts 18:24–28.)

APOSTASY.

Falling away from true faith in God. Our worst enemy, Satan, causes apostasy. Sometimes apostasy happens because people listen to false teachers. These teachers do not teach the true Word of God. Instead, they say what people want to hear. Sometimes, believers fall away from faith during hard times. Love of worldly things can make believers turn away, too. Apostasy won't happen to you if you keep your mind on God's truth, love Him more than the things you own, and have faith that He is the one true God.

Hebrews 3:12
Luke 22:31–32
2 Timothy 4:3–5
Matthew 13:21
2 Timothy 4:10
Ephesians 4:13–16

A
b
c
d
e
f
g
h
i
j
k
l
m
n
o
p
q
r
s
t
u
v
w
x
y
z

John, holding a pen, writes the vision God gave him on an island called Patmos. Part of his vision was of four horses and their riders, who caused terrible suffering on the earth.

A
b
c
d
e
f
g
h
i
j
k
l
m
n
o
p
q
r
s
t
u
v
w
x
y
z

APOSTLE.

A disciple; one who is called by Jesus. The original twelve apostles were Peter, Andrew, James the son of Zebedee, John, Philip, Bartholomew, Thomas, Matthew, James the son of Alphaeus, Thaddaeus, Simon, and Judas. It was their job to share what Jesus taught. Jesus gave His apostles the power to cast out evil spirits and to heal the sick. Saul, who was later called Paul, became an apostle after he met Jesus on the Damascus Road.

Matthew 10:2–4
John 15:16
Matthew 10:1
Acts 9:1–30

AQUILA.

A Christian teacher during Paul's time. Aquila and his wife, Priscilla, worked with Paul at Corinth. They continued Paul's work at Ephesus. Aquila was also involved with the church at Rome.

Acts 18:2
Acts 18:24–26
Romans 16:3

ARABIA.

A hot, dry desert area in the Middle East. Arabia is southeast of Palestine. It is about 1,400 miles long and 800 miles wide. The queen of Sheba came from Arabia. She brought gold and precious jewels to King Solomon and tested his wisdom by asking him hard questions.

1 Kings 10:1–15

ARCHANGEL.

A most powerful angel. Only one archangel, Michael, is mentioned in the Bible. The prophet Daniel described him as "the great prince." It is the archangel who will announce the return of Jesus. In the end-times, Michael will fight with Satan and win. The Bible tells about it: "A war broke out in heaven. Michael and his angels were fighting against the dragon and its angels. But the dragon lost the battle. It and its angels were forced out of their places in heaven and were thrown down to the earth. Yes, that old snake and his angels were thrown out of heaven! That snake, who fools everyone on earth, is known as the devil and Satan."

Daniel 12:1
1 Thessalonians 4:16
Revelation 12:7–9 CEV

ARK, NOAH'S.

Noah's big wooden boat. Noah, his family, and assorted animals lived on the ark for about a year. The ark saved them from God's big flood. God used the flood as a way to destroy all the rest of the humans because they were wicked. Noah followed God's directions when he built the ark. Then he and his family entered the ark with every kind of animal. Rain fell on the earth for forty days and nights. Before long, the ark floated away. The flood covered the earth for 150 days. Finally, God sent a wind to dry up the water, and He also stopped the rain. The ark ended up on top of the mountains called Ararat. When the water was totally gone, Noah, his family, and all the animals went safely to dry land.

Genesis 6:14–16
Genesis 6:18–20
Genesis 7:17
Genesis 7:24
Genesis 8:1–4
Genesis 8:18–19

This model of Noah's ark, with elephants, giraffes, and other animals in front, gives an idea of how big the real thing was!

The gold-plated ark of the covenant had a solid gold top with two big angels called "cherubim." The whole lid was called the "mercy seat."

ARK OF THE COVENANT.

A wooden chest containing the Ten Commandments. The Ten Commandments were carved on two stone tablets. God said to put them into the ark of the covenant. The New Testament book of Hebrews talks about some manna and Aaron's rod also being in the ark of the covenant. God wanted a jar of manna to be placed before the ark to remind the people that He took care of them in the wilderness. Aaron's rod or staff was also kept there as a sign to those who rebelled against the Lord. God gave instructions for making the ark. When it was done, the ark was a holy symbol. It showed that God was with His people. At first, the ark was stored in the tabernacle. Then the Israelites took it into battle. The Philistines captured it. Later, it was in the temple in Jerusalem. King Nebuchadnezzar of Babylon might have stolen it from there. Some people believe it still exists and is hidden in the Middle East. No one knows for sure what happened to it. It's one of the world's great mysteries.

Exodus 34:28
Deuteronomy 10:3–4
Hebrews 9:4
Exodus 16:32–34
Numbers 17:10
Exodus 25:10–22
Exodus 26:33
1 Samuel 4:1–5
1 Samuel 4:10–11
1 Kings 8:1–9
2 Chronicles 36:7, 18

ARMAGEDDON.

A name for the valley between Mount Carmel and the city of Jezreel. In Bible times, many battles were fought there. Armageddon is named as the site of the greatest battle of all: In the end-times, good will fight evil at Armageddon. Good will win.

Revelation 16:14–16
Revelation 17:14

ARTAXERXES I.

A king of Persia. Artaxerxes followed the reign of King Cyrus. Both Ezra and Nehemiah served in his court. Artaxerxes allowed Ezra to lead a group of Jews back to Jerusalem to settle there. Years later, he allowed Nehemiah to return to Jerusalem to rebuild its walls.

Ezra 7:1–7
Nehemiah 2:1–10

ASA.

The third king of Judah. Asa reigned from about 911–869 BC. He destroyed places where people worshipped idols. He also brought a time of peace to Judah. Asa was a faithful and obedient servant of God. Then, one day, he got sick with a foot disease. Because he trusted only in his doctors and not in the Lord, he died. Asa had been king for forty-one years.

2 Chronicles 14:2–8
2 Chronicles 16:12–14

ASAPH.

A choir leader and writer of psalms (songs). Asaph was a Levite. He wrote a dozen of the psalms. Take a look at Psalm 50 and Psalms 73–83.

A b c d e f g h i j k l m n o p q r s t u v w x y z

A
b
c
d
e
f
g
h
i
j
k
l
m
n
o
p
q
r
s
t
u
v
w
x
y
z

ASCENSION OF CHRIST.

Jesus' return to heaven after He rose from the dead. Jesus was crucified and then buried in a tomb. Three days later, He came to life again. He stayed on earth for forty days. After that, He went up (ascended) into heaven to be with God. Jesus' ascension happened in a place called the Mount of Olives. The apostles were there when it happened. "While they were watching, he was taken up into a cloud. They could not see him, but as he went up, they kept looking up into the sky. Suddenly two men dressed in white clothes were standing there beside them. They said, 'Why are you men from Galilee standing here and looking up into the sky? Jesus has been taken to heaven. But he will come back in the same way that you have seen him go.' "

Acts 1:3
Luke 24:1–51
Acts 1:9–11 CEV

ASHES.

The powder left after something burns. Ashes are a symbol of sadness and of being sorry. In Bible times, people who sinned were sometimes sprinkled with ashes. This was a sign to God that they wanted to be pure enough to worship Him again.

Hebrews 9:13

ASIA.

In New Testament times, it was a region east of the Aegean Sea. Asia was part of the Roman Empire. Major cities in Asia included Ephesus, Smyrna, and Pergamum. Later, this area of the world was called Asia Minor and then Turkey. The apostle Paul preached in Asia.

Acts 19:10

ASSEMBLY.

People gathering to worship. Hebrews 10:25 says, "Some people have gotten out of the habit of meeting for worship, but we must not do that. We should keep on encouraging each other, especially since you know that the day of the Lord's coming is getting closer" (CEV).

ASSURANCE.

Totally believing in God's promises. We can be sure that God will not turn away from us if we seek Him and trust Him. God promised: "I will bless those who trust me. They will be like trees growing beside a stream—trees with roots that reach down to the water, and with leaves that are always green. They bear fruit every year and are never worried by a lack of rain." That's assurance!

Psalm 9:10
Jeremiah 17:7–8 CEV

ASSYRIA.

An ancient kingdom located between the Tigris and Euphrates rivers. Between 900 and 700 BC, it was a very powerful place. The Assyrian people were mean. They did terrible things to their enemies and worshipped false gods. Old Testament prophets like Isaiah, Ezekiel, and Hosea spoke out against them.

Isaiah 10:5
Ezekiel 16:28
Hosea 8:9

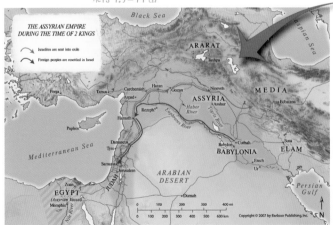

THE ASSYRIAN EMPIRE DURING THE TIME OF 2 KINGS

Israelites are sent into exile

Foreign peoples are resettled in Israel

Black Sea · Caspian Sea · ARARAT · Tushpa · MEDIA · Perga · Tarsus · Carchemish · Haran · Gozan · Nineveh · ASSYRIA · Asshur · Ecbatana · Arpad · Rezeph · Habor River · Ephrates River · Tigris River · Hamath · Paphos · Damascus · Babylon · Cuthah · Susa · Tyre · BABYLONIA · Erech · ELAM · Ur · Mediterranean Sea · Samaria · Jerusalem · JUDAH · ARABIAN DESERT · Zoan · Dumah · Persian Gulf · EGYPT · (Assyrian Vassal) · Memphis · Nile River

0 100 200 300 400 mi
0 100 200 300 400 500 600 km
Copyright © 2007 by Barbour Publishing, Inc.

The ruins of the Parthenon (center), built about 500 years before Jesus, are one of the most familiar images of Athens today.

ATHALIAH.

The daughter of King Ahab and his wife, Jezebel. Athaliah was queen of Judah from about 841–835 BC. She became queen by murdering all but one of her relatives who were in line to become king.

2 Kings 11:1–3

ATHEISM.

Refusing to believe that the one true God—or any other god—exists. What does the Bible say about atheism? "Only a fool would say, 'There is no God!' People like that are worthless! They are heartless and cruel and never do right."

Psalm 53:1 CEV

ATHENS.

An important city of ancient Greece. The apostle Paul traveled to Athens on his second missionary journey. He found it full of idols (statues of false gods). There was even an altar to "the unknown god." Paul taught and argued with the people of Athens. He wanted to teach them about the real God.

Acts 17:22–23

ATONEMENT.

Settling differences between God and man through a sacrifice. In Old Testament times, *atonement* meant making animal sacrifices to God. Today, believers don't make animal sacrifices. When Jesus died on the cross, He was the ultimate sacrifice to God. He died so everyone who believed in Him could be forgiven for their sins. Christ's atonement, His dying on the cross, is our foundation for peace.

2 Corinthians 5:21
Ephesians 2:13–16

AUGUSTUS.

A title of honor used for emperors of the Roman Empire. The title *Augustus* meant "his reverence." A well-known Roman emperor named Caesar Augustus wanted to know how many people lived in the Roman Empire. He ordered all the people to go to Bethlehem to be counted. Jesus' parents went to Bethlehem to be counted. While they were there, Jesus was born.

Luke 2:1–7

B

b
c
d
e
f
g
h
i
j
k
l
m
n
o
p
q
r
s
t
u
v
w
x
y
z

BAAL.

The main false god of the Canaanites. Baal worship was wicked. The Canaanites believed that Baal made crops grow and livestock reproduce. There were Baal priests and prophets. And some of God's people even worshipped Baal. In doing So they broke the Second Commandment. This made God very angry. He sent His prophet Elijah to prove that there was just one true God. Many of the people turned from their evil ways. The rest of them were killed. (Read more about it in 1 Kings 18:1–40.)

Exodus 20:4–5

BABYLON.

The capital city of the Babylonian Empire. Nimrod the hunter built Babylon. He was a mighty warrior whose strength came from God. Babylon was on a plain between the Tigris and Euphrates rivers. It was where the Tower of Babel was built. In its time, Babylon was a magnificent city with rich and powerful leaders. One of them was King Nebuchadnezzar. His forces attacked Jerusalem in 587 BC. They took the Jewish people captive. Then the Jews were kept as slaves in Babylon. *Babylon* means "gate-

In this ancient idol, Baal holds a blossoming branch.

way of the gods." Its ruins still exist, not far from Baghdad, Iraq.

Genesis 10:9–10
Genesis 11:1–9
Daniel 4:1–3, 30
2 Chronicles 36:5–21

BACKBITING.

Saying bad things about others behind their backs. The Bible says that backbiting is not good behavior for anyone, especially Christians.

Romans 1:30
Proverbs 25:23

BACKSLIDING.

Knowing God, then turning away from Him. Backsliding is bad because it keeps us away from God. Some people backslide because they don't grow in their faith. Others backslide when they lose their faith in bad times. Sometimes people love the things they own more than they love God. That causes backsliding, too.

Isaiah 59:2
2 Peter 1:5–9
Matthew 13:20–21
1 Timothy 6:10

BALAAM.

A prophet with a talking donkey. Moab's king hired Balaam to curse God's people. But God spoke to Balaam through his donkey, and Balaam blessed the Israelites instead.

Numbers 22–24

BANQUET.

A totally awesome feast! Imagine long tables filled with mouthwatering treats. That's a banquet. Read what Jesus said about banquets in Luke 14:12–15.

A visitor to the Holy Land is baptized in the Jordan River, the same river that John the Baptist used in the time of Jesus.

BAPTISM.

A Christian ceremony of faith where people are dipped in water, or water is poured or sprinkled on their heads. Baptism is a ceremony that proves our faith in Jesus Christ. It is a symbol that we are washed clean of our sins. The word *baptize* comes from the Greek word *baptizo*. It means to dunk, dip, or plunge. In the New Testament, you can read about John the Baptist. He baptized many people, including Jesus. Jesus had no sin, so He really didn't need to be baptized. But He had John baptize Him to set an example for us.

Matthew 3:4–17

BARABBAS.

A famous criminal. Barabbas was in jail when Jesus was arrested. Barabbas was a murderer. He was sentenced to die for his crime. Jesus was brought to Pontius Pilate, the Roman governor of Judea, to be judged. A great mob of people wanted Barabbas released from jail. So Pilate gave them a choice: Barabbas or Jesus. Barabbas was set free, and Jesus was sent to be crucified.

Mark 15:6–15

BARAK.

A general in the prophetess Deborah's army. Barak and Deborah battled the Canaanites. The Canaanites were fighting with the Israelites after they entered the Promised Land. Who won the battle? Barak and his army did. Read all about it in Judges 4.

BARBARIAN.

Someone who is wild and ill-mannered. In Bible times, the Greeks called citizens of other nations barbarians.

Romans 1:14 KJV

BARLEY.

A grain, like oats. Barley was used as food for livestock. Poor people ground up barley and made bread out of it.

1 Kings 4:28
John 6:9

Crowds shout for the criminal Barabbas to be released, instead of the innocent Jesus.

BARNABAS.

A good friend to the apostle Paul. Barnabas's real name was Joses, but the apostles called him Barnabas. The name Barnabas means "one who encourages others." Barnabas was a good man. His friend Paul had not always been a Christian. Paul met Jesus on the road to Damascus. From that day on, Paul believed in Him. Jesus' disciples were not sure about Paul. They didn't trust him. It was Barnabas who convinced them that Paul was a new and true follower of Jesus.

Acts 4:36 CEV
Acts 9:1–19
Acts 9:26–28

BARREN.

Not able to have a child. God sometimes works miracles for women who are barren. In Bible times, He blessed with children several barren women. They were Sarah, Rachel, Hannah, and Elizabeth.

Genesis 29:31
1 Samuel 1:5, 20
Luke 1:7, 57–58

Bartholomew

BARTHOLOMEW.

One of Jesus' disciples. Some people who study the Bible believe that Bartholomew was also called Nathanael.

Mark 3:16, 18
John 1:45–49

BARTIMAEUS.

A blind beggar healed by Jesus. Bartimaeus was sitting on the roadside when Jesus and His disciples walked by. "Have pity on me!" he cried out. A crowd following Jesus told Bartimaeus to be quiet. But he kept calling to the Lord. Jesus stopped. "What do you want?" He asked. "I want to see!" Bartimaeus replied. Because Bartimaeus had faith, Jesus touched his eyes and healed him. (Find out more in Mark 10:46–52.)

BARUCH.

A friend of the prophet Jeremiah. Baruch was a scribe. Scribes were like secretaries. The Lord told Jeremiah what to say. Then Jeremiah told Baruch, and Baruch wrote it down.

Jeremiah 36:4–32

BATHSHEBA.

King Solomon's mom. King David saw Bathsheba and thought she was beautiful. The problem was that Bathsheba was married to someone else—Uriah, a soldier in David's army. So David did a terrible thing. He made sure that Uriah was killed while fighting in a battle. Once Uriah was dead, David was free to marry Bathsheba. Bathsheba and David had four sons. One of them was Solomon who grew up to be a king of Israel.

2 Samuel 11:14–17
2 Samuel 12:24

BEAR.

A big, heavy mammal. Bears were well-known in Bible lands and times. David killed a bear to protect his father's sheep.

1 Samuel 17:34–35

BEARD.

Hair on a man's face. In Bible times, Jewish men were proud of their beards. If someone shaved his beard, it was a sign of suffering or sadness.

Jeremiah 48:37–38

BEATITUDES.

Blessings! When Jesus gave the Sermon on the Mount, He blessed the people. These blessings are called the Beatitudes. Jesus said: "Blessed are the poor in spirit, for theirs is the kingdom of heaven. Blessed are those who mourn, for they will be comforted. Blessed are the meek, for they will inherit the earth. Blessed are those who hunger and thirst for righteousness, for they will be filled. Blessed are the merciful, for they will be shown mercy. Blessed are the pure in heart, for they will see God. Blessed are the peacemakers, for they will be called sons of God. Blessed are those who are persecuted because of righteousness, for theirs is the kingdom of heaven. Blessed are you when people insult you, persecute you and falsely say all kinds of evil against you because of me. Rejoice and be glad, because great is your reward in heaven".

Matthew 5:1–12 NIV

BEERSHEBA.

A well where Abraham and Abimelech sealed a promise. The name means "well of the oath." (An *oath* is a promise.)

Genesis 21:30–32 NIV

BEGGAR.

A poor person asking for help. God commanded the Israelites to take care of the poor. There are stories in the Bible about Jesus and His disciples helping beggars. Peter healed a poor beggar who could not walk and was asking for money. Jesus healed Bartimaeus, a blind beggar, on the road to Jericho.

Acts 3:2–3
Deuteronomy 15:7–11
Acts 3:6–10
Luke 18:35–43

BEGOTTEN.

A natural child of someone. John 3:16 tells us that Jesus is God's "only begotten Son." That means that He is the one-and-only, one-of-a-kind Son of God. Check out how special Jesus is by reading John 3:16–18.

In this painting, almost 400 years old, King Belshazzar reads "the handwriting on the wall."

a B c d e f g h i j k l m n o p q r s t u v w x y z

BEHEMOTH.
A giant Bible beast. The behemoth was a beast that is described in the book of Job. No one knows for sure what the behemoth was. Some people think it might have been an elephant or hippopotamus or even a dinosaur.

Job 40:15–24

BELIAL.
Wicked, or the wicked one. *Belial* can mean "wickedness" or "wicked people".

1 Kings 21:10 KJV

BELIEVE.
To trust with all your heart that something is real. Jesus said that anything is possible if we believe. Although we can't see Jesus, we trust that He is real. Believing helps us stay strong when times are bad. Belief in Jesus Christ is what allows us to be saved.

Mark 9:23
John 20:29
John 6:35
Acts 16:31

BELSHAZZAR.
The last king of Babylonia (Daniel 5:1). Belshazzar was a bad guy. He worshipped false gods. He also had wild parties. At one, a mysterious hand appeared in the room. It wrote a message on the wall. The message said that Belshazzar's reign as king would end soon. It did. That very night the king was killed.

Daniel 5:2–5
Daniel 5:25–28
Daniel 5:30

21

Benevolence

BENEVOLENCE.

Being generous toward others. The apostle Paul said it is good to show benevolence toward the poor and needy. It is also good to be generous to those who serve God. The Bible says we should even show benevolence to our enemies: "If your enemy is hungry, give him food to eat; if he is thirsty, give him water to drink."

Galatians 2:10
Philippians 4:14–17
Proverbs 25:21 NIV

BENJAMIN.

Joseph's little brother. Benjamin was the youngest of twelve brothers. His dad was Jacob. Benjamin and Joseph were their dad's favorites because they were the sons of Rachel, the wife Jacob loved the most. Benjamin's brothers were jealous of Joseph, so they did a disgusting thing. They sold Joseph as a slave and lied about it. Years later, Joseph saw his brothers again, and he forgave them. He was especially happy to see his baby brother Benjamin. Joseph loved him very much. A tribe of Israel was named after Benjamin. All of its people were his ancestors. They were known as the Benjamites.

Genesis 37:3; 42:38
Genesis 29:30; 35:24
Genesis 37:28, 31–32
Genesis 45:14
Numbers 1:36–37
Judges 20:15

BEREA.

A city in Macedonia. Today, Macedonia is called Greece. Paul visited Berea during his second missionary journey. The people there were excited to learn about God and study the scriptures.

Acts 17:10–11

BESIEGE.

To surround with soldiers. In Bible times, many cities had walls. When armies went to war with these cities, they surrounded the walls with soldiers or besieged them. When that happened the citizens were trapped inside.

Deuteronomy 20:12

BETHANY.

A village at the foot of the Mount of Olives near Jerusalem. Jesus went to Bethany often. His good friends Mary, Martha, and Lazarus lived there. Bethany is where Jesus brought Lazarus back to life after he had been dead for four days. After He died and came back to life, Jesus ascended (went up) into heaven from Bethany.

Mark 11:1
John 11:1
John 11:17–44
Luke 24:50–51

BETHEL.

A city about twelve miles north of Jerusalem. Bethel is where Jacob had his famous dream about a ladder that stretched from earth to heaven. Before Jacob's dream, Bethel was known as Luz. Then Jacob renamed it Bethel. The Israelites often went to this city to talk to and worship God.

Genesis 28:10–12
Genesis 28:18–19
Judges 20:18; 21:2

BETHLEHEM.

The place where Jesus was born. Bethlehem is also where King David grew up. Sometimes, it's called "the city of David." So why was Jesus born there? Wasn't He from Nazareth? In Bible times, people had to travel to their hometowns to be counted. It was the only way to know how many lived in a certain region. Jesus' mom, Mary, and his adopted dad, Joseph, lived in Nazareth. But Joseph's hometown was Bethlehem. So Joseph and Mary walked from Nazareth to Bethlehem to be counted. When they got there, Jesus was born.

1 Samuel 16:1–13
2 Samuel 5:7
Luke 2:1–11

BETHSAIDA.

A fishing village on the shore of the Sea of Galilee. It was the home of Jesus' disciples Andrew, Peter, and Philip.

John 1:44

BETROTHAL. —————

A marriage agreement. In Bible times, the groom made an agreement with the bride's parents. The groom agreed to marry their daughter and take her as his wife. If a couple was betrothed, they were legally married. Mary and Joseph, Jesus' parents, were betrothed.

Matthew 1:18–19

BIBLE. —————

The written Word of God. The Bible is split into two parts, the Old Testament and the New Testament. The parts are a collection of sixty-six books. They were written by more than forty different authors. The authors weren't all rich or famous. Some were ordinary men. Others were prophets. Some were kings. God inspired the authors to write. The words are His. We can believe everything in the Bible is true. The Bible took a very long time to write—about 1,500 years! The oldest books (from Genesis to Deuteronomy) were probably written between 1446 and 1406 BC. The newest book (Revelation) was written around AD 95.

The Bible begins with the creation of the earth (Genesis 1). It ends with some ideas about how life on earth will end (the book of Revelation). The last spoken words of the Bible are Jesus' promise that He is coming back some day. There are thirty-nine books in the Old Testament and twenty-seven books in the New Testament. All of them were written by hand. Finally, in AD 1454, the Bible was printed on a printing press. It was the first book ever printed.

2 Timothy 3:16
Revelation 22:20

a
B
c
d
e
f
g
h
i
j
k
l
m
n
o
p
q
r
s
t
u
v
w
x
y
z

A Jewish rabbi (religious leader) carefully repairs a scroll of the Old Testament. He's doing what "scribes" did in ancient times—preserving the Bible we read today.

BILDAD.

One of Job's friends. Bildad was the second friend to comfort Job in his time of trouble. He told Job that all suffering is because of sin. But Bildad was wrong. See what Jesus said about that in John 9:1–3.

Job 2:11
Job 8; 18; 25

BIRTHRIGHT.

Wealth for an oldest son. In Bible times, the oldest son was sometimes given many good things. For example, he would get a double share of everything his dad owned when his dad died. Then he would take over as the leader of the family. This was his birthright. If the son behaved badly, his birthright could be taken away. One son who did not respect his birthright was Esau. He sold it to his younger brother, Jacob, for a single bowl of stew!

Deuteronomy 21:17
Genesis 25:29–34

BLASPHEME.

To curse or show disrespect toward God. Blasphemy is a very bad sin. In fact, in Bible times if a person blasphemed God, he could be put to death. The Jewish leaders accused Jesus of blasphemy. Jesus said that He was the Son of God. But the leaders believed that He was just an ordinary man. Jesus was crucified on the cross because He claimed to be God's Son. The Bible says there is one sin that will never be forgiven—to blaspheme the Holy Spirit.

Exodus 22:28
Leviticus 24:15–16
Matthew 9:3
Mark 3:28–29

BLESS.

To give honor, glory, or favor. God blesses us by giving us His goodness. Jesus said that God blesses those who depend on Him, those who are sad, those who are gentle, and those who obey. People who are kind and have pure hearts are blessed. Peacemakers are blessed, too. So are people who are disapproved of for doing what is right. (Check out Matthew 5:1–10.) As Christians, we should ask God to bless anyone who mistreats us. Jesus blessed kids. And we can bless God by praising His goodness, and others by being kind to them.

Romans 12:14
Mark 10:16 NIV
Psalm 103:1

BLIND.

Not able to see. *Blind* usually means that you can't see with your eyes. But it can also mean that you can't "see" with your spirit. People with blind spirits put their faith in things other than God. They like to go their own way and disobey God's rules. Satan causes spiritual blindness. He loves it when you can't "see" God.

Matthew 9:27
Ephesians 4:18
2 Corinthians 4:4

BLOOD.

The red stuff flowing through your body. In Old Testament times, a person killed a healthy, perfect animal when the person sinned. This was called a sacrifice. The animal's blood was a symbol of the person's blood, or life. Then the person did not have to die for a sin, because the animal took his place. In New Testament times, Jesus sacrificed His own blood and life to pay for *our* sins. Jesus is sometimes called the Lamb of God. He was a perfect sacrifice in every way. Today, when people take communion, they remember that Jesus gave His blood and His life so that God would forgive us for our sins.

Leviticus 17:11
1 Peter 1:18–19
Hebrews 9:14
1 Corinthians 11:25

BOANERGES.

An Aramaic word that means "Sons of Thunder." Boanerges was the name Jesus gave to his disciples James and John. It isn't clear just what Jesus meant—maybe that James and John were powerful when they preached.

Mark 3:17

BOAZ.

An ancestor of Jesus. Boaz was a rich man from Bethlehem. He married Ruth. Their son was Obed. He had a son named Jesse. Jesse was the father of King David. Boaz, Obed, Jesse, and King David were all ancestors of Jesus Christ.

Ruth 4:17
Luke 3:23–32

BODY OF CHRIST.

Another name for Christ's church. The apostle Paul called the church Christ's body. Jesus' spirit is always in His body, the church. He rules over it. He is the head of everything in it. The next time you go to church, look around you. All the people there, including you, are members of the body of Christ. Now, imagine all the Christian churches in the whole, wide world. They are members of the body of Christ, too. The Bible says that the members of the body of Christ should help and care for one another. That means all Christians should look out for one another.

Colossians 1:24
Ephesians 1:22–23
1 Corinthians 12:25–27

BOLDNESS.

The ability to be strong in hard situations. Christians should be bold when they honor God. When you pray, ask God to help you speak boldly whenever you tell others about Him. Peter and John were bold when they taught about Jesus. As they faced their enemies, they prayed: "Lord, listen to their threats! We are your servants. So make us brave enough to speak your message."

Ephesians 6:18–20
Acts 4:13
Acts 4:29 CEV

BONDAGE.

Being a slave to someone or something. Bondage is when people are held against their will. When you are in bondage, you are stuck. You can't get out. Bondage can happen to your heart, too. Sin can make your heart feel like a slave. It holds on to you and doesn't leave any room in there for God. The only way out is through Jesus. If you trust in Him, you won't have to worry about sin taking over your heart.

John 8:34
Romans 6:18

BOOK OF LIFE.

God's list of who's going to heaven. The Book of Life is God's list of people who love Him. Are you on that list? You are if you've asked Jesus to forgive you for your sins and live in your heart. Be very happy that your name is on the list. It means that someday you will live with God in heaven.

Malachi 3:16–18
Philippians 4:3
Luke 10:20
John 6:40

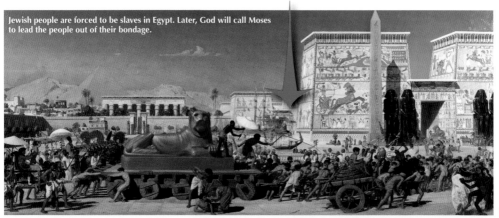
Jewish people are forced to be slaves in Egypt. Later, God will call Moses to lead the people out of their bondage.

BOOK OF THE LAW. ——
The law according to Moses. The Book of the Law is a name for the first five books of the Old Testament—Genesis, Exodus, Levit-icus, Numbers, and Deuteronomy. These books are called the Pentateuch. God told these laws to Moses, and Moses wrote them down. Then he gave them to the priests, and they read the laws to the people.

Deuteronomy 31:9–11

Jesus once compared Himself to the brass serpent: "As Moses lifted up the serpent in the wilderness, even so must the Son of man be lifted up" (John 3:14 KJV).

BORN AGAIN. ——
New life as a believer in Jesus Christ. God gives everyone the chance to be forgiven for their sins. To be forgiven, you must believe that Jesus died for you. When He was crucified, Jesus took all the punishment that you deserve when you break God's rules. Wow! How many friends do you know who would do *that* for you? Another word for "born again" is *saved*: "If you confess with your mouth, 'Jesus is Lord,' and believe in your heart that God raised him from the dead, you will be saved." To get into heaven, you must be born again.

Acts 13:38–39
1 Corinthians 15:3
John 3:3
Romans 10:9 NIV

BOWELS. ——
Your inside parts. The bowels are part of the human digestive system. In Bible times, they were thought to be the center of a person's feelings and emotions.

Job 30:27–28 KJV

BRASS SERPENT. ——
A metal snake God used to heal people bitten by real snakes. Some of the Israelites were disrespectful. They were so bad that God sent poisonous snakes to bite them. The people ran to Moses for help. They asked him to tell God to send the

a
B
c
d
e
g
h
i
j
k
l
m
n
o
p
q
r
s
t
u
v
w
x
y
z

snakes away. God told Moses to make a snake out of brass and put it on top of a pole. Anyone who was bitten should look at the snake. It would heal them of their snake bites.

Numbers 21:4–9

BREAD.

Something good to eat. In Bible times, *bread* was a word that meant "food." Bread was made from flour and baked in loaves. When the Israelites were in the desert and hungry, God fed them by sending a special kind of bread, called manna, that fell from the sky like dew. Jesus described Himself as the Bread of Life. He said: "I am the bread of life. He who comes to me will never go hungry, and he who believes in me will never be thirsty." In the New Testament, you'll find a story about Jesus feeding over 5,000 people with just five loaves of bread.

Exodus 16
John 6:35 NIV
Matthew 14:15–21

BREASTPLATE.

A vest worn by Jewish high priests. The breastplate was made of cloth and held twelve precious stones. The stones carried the names of the twelve tribes of Israel.

Exodus 28:15–30

BREATH OF GOD.

A way of saying that God is the source of life. God's breath has power to do great things. When God created the first man, Adam, He gave him life by breathing into his nostrils. After Jesus was raised from the dead, He went to be with His disciples. He breathed on them, and they received the Holy Spirit.

Job 33:4
2 Samuel 22:16
Genesis 2:7
John 20:22

BRIDE.

A newly married woman. In the New Testament, the church is called the bride of Christ. That means that Christ loves the church with all His heart. The Bible says: "As a bridegroom rejoices over his bride, so will your God rejoice over you."

Ephesians 5:25–35
Isaiah 62:5 NIV

BURNING BUSH.

A fiery, talking shrub. One day, Moses saw a bush on fire. It wasn't burning up, so Moses went to check it out. When he got to the bush, it talked to him. "Moses! Moses!" The voice was God's. God said He was concerned about His people in Egypt. He told Moses to lead them out of Egypt and into a better place. God described this new place as "a good and spacious land, a land flowing with milk and honey."

Exodus 3:8 NIV

BURNT OFFERING.

A gift for God. In Old Testament days, people made burnt offerings to God. They killed a healthy, perfect animal. Then parts of the dead animal—its fat, the lower part of its liver, and its two kidneys—were placed on an altar. These parts were burned, making a smoky fire. A burnt offering was a holy ceremony, a gift to God.

Leviticus 1:1–8

a
B
c
d
e
f
g
h
i
j
k
l
m
n
o
p
q
r
s
t
u
v
w
x
y
z

CAESAR. ——————

A title used for Roman kings or emperors. One famous Roman emperor was Caesar Augustus. This Caesar was responsible for Jesus being born in Bethlehem. Jesus had to be born there—the prophets said so. They spoke for God, and God said that Bethlehem was the place. Caesar didn't know he was helping God. He ordered his citizens to return to their hometowns to be counted. He wanted to find out how many people lived in his empire. Jesus' parents–to–be lived in Nazareth. So they had to go to Bethlehem to be counted. While they were there, Jesus was born.

Micah 5:2
Luke 2:1–11

CAESAREA PHILIPPI. ———

A city at the foot of Mount Hermon. Caesarea Philippi was in northern Palestine. It is where Peter said that Jesus was the Messiah.

Matthew 16:13–16

CAIAPHAS. ——————

The Jewish high priest who said Jesus should die. Caiaphas ruled over the trial of Jesus. He accused Jesus of blasphemy and suggested that He be killed. In those days, it was a crime to be disrespectful toward God—a crime that could end in death. Jesus called Himself the Son of God. The Jewish leaders did not believe Him and wanted Him to die.

John 18:14
Matthew 26:57–68

A statue of Caesar Augustus.

CAIN.

The oldest son of Adam and Eve. Cain did not get along with his younger brother, Abel. Cain was jealous because Abel's offerings always pleased God. Cain gave the Lord only what he wanted to give Him. Before long, Cain's jealously led to anger. One day, he took Abel out into a field and killed him! God punished Cain by sending him away. He made him a "restless wanderer on the earth."

Genesis 4:3–11
Genesis 4:12 NIV

CALEB.

An Israelite spy. Caleb was one of twelve spies sent to check out Canaan. Canaan was land that God promised to Abraham's ancestors. Moses sent the spies to see what Canaan was like. Caleb reported back that the Israelites should attack the Canaanites and take their land. None of the other Israelites, except for Joshua, agreed with Caleb. It was forty long years before they took Caleb's and Joshua's advice. Finally, they went into the Promised Land. By then, Caleb was an old man.

Genesis 15:3–7
Numbers 13:17–20
Numbers 13:30
Numbers 14:6–10
Joshua 14:6–14

An angry Cain kills his younger brother, Abel, in the first murder in human history.

CALF.

A baby cow. Calves were often sacrificed as offerings to God. Aaron made an idol, or false god, that looked like a golden calf. The Israelites made God mad when they bowed down and worshipped it.

Leviticus 9:8
Exodus 32:1–10

CALLING.

God's purpose for someone. Everyone has a purpose. For example, the apostle Paul said that God chose him to be a disciple. Paul's calling was to be a preacher, an apostle, and a teacher. What special skills do you have? If your skills are good and right, then they might be your calling. Use them to honor God.

2 Timothy 1:1
2 Timothy 1:11
2 Thessalonians 1:11–12

CALVARY.

The hill where Jesus was crucified. The word *Calvary* comes from a Latin word that means "skull." That is why Calvary is sometimes called "the Skull." It is also called "Golgotha." The hill was just outside the city walls of ancient Jerusalem. If you go to Jerusalem today, you can visit the place where Jesus was crucified. A church marks the site. It is called the Church of the Holy Sepulchre.

John 19:16–17
Mark 15:22
Luke 23:33

CAMEL.

An animal with a humped back, used for transportation. Camels love the desert climate of the Middle East. They are strong, tough animals. Camels were used in Bible times like horses were in the American Wild West. They carried people and baggage from place to place.

Genesis 24:32

A camel caravan in the 1900s.

CAMP.

A tent village. Tents were homes for nomads—people who regularly traveled from one place to another. The Israelites lived in tent camps when they wandered in the wilderness.

Numbers 33:1–49

CANA.

A village where Jesus did his first miracle. He turned water into wine at a wedding feast there.

John 2:1–11

CANAAN.

The Promised Land. Canaan was mainly between the Mediterranean Sea and the Jordan River. Today, this area is Israel, the West Bank, the Gaza Strip, and parts of Lebanon and Syria. Canaan was named after Noah's grandson, Canaan. His ancestors lived on the land for many years. They were known as the Canaanites. Because God owns the earth, He gets to decide where people live. God promised the land of Canaan to Abraham's ancestors. That promise was made true when Joshua led the Israelites to take the land away from the Canaanites.

Genesis 10:1, 6–20
Genesis 15:3–7
Joshua 10–12

CAPERNAUM.

A city on the shore of the Sea of Galilee. Capernaum was Jesus' home during His ministry. His disciples Andrew, Peter, and Philip moved from their hometown of Bethsaida to Capernaum where disciples Matthew, James, and John lived. All of these men, except Matthew the tax collector, were fishermen. Jesus did many miracles in Capernaum. He healed people, and He cast out demons. He sometimes taught in the synagogue there. Although the people of Capernaum saw His miracles, they did not believe in Him. Jesus scolded them for not having faith.

Matthew 4:13
John 1:44
Matthew 4:18–22
Matthew 9:9
Matthew 8:5–17
Mark 1:21
Matthew 11:23–24

CANAAN DURING THE TIME OF THE PATRIARCHS

- attack route of the four kings
- return route of the four kings
- Abram pursues the four kings
- Jacob's entry into Canaan
- Esau's pursuit of Jacob
- o allied rebel city
- ✳ clash of forces
- altar built by Abraham, Isaac, or Jacob

Copyright © 2007 by Barbour Publishing, Inc.

CAPTIVITY.

Being kidnapped and held against your will. Citizens of countries that lost wars were often taken away. In Old Testament times, the Assyrians took citizens of Israel into captivity. The Babylonians held the citizens of Judah captive.

2 Kings 15:29
2 Chronicles 36:6–7, 20

CARNAL.

To love things of the world more than God. Satan wants people to act in a carnal way. Paul accused the Corinthians of being carnal, or worldly. He said, "You are jealous and argue with each other. This proves that you are not spiritual and that you are acting like the people of this world."

Romans 8:5
1 Corinthians 3:1
1 Corinthians 3:3 CEV

CASTAWAY.

Someone or something that is worthless or rejected. Paul said that he kept himself in control so he wouldn't give in to Satan's ways. He did not want to risk being a castaway—rejected—after preaching the Word of God to others.

1 Corinthians 9:27 KJV

CEDAR.

An evergreen tree. Cedar trees have reddish wood that smells good. Cedar wood was used to build the temple in Jerusalem.

1 Kings 5:1–10

CENSUS.

A counting of the people. A census is taken to find out how many people live in a certain place. It was a census that brought Mary and Joseph to Bethlehem. They went there to be counted. In Old Testament times, David got in trouble with God by taking a census of Israel and Judah's fighting men. It seems like David was trusting in his army more than in God.

Luke 2:1
2 Samuel 24

CENTURION.

An army man living in ancient days. Centurions were Roman military officers. They commanded a group of about 100 soldiers. A centurion was at the foot of the cross when Jesus died. The Bible says: "With a loud cry, Jesus breathed his last. The curtain of the temple was torn in two from top to bottom. And when the centurion, who stood there in front of Jesus, heard his cry and saw how he died, he said, 'Surely this man was the Son of God!' "

Acts 10:1, 22
Mark 15:37–39 NIV

CHAFF.

The worthless coverings of a grain seed. Chaff is what's left after the seed is separated from the plant. The Bible compares wicked people to chaff.

Psalm 1:4

This model of a Roman soldier was made around the time of Jesus.

a
b
C
d
e
f
g
h
i
j
k
l
m
n
o
p
q
r
s
t
u
v
w
x
y
z

Chariot

Egyptian pharaoh Ramses II rides to battle in a chariot in this painting from the 1800s.

CHARIOT.

A two-wheeled cart pulled by horses. Rulers rode in chariots. Chariots were also used as vehicles in wars.

Genesis 41:42–43
Deuteronomy 20:1

CHEEK.

The side of your face. To hit someone on the cheek is a serious insult. What did Jesus say about it? "If someone slaps you on one cheek, don't stop that person from slapping you on the other cheek." He didn't mean that we should go around allowing people to hit us. Jesus wanted us to react to insults with kindness.

Job 16:10
Luke 6:29 CEY

CHERUBIM.

Heavenly winged creatures. You can read about cherubim in the Old Testament. After God sent Adam and Eve from the Garden of Eden, the cherubim showed up. They guarded the entrance so Adam and Eve couldn't return. Ezekiel saw cherubim. He told us what they look like: "Each of the winged creatures had four faces: the face of a bull, the face of a human, the face of a lion, and the face of an eagle." The ark of the covenant had golden cherubim statues on its lid.

Genesis 3:24
Ezekiel 10:14 CEY
Exodus 25:18–20

CHILDREN.

Kids like you! Children are blessings from God. Jesus loves children. He enjoyed having them around. He held them in His arms and blessed them. Jesus said the kingdom of heaven belongs to people who trust Him like little children. When Jesus came to Jerusalem, the children praised Him. They shouted, "Hosanna to the Son of David." *Children* is also a word used for those who accept Jesus as their savior. The Bible says: "To all who received him, to those who believed in his name, he gave the right to become children of God."

Psalm 127:3
Mark 10:13–16
Matthew 19:14
Matthew 21:15 NIV
John 1:12 NIV

32

CHRISTIAN.

A person who follows Christ. The word *Christian* doesn't show up in the Bible until the book of Acts. Christ's followers were first called Christians in Antioch, a city that's now part of the country of Turkey.

Acts 11:25–26

CHRONICLES, FIRST AND SECOND BOOKS OF.

Two books of the Old Testament. First and Second Chronicles are history books. They tell about the early history of Israel. If you read these books, you will learn about ancient kings. First Chronicles tells about the death of King Saul. It also tells about the reign of King David. Second Chronicles tells about King Solomon and kings who reigned after his death.

1 Chronicles 10–29
2 Chronicles 1–9

CHURCH.

God's people. When you think of the word *church*, you probably think of a building. But the true church is not the building; it is the people. It is all the people who belong to Christ. The word *church* means "an assembly." God's people often assemble in a church building to worship Him. Jesus is the head of the church. The church's purpose is to help Christians grow in their faith and serve others around them.

Ephesians 5:21
Ephesians 1:22
Ephesians 4:11–13

CIRCUMCISION.

A religious ceremony performed on boys. Circumcision was a symbol of God's agreement with the Israelites. Israelite boys were circumcised eight days after they were born. The word has another meaning. In the New Testament, *circumcision* can mean putting off sin.

Genesis 17:3–14
Leviticus 12:3
Colossians 2:11

CITY OF DAVID.

A nickname for Jerusalem and for Bethlehem. King David took part of Jerusalem from the Jebusites. He named it after himself—the City of David. Bethlehem, too, has been called the City of David. It is where King David was born. Jesus Christ was born there, too.

2 Samuel 5:6–7
2 Samuel 5:9
Luke 2:1–11

CLAY.

Soil used for making bricks and pottery. The Bible teaches that we are like clay in God's hands. He made us, and He forms us into what He wants us to be.

Jeremiah 18:1–6
Isaiah 64:8

CLEAN.

Pure. *Clean* means acceptable to God. In the Old Testament, certain animals were thought of as "clean" or "unclean." Clean animals were okay to eat. Unclean animals were not okay to eat, or even touch. It had nothing to do with how dirty they were! (Read more about it in Leviticus 11.) For people, *clean* means "holy" or "blameless."

Psalm 24:3–4

CLOUDS.

Water vapor floating in the air. Look up to the sky, and think of God! Clouds are His symbol of protection. Psalm 104:3 says that God "makes the clouds his chariot and rides on the wings of the wind" (NIV). God showed Himself to the Israelites in clouds over the desert. And when Jesus comes to earth again, He will come on the clouds.

Job 35:5
Genesis 9:14–15
Exodus 16:10
Matthew 24:30

COCK.

A rooster. In ancient times, men kept watch in three- or four-hour blocks throughout the night. The cock crowed during the third watch of the night. The third watch was the last watch, just before sunrise.

Mark 13:35

a
b
C
d
e
f
g
h
i
j
k
l
m
n
o
p
q
r
s
t
u
v
w
x
y
z

COLOSSIANS, LETTER TO THE. ———

A New Testament book written by the apostle Paul. Colossians is a letter Paul wrote to Christians in the city of Colosse. The people of Colosse were called Colossians. Paul's letter is about the greatness of Christ. He encouraged the Colossians to be more like Jesus. He asked them to be kind and forgiving toward one another.

Colossians 3:1–14

COLT. ———

A young donkey. Jesus rode a colt into Jerusalem on the day we celebrate as Palm Sunday.

Matthew 21:1–7

COMFORTER. ———

Another name for the Holy Spirit. The Comforter, or Holy Spirit, is our Helper. Jesus said, "I will ask the Father, and He will give you another Helper, that He may be with you forever." The Holy Spirit teaches us and gives us advice. He reminds us of what Jesus would do.

John 14:16 NASB
John 14:26

COMMANDMENT. ———

A rule made by someone in control. Do you know the Ten Commandments? They are ten rules that God gave to Moses for His people. Jesus wants us to obey God's commandments. He said

The Good Samaritan shows compassion to a wounded enemy in this stained glass window scene from a church in England.

that the greatest commandment is to love God with all your heart and with all your soul and with all your mind. The second greatest commandment is to love your neighbor.

Exodus 34:28
Matthew 19:17
Matthew 22:37–39

COMMISSION. ———

A special assignment given by someone in charge. A commission is a responsibility. Your parents might give you a commission to care for a younger brother or sister. Jesus has a Great Commission for all of His followers. He wants us to make disciples of people everywhere.

Matthew 28:19–20

COMPASSION. ———

Kindness to and forgiveness for others. God is compassionate. So is His Son Jesus. Jesus is a Savior who cares deeply about people. He expects us to show compassion toward others, too, just as He did.

Psalm 86:15
Matthew 15:32
Matthew 18:33

CONCEIT. ———

Thinking you're the greatest. Conceit is having a blown-up opinion of yourself. Paul warned Christians about conceit. He said, "Live in harmony with one another. Do not be proud, but be willing to associate with people of low position. Do not be conceited."

Romans 12:16 NIV

CONDEMNATION. ———
Being guilty of sin and deserving punishment. Everyone is guilty of sin—kids and grown-ups, too. The Bible says that we all are sinners and deserving of punishment; but Christ died for us so we would be forgiven of our sins. If Jesus hadn't come, we would all be condemned. That means none of us would ever get to heaven. Jesus came to save us from condemnation. If we truly believe in Him, we will not be condemned. Instead, Jesus promises we will live with Him forever.

Romans 5:8
John 3:17–18

CONFESS. ———
To admit your sins *and* your faith. It is important to confess to God the wrong things you do. The Bible says: "If you don't confess your sins, you will be a failure. But God will be merciful if you confess your sins and give them up." *Confess* also means to tell others about your faith in God. Have you shared your faith with friends and family? It's a good thing to do.

1 John 1:9
Proverbs 28:13 CEV
Romans 10:8–10

CONGREGATION. ———
A gathering of people. A congregation is often thought of as a group of people worshipping God. The next time you go to church, look around at all the people. They and you make up a congregation!

Acts 13:43

CONSECRATE. ———
To bless something and give it to God for His use. Men were consecrated before they became priests. Altars were consecrated, too. God wants all believers to be consecrated. This means they should be pure so they can do good works for Him. Second Timothy 2:21 says that people "who stop doing evil and make themselves pure will become special. Their lives will be holy and pleasing to their Master, and they will be able to do all kinds of good deeds" (CEV).

Exodus 28:40–41
Exodus 29:37

CONSOLATION. ———
Comfort and encouragement. Jesus Christ and the Holy Spirit give us consolation. When we put all our faith in them, they make us feel better. The psalms often sing praises to God for His comfort and encouragement. For example, Psalm 94:19 says, "And when I was burdened with worries, you comforted me and made me feel secure" (CEV).

Romans 15:5

CONTENT. ———
Peaceful and worry-free. There is a secret to being content all the time. The secret is to put your faith in God. God will bless you with peace that no one can completely understand. This peace will control the way you think and feel. Don't worry about not having enough. Instead, be content with what you have. Whenever you are worried, always remember that God is with you.

Philippians 4:12–13
Philippians 4:7
Hebrews 13:5

CONTENTION. ———
Strong disagreement between two people. When disagreements happen, people often get hurt. Disagreements can keep people apart, even in the church. Christians should be at peace with one another. They should try hard to work out their disagreements.

Acts 15:39
Romans 12:18–21

CONTRITE. ———
Feeling sorrow for your sins. God wants His people to be contrite. When people are contrite, they are truly sorry for their sins. Being sorry helps you to be gentle and kind.

Isaiah 66:2
2 Corinthians 7:10

a b C d e f g h i j k l m n o p q r s t u v w x y z

a
b
C
d
e
f
g
h
i
j
k
l
m
n
o
p
q
r
s
t
u
v
w
x
y
z

CONVERSATION. ———

How people act or behave. Did you think *conversation* means to talk with someone? It does! But in ancient days, it was a word that meant behavior. Paul had a special message about conversation for young people. He said: "Don't let anyone make fun of you, just because you are young. Set an example for other followers by what you say and do, as well as by your love, faith, and purity."

1 Timothy 4:12 CEV

CONVICTION. ———

Being aware of your sin and the guilty feelings it brings. Sin and guilt are not hidden from God. So when your conscience tells you that you've done something wrong, listen to it! The Holy Spirit might be convicting you of sin. The Holy Spirit is God's Helper in charge of conviction. He makes you aware of your sin and allows you to feel guilty. If you admit your sin to God and are sorry, He will forgive you.

Psalm 69:5
John 8:1–11
1 John 1:9

CORBAN. ———

A special offering promised to God. The Pharisees were sneaky. They got away with not helping their elderly parents. Instead of giving their parents the things they needed, the Pharisees said those things were "Corban"— promised to God. So they broke a very important commandment: Honor your father and mother. (See Mark 7:9–13.)

CORINTH. ———

A big seaside city near Athens, Greece. Corinth was known for how badly its people behaved. The apostle Paul lived in Corinth for eighteen months. He taught there and tried to convince people to believe in Jesus. Many of the people believed and were baptized.

Acts 18:1–11

The ruins of a temple to the Greek god Apollo are a familiar image of modern Corinth.

CORINTHIANS, FIRST AND SECOND LETTERS TO THE. ———

Paul's letters to the church at Corinth. These letters are in the New Testament. Paul wrote them to new Christians. The people in Corinth, known as Corinthians, needed to stop their old, bad behavior. In 1 Corinthians, Paul told them how Christians should behave. He also wrote about the importance of love. In 2 Corinthians, Paul wrote about hard times and suffering, including his own.

1 Corinthians 13:1–13
2 Corinthians 11:24–33

CORN. ———

Grain. In Bible times, corn was more than yellow kernels on a cob. In some versions of the Bible, the word *corn* meant different kinds of grain—millet, wheat, and barley.

Matthew 12:1 KJV

CORNELIUS. ———

One of the first Gentiles to become a Christian. Cornelius was a Roman soldier. Jews weren't allowed to have anything to do with Gentiles like Cornelius. But Cornelius loved God, who told him to call for the apostle Peter. The Holy Spirit told Peter to accept Cornelius as a Christian. After that, other Gentiles became Christians and were baptized. (Read all about it in Acts 10.)

COUNCIL. ———

The highest court in New Testament times. The Jewish high council was called the Sanhedrin. It included seventy-one priests, scribes, and elders. The council accused Jesus of blasphemy. It also ordered Peter and John to stop preaching what Jesus taught. Paul was brought before the council, too, because he believed in Jesus Christ.

Luke 22:66–71
Acts 4:5–21
Acts 22–24

COUNTENANCE. ———

The expression on your face. Your face can show a lot about

how you feel. What is your countenance like today?

Daniel 5:6 KJV

COURAGE.

Bravery. If you search the Bible, you will find the words "be strong and courageous" many times. (For example, see 1 Chronicles 28:20.) You can get courage by trusting in God. The Bible says: "Be strong and of good courage; do not be afraid, nor be dismayed, for the LORD your God is with you wherever you go".

Joshua 1:9 NKJV

COURT.

A yard or patio attached to a building. You might have a patio attached to your house. Your school might have a courtyard. The tabernacle and the temple in Jerusalem both had courts, or courtyards.

Exodus 27:9
1 Kings 6:3, 36

COVENANT.

An agreement or promise. God often made covenants with His people. He promised to bless them if they obeyed and followed Him. God made a covenant with Noah after the big flood. He said, "Never again will all life be cut off by the waters of a flood; never again will there be a flood to destroy the earth." God put a rainbow in the sky. It was a symbol of His covenant. Jesus said that His blood was a covenant. He promised that those who believe in Him will be saved from condemnation.

Genesis 22:15–18
Genesis 9:11 NIV
Genesis 9:12–17
Matthew 26:28
John 10:9

COVETOUSNESS.

Being really greedy for something someone else has. The Tenth Commandment says: "Do not want anything that belongs to someone else. Don't want anyone's house, wife or husband, slaves, oxen, donkeys or anything else." Think about the "anything else" part. Have you ever coveted (wanted) something that didn't belong to you?

Exodus 20:17 CEV

CREATION.

God's awesome handiwork. Before the beginning of time, before there was anything else, there was God. Can you imagine? There was only God. From nothing, He created the universe. He made the earth and the sky. He separated light from darkness. He made every living thing: plants, animals, and people. Read Genesis 1 and 2. They tell about God's creation. When God was done, He looked around, and He liked what He made. He said it was all good. And He'd finished it in six days! Do you know what God did on the seventh day? The Bible says, "He blessed the seventh day and made it special, because on that day he rested from his work."

Genesis 1:1–2
Genesis 2:3 CEV

a
b
C
d
e
f
g
h
i
j
k
l
m
n
o
p
q
r
s
t
u
v
w
x
y
z

Surrounded by angels, God gives life to Adam in this classic painting by Michelangelo. It's on the ceiling of the Sistine Chapel in the Vatican in Rome.

CREATOR. —————

God. He is the Great Creator. He made *everything*: the universe, sky, earth, and all living things. God rules over His creation. When Job was suffering, he wondered why God wasn't helping him. God answered Job. He reminded Job that He is the Great Creator. Read all about it in God's own words in Job 38:4–41 and 39:1–30. You'll be amazed by all the things God can do.

Genesis 1; 2:1–4
Psalm 47:1–9

CRETE. —————

A big island in the Mediterranean Sea. When Paul was held prisoner by the Roman authorities, He was put on a ship to Rome. The ship sailed along the shore of Crete. Soon after, there was a big shipwreck. You can read about the shipwreck in Acts 27:14–28:10.

CROSS.

—————

What Jesus was crucified on. The cross was made out of two rough and heavy wood posts. One post was long. When it was stuck into the ground, it was like a very tall fencepost. The other post was shorter. It was attached crosswise near the top of the long post. Jesus had to have help to carry the cross to the place where He was crucified. Then Jesus' hands and feet were nailed to it. The long post was set upright into the ground, and Jesus was left hanging there to die. Jesus hung on the cross for six hours before He died. Today, we remember that day as Good Friday. Jesus died on the cross so we would be forgiven for our sins.

Matthew 27:32
Luke 23:33
John 19:30–33
Romans 6:6–11

CROWN. —————

A royal headpiece. Leaders, like kings and queens, wore crowns. They were often made of precious metals and jewels. Just before Jesus was crucified, the Roman soldiers made an ugly crown out of branches with sharp thorns. They made Jesus wear it. Then they mocked Him because He said that He was the King of the Jews.

2 Kings 11:12
1 Chronicles 20:2
John 19:1–3
Luke 23:3

Hundreds of artists have painted pictures of Jesus' crucifixion. This one, from 1627, is by Francisco de Zurbarán.

CRUCIFIXION.—

Putting someone to death on a cross. That's the way Jesus died. In ancient days, many criminals were sentenced to death by crucifixion. A criminal's hands and feet were nailed to a big, wooden cross. The bottom of the cross was stuck into the ground. Then the criminal hung on the cross until he died. It was a terrible death. Often, criminals hung there for days before their bodies gave out. Jesus died after only six hours on the cross. Read all about it in Matthew 27:11–54. Jesus was an innocent man who was crucified. He allowed Himself to die an awful death so we would be forgiven for our sins.

1 Peter 1:19
Revelation 1:5–6

a b **C** d e f g h i j k l m n o p q r s t u v w x y z

CUBIT.

An ancient measurement. A cubit was the length from a man's elbow to the tip of his middle finger—about 18 inches. Noah's ark was 300 cubits long, 50 cubits wide, and 30 cubits high. That comes out to about 450 feet long, 75 feet wide, and 45 feet high. Try measuring some of your stuff using cubits.

Genesis 6:15

CURSE.

To call for evil on someone else. To curse also means to swear at or about somebody. That's not a very nice thing to do! In Old Testament times, a king named Balak hired a man named Balaam to curse—dump evil—on God's people. But God spoke to Balaam through his donkey, and Balaam blessed the Israelites instead. Jesus taught that Christians should react to curses with kindness.

Numbers 22–24
Luke 6:28

CYRUS.

An important king of the Persian Empire. When his army defeated the Babylonians, Cyrus took their land. Afterward, he allowed the Jewish prisoners in Babylonia to go home to Jerusalem.

2 Chronicles 36:22–23

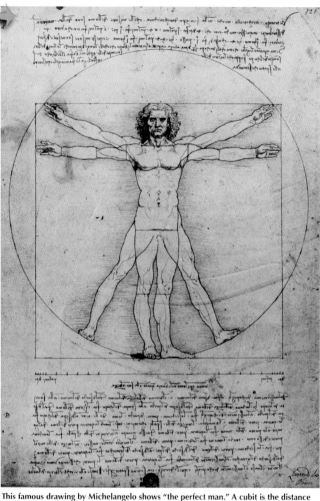

This famous drawing by Michelangelo shows "the perfect man." A cubit is the distance from his elbow to the tip of his middle finger.

a
b
C
d
e
f
g
h
i
j
k
l
m
n
o
p
q
r
s
t
u
v
w
x
y
z

DAGON.

The chief false god of the Philistines. Some believe it had the upper half of a man's body and the tail of a fish. When the Philistines captured Samson, they gave Dagon the credit. When they stole God's ark of the covenant, they set it in their temple next to a statue of Dagon. The false god fell flat on its face in front of the holy ark. (Read all about it in 1 Samuel 5:1–5.)

Judges 16:23

DAMASCUS.

The capital city of Syria, northeast of Jerusalem. Damascus is one of the world's oldest cities. You'll find it mentioned often in the Bible. It existed all the way back to the book of Genesis. It still exists today. Damascus was where Saul became a Christian. Saul, later called Paul, is known as one of the greatest apostles of all time.

Genesis 14:15
Acts 9:1–25

DAMNATION.

Forever punished in hell. Damnation happens to those who don't believe in Jesus. The Bible says that in the end-times everyone will be judged. Those who have done right by trusting Jesus will go to heaven. Everyone else will be punished in hell.

Mark 16:16
John 5:28–29

DAN.

Jacob's fifth son. Dan's ancestors formed the tribe of Dan. They were known as the Danites. The Danites lived in a region called Dan.

Genesis 30:6
Judges 18:16
Judges 20:1

DANIEL.

An Old Testament prophet. Daniel was loyal to God in a time when many people worshipped false gods. He was very wise. God gave Daniel the gift of explaining people's dreams. He could predict things that would happen in the future. Daniel is well-known for being thrown into a den of lions because he refused to pray to King Darius. A stone was rolled in front of the den so Daniel couldn't get out. God sent an angel to watch over Daniel. It shut the lions' mouths so they couldn't eat him. In the morning, the king checked the den. He was amazed to find Daniel alive and well.

Daniel was saved because he trusted God. (Check out Daniel 6:1–23.)

Daniel 4

Miraculously tamed lions are more like pet cats for the godly prophet Daniel.

DANIEL, BOOK OF.

An Old Testament Bible book. Daniel was a prophet. He had the gift of knowing what would happen to God's people in the future. Part of the book of Daniel is about his dreams. In this Bible book, you'll find some well-known stories. There's the story of King Nebuchadnezzar's big gold statue. And the story of what happened to three men who were thrown into a fiery furnace for not

40

DRAGON.

A name for a made-up sea creature or winged lizard. Satan is described as "the great dragon" in Revelation 12:9. An angel will capture the great dragon (Satan) and keep him prisoner for 1,000 years.

Revelation 20:1–3 NIV

DREAM.

A movie in the mind. God often used dreams to speak to people, even to tell the future. Joseph and Daniel were famous for explaining people's dreams.

Genesis 40–41
Daniel 2

DROUGHT.

A period of no rain. Have you known a time when it didn't rain for weeks or months? That's a drought. Without rain, the grass turns brown. Flowers die. Nothing grows. Your soul can have a drought, too. If you trust in worldly things, your faith and goodness cannot grow. If you trust in the Lord, your soul will be like a tree planted near a river. It will have plenty to drink, and it will be good and strong in the Lord.

Jeremiah 17:5–8

DRUNKENNESS.

Drinking too much alcohol. Not only is drinking bad for your heath, but it can get you into a lot of trouble. The Bible warns about drunkenness. It can lead people to sin. Instead of filling up on alcohol, people should fill up on the Spirit of God.

Proverbs 23:21
Ephesians 5:18

DUMB.

Unable to speak, or mute. Sometimes people are mute for their whole lives. Others are mute only for a little while—like Zacharias, who was not able to speak after he saw a vision of an angel in the temple. When Zacharias doubted Gabriel's message, the angel said Zacharias would be "dumb, and not able to speak, until the day that these things shall be performed."

Luke 1:11–22

DUST.

Dry powdery earth. God made Adam from dust. When people die, after many years in the ground, their bodies become dust again. In Old Testament times, people put dust on their heads when they felt sad or embarrassed.

Genesis 2:7
Genesis 3:19
Job 2:12

Jacob dreams of angels on a stairway to heaven (Genesis 28:10–16).

a
b
c
D
e
f
g
h
i
j
k
l
m
n
o
p
q
r
s
t
u
v
w
x
y
z

45

b
c
d
e
f
g
h
i
j
k
l
m
n
o
p
q
r
s
t
u
v
w
x
y
z

EARNEST.

A promise. If you borrow money, you might give the lender something of value to seal the deal. It is a promise that you will pay all of what you owe. God sent His Holy Spirit as a kind of "earnest" payment to believers. The Holy Spirit is God's promise that we will have all of Him someday. Believers will go to heaven and belong only to God.

2 Corinthians 1:22 KJV

EARTHQUAKE.

A rough shaking of the ground. There was a big earthquake on the first Easter. It happened after Jesus died and was put in His tomb. He was dead for three days when the big earthquake shook the ground. It was an angel of the Lord coming down from heaven. He moved the boulder that sealed the entrance to Jesus' tomb. In Bible times, an earthquake was used as a symbol of God's anger and judgment.

Matthew 28:2
Judges 5:4

EASTER.

The day that Christians celebrate Jesus' rising from the dead. The story of Jesus' resurrection is a wonderful one. After He was crucified on the cross and died, His body was put into a tomb. The tomb was a burial cave carved into the side of a big rock. A huge stone was rolled in front of the entrance to close it up forever. Jesus had promised that after He was dead for three days, He would come back to life. The Jewish leaders didn't want people to believe that Jesus had such power. They worried that Jesus' disciples would steal His body to make it look like He came back. So they talked to Pilate, the Roman governor, and he gave them some guards. They made the tomb as secure as they could and set the guards to watch over it. On the third day, an earthquake shook the earth. An angel came down from heaven. The guards were so afraid that they shook like jelly. They were so scared they could not move. The angel rolled the stone away from the tomb and sat on it. The tomb was empty. Jesus' body was gone! Jesus was alive again, and He appeared to many people. Just as He'd said, He was the Son of God. Read more about Jesus rising from the dead in Matthew 28 and John 20.

Matthew 27:57–66

EBENEZER.

A battleground and a stone. Ebenezer is where the Philistines defeated Israel's army. Later, Israel defeated the Philistines. Samuel built an altar on the battleground. He named it Ebenezer, which means "the stone of help."

1 Samuel 4:1–2
1 Samuel 7:10–12

ECCLESIASTES, BOOK OF.

A book in the Old Testament. Ecclesiastes is a book of wisdom. It was probably written by King Solomon. The book is about both the sadness and joy of life. It says that joy doesn't come from things of this world. Instead, it comes from faith in God. If we worship and obey Him, we will find joy. Think about how the seasons change. The book of Ecclesiastes tells about the seasons of human life. It teaches that there is a time for everything. Read all about it in Ecclesiastes 3:1–8. These Bible verses teach us a lot about living. In modern times, people have even written songs about them.

EDIFICATION.

The process of growing in the Christian faith. One of the ways we grow in faith is to encourage and help one another as Christians. You can help other Christians by reminding them about what Jesus taught. Christians should try to live in peace and help each other have a strong faith.

1 Thessalonians 5:9–11
Romans 14:19 CEV

EGYPT. —————
A country in North Africa on the Nile River. Many key Bible events took place in Egypt. Abram went there during a famine in Canaan. Jacob's family lived in Egypt. His ancestors became the Hebrew nation. The Hebrew people were held as slaves in Egypt for 400 years. God told Moses to go and set them free. In New Testament times after baby Jesus was born, King Herod wanted Him killed. An angel told Mary and Joseph to take Jesus to Egypt and hide. Today, Egypt is a major country in Africa. It is often in the news. Almost 80 million people live there.

Genesis 12:10
Genesis 46:6
Exodus 3:7–10
Matthew 2:13–14

Sand, camels, and pyramids are among the well-known features of Egypt.

EHUD. —————
The second judge of Israel. For eighteen years, Eglon, king of Moab, ruled the Israelites. Then the Lord sent Ehud to save them. Ehud killed Eglon and set the Israelites free. After that, the Israelites had peace for eighty years.

Judges 3:14–29
Judges 3:30

ELDER. —————
A leader. In Old Testament times, elders were leaders of a family or a tribe. God told Moses to gather seventy elders of the tribe of Israel to help him lead the people out of Egypt. In New Testament times, elders were church leaders who served as pastors or teachers. Today some church leaders are still called elders.

Numbers 11:16–17
1 Timothy 5:17

ELEAZAR. —————
Aaron's third son. Eleazar followed in his father's footsteps as Israel's high priest. He helped divide the land of Canaan among the twelve tribes of Israel.

Exodus 6:23
Numbers 20:25–28
Joshua 14:1

ELECT. —————
Special ones chosen by God. Some believe the Bible teaches that even before we were born, God decided whether we would believe in Him and be saved.

Saved means to live forever with God. The Bible says that God wants everyone to be saved. Those who refuse to believe in Jesus will be lost. They will not go to heaven. God's chosen people should try to behave like Jesus. They should love God, live according to His rules, and be loving. They should do good things.

Romans 8:29
2 Peter 3:9
John 5:39–40
Romans 8:29
Ephesians 1:4 CEV
Ephesians 2:10

ELI. —————
A high priest of Israel. Eli was like an adopted dad to the prophet Samuel. From the time he was very young, Samuel lived with Eli. Samuel's birth mom, Hannah, trusted him with Eli. She wanted Samuel to learn from Eli how to serve the Lord. Samuel was a good boy. But Eli's own sons, Phinehas and Hophni, were evil. Although they were priests, they refused to obey God. Eli was angry when he discovered the bad things his sons were doing. He gave them a good talking-to, but they did not listen. God was angry, too. He allowed Eli's sons to be killed in a battle with the Philistines. When Eli found out, he fell off his chair and died. He was ninety-eight years old.

1 Samuel 2:11–12
1 Samuel 1:3
1 Samuel 2:22–26
1 Samuel 4:11
1 Samuel 4:17–18

a b c d E f g h i j k l m n o p q r s t u v w x y z

a
b
c
d
E
f
g
h
i
j
k
l
m
n
o
p
q
r
s
t
u
v
w
x
y
z

ELIHU.

Job's friend. Elihu spoke to Job in his time of trouble. He was angry at Job's other three friends because they had falsely accused Job. And he was angry at Job because he seemed stuck-up, felt sorry for himself, and blamed God for his suffering.

Job 32-37

ELIJAH.

A prophet and God's friend. God told Elijah to give a message to a wicked king named Ahab. The message was that no rain would fall on the king's land for three years. That made Ahab mad, and he took it out on Elijah. So God told Elijah to hide near the Jordan River. While Elijah was there, God sent ravens to feed him. They brought bread and meat every day. Later, Elijah had a contest with King Ahab. Ahab worshipped a false god, and Elijah worshipped the real God. The contest proved that Elijah's God, the real God, was the most powerful. At the end of his life on earth, Elijah went to heaven in a very special way. God sent a chariot and horses made out of fire. They carried Elijah away in a whirlwind.

1 Kings 17:1
1 Kings 17:5
1 Kings 17:6
1 Kings 18:16-39
2 Kings 2:11

ELIZABETH.

Zachariah's wife and John the Baptist's mom. Elizabeth was a relative of Jesus' mother, Mary. Both women were expecting babies at the same time. They knew their babies were special, because angels from the Lord said so. Elizabeth and Mary both believed that the baby inside Mary was the Messiah and Savior. The women celebrated because soon Jesus would be born. Elizabeth

An angel brings bread to the sad and tired prophet Elijah (1 Kings 19).

had her baby first. Jesus was born about six months later.

Matthew 1:20-21
Luke 1:11-13 KJV
Luke 1:39-55

ELISHA.

An Old Testament prophet who saw Elijah disappear in a whirlwind. Elisha was the prophet Elijah's assistant and learned from him. After a few years, God decided to take Elijah to heaven. As Elisha watched, a chariot of fire came and got Elijah. It disappeared into a whirlwind. Elisha took Elijah's place as leader of the prophets. He served as a prophet to four kings.

2 Kings 2:11
2 Kings 2:15

EMMANUEL.

Another name for Jesus. Emmanuel means "God with us." It is sometimes spelled Immanuel. This title was given to Jesus before He was born. The prophet Isaiah predicted Jesus' birth. God told Isaiah, "The virgin will be with child and will give birth to a son, and will call him Immanuel". The Gospel of Matthew mentions Isaiah's prediction again. It says that when Jesus was born, Isaiah's prediction from God came true. The name Emmanuel is a symbol that God came to earth in the person of Jesus Christ.

Isaiah 7:14 NIV
Matthew 1:22-23
1 John 4:2

EMMAUS. ——————
A village near Jerusalem. After Jesus rose from the dead, He appeared to two of His disciples on the road to Emmaus.

Luke 24:13-31

ENMITY. ——————
Active anger toward something or someone. It is another word for hate. Hate is a sin. People who hate don't have Jesus in their hearts.

James 1:20

ENOCH. ——————
A great-grandfather of Noah. Enoch was the first son of Cain. Enoch is also the name of a city. Cain built the city and named it after his son. Enoch lived 365 years! His body didn't die like a normal person's does. God just took him away. This strange event is written about in the New Testament, Hebrews 11:5. Because he was so faithful to God, Enoch didn't have an ordinary death. Enoch had a son named Methuselah. He lived for 969 years!

Genesis 5:22-29
Genesis 4:17

EPHESIANS, LETTER TO THE. ——————
A New Testament book written by the apostle Paul. Ephesians is a letter that Paul wrote to Christians at the church in Ephesus. The people who lived in Ephesus were called Ephesians. Paul's letter is about Jesus being Lord of everything, especially His church. The letter talks about salvation. Paul reminded the Ephesians that Jesus' death made it possible for all of us to have eternal life. That means that our souls will live forever with God. The letter to the Ephesians encourages Christians to try to be like Jesus. It tells us to keep our faith, especially during hard times.

Ephesians 2:3-6
Ephesians 4-6

EPHOD. ——————
Clothing for the priest. An ephod was a beautiful sleeveless covering made from linen. In Old Testament times, high priests wore ephods.

Exodus 39:2
1 Samuel 2:28

EPHRAIM. ——————
A son, a nation, a forest, and a village. Ephraim has four different meanings. It is the name of Joseph's son, the leader of one of the twelve tribes of Israel. It is also a name for the nation of Israel. Ephraim is also the name of a forest and the name of a village where Jesus and His disciples went.

Joshua 14:4
Judges 3:27
2 Samuel 18:6
John 11:54

EPISTLE. ——————
A letter. Many of the New Testament books are sometimes called epistles. Paul wrote fourteen epistles. John wrote three. Peter wrote two. James and Jude each wrote one.

ESAU. ——————
Jacob's brother. Esau was Isaac's oldest son. As the oldest, he had a special position in the family. This was called his birthright. Esau had a younger brother named Jacob. One day, Esau decided to sell his birthright to his younger brother. Can you guess how much he sold it for? Jacob paid Esau with one bowl of stew! (Read more about it in Genesis 25:29-34).

Deuteronomy 21:17

Red-haired hunter Esau talks with his younger twin Jacob, making a stew.

ESTHER. ——————
Queen of Persia. The Old Testament book of Esther tells of a famous queen. Esther—also called Hadassah—was a Jewish orphan girl who was raised by her cousin Mordecai. When she grew up, she became the queen of Persia. Esther saved her people, the Jews, from an evil

a
b
c
d
E
f
g
h
i
j
k
l
m
n
o
p
q
r
s
t
u
v
w
x
y
z

49

a
b
c
d
E
f
g
h
i
j
k
l
m
n
o
p
q
r
s
t
u
v
w
x
y
z

man named Haman; he was an aide to the Persian king. Haman planned to kill all the Jews. When Esther found out about it, she was able to save them. In the end, Haman was hanged. The story of Esther shows that God protects and takes care of His people.

Esther 2:7
Esther 2:17
Esther 3:5–6

Beautiful Queen Esther eats with her husband, King Ahasuerus of Persia.

ETERNAL LIFE. ———

Life without end. Jesus said: "I am the resurrection and the life. He who believes in me will live, even though he dies; and whoever lives and believes in me will never die. Do you believe this?" If you believe that Jesus died on the cross for your sins, then you will have eternal life. Eternal life means that your soul will live forever with God in heaven and then on the new earth. Although your body will die someday, your soul —your personality, what makes you you—will always be with God. While you are here and alive, get to know God by reading your Bible. He loves you now, and He will love you forever.

John 11:25–26 NIV
John 3:16
Jude 1:21

ETHIOPIA. ———

An ancient nation south of Egypt. Ethiopia was also called Cush. The land was known for its precious stone topaz. In Bible times, the apostle Philip taught an

Ethiopian servant about Jesus. Read the story in Acts 8:26–38.

Genesis 2:13
Job 28:19

EUPHRATES. ———

An important river. It forms in Turkey and flows through Syria and Iraq where it joins the Tigris River. You might have studied this river in school. Did you know that its history began in the first book of the Bible? The Euphrates River flowed from the Garden of Eden. It is also mentioned in the last book of the Bible, the book of Revelation. The Euphrates River will continue to exist when Jesus comes back to earth some day.

Genesis 2:10–14
Revelation 16:12

EUTYCHUS. ———

Eutychus fell asleep while the apostle Paul was preaching. He was sitting in a window, and he fell three stories to the ground. He was picked up, dead, but Paul put his arms around Euty-

chus and said, "Don't worry! He's alive." Eutychus was indeed alive. His friends were happy, and later they took him home.

Acts 20:9–10 CEV
Acts 20:12

EVANGELIST. ———

A preacher of the Gospel. Evangelists spread the good news that Jesus died so we might have eternal life. The New Testament calls Philip an evangelist.

John 3:16
Acts 21:8

EVE. ———

The first woman on earth. Eve is sometimes called the mother of the human race. God made her from one of Adam's ribs. Adam was the first man on earth. God made Eve so Adam wouldn't be lonely. Adam and Eve lived in a garden called Eden. They had no worries. God gave them everything they needed. He told them they could eat the fruit from all of the trees except one—the tree of the knowledge of good and evil. One day, a talking snake showed up in the garden. It was Satan in disguise. He told Eve to eat the forbidden fruit. She did, and she also gave some to Adam. God was very angry that Eve and Adam had disobeyed. He took away all of the good things He had given them. God told them they would have to work hard for the rest of their lives. Then he sent them out of the garden forever.

Genesis 3:20
Genesis 2:21–22
Genesis 2:17
Genesis 3:1–6
Genesis 3:19
Genesis 3:23

Eve holds the "forbidden fruit." (The Bible never says it was an apple!)

Evil.

Bad stuff caused by Satan. Evil is the opposite of good. Satan is called the evil one. When someone trusts in God, Satan tries to take that trust away. Satan loves it if he can get people to turn from God. He will do his best to get you to do bad things. So watch out! The Bible says we shouldn't have anything to do with evil. Stay close to God and do only what is good. If you trust God, He will protect you from evil.

Matthew 13:19
1 Thessalonians 5:22
2 Thessalonians 3:3

Exodus, Book of.

An Old Testament book. Exodus is a history book about the Hebrew people. It tells how they were led out of slavery in Egypt and survived in the wilderness. Many well-known Bible stories come from Exodus. There's a talking bush in Exodus. Exodus 7–12 tells about the ten plagues—terrible things that happened to the Egyptians. In these chapters, you'll read about frogs, locusts, and flies invading the land. You'll learn about Moses making a path through the middle of a sea! There's even a story about a kind of bread—manna—that settled on the ground like dew. And in Exodus 20, you can read about the Ten Commandments.

Exodus 3
Exodus 14
Exodus 16

Ezekiel.

Ezekiel was a priest and a prophet. God allowed him to "see" things that would happen in the future. He wrote the Old Testament book called Ezekiel. His book predicted things that were to come. Most of Ezekiel's predictions were about Israel and the Jewish people. Some of his predictions have not yet come true. They are about the end-times when Jesus will come back to earth.

Ezekiel 1:3

Ezra.

Ezra was a priest and a scribe. Scribes wrote everything—from the king's simple orders to whole books. They also practiced law. Ezra wrote the book of Ezra that is part of the Old Testament. His book is about events in ancient Jerusalem. It tells about the lives of the Jewish people after they were held as slaves in Babylonia and Persia. During Ezra's time, the Jews returned to worshipping God and the temple in Jerusalem was rebuilt.

Ezra 7:6
Ezra 7:10

The people of Israel leave Egypt in a huge escape called "the exodus."

51

FABLE.

A story that teaches a lesson. In some fables, animals and things behave like people. You can read a Bible fable about talking trees in Judges 9:7–15.

FAITH.

Confidence in something you've been told. Faith is another word for trust. When you trust someone, you are absolutely sure that you can depend on him or her. Faith means believing in God even though you can't see Him. He's like the air you breathe. You can't see it, but you know by faith that it's there. Jesus said that anything is possible by putting your faith in God. There is one thing that we can surely have faith in: Jesus was sent by God to save us from our sins. If we have faith in Him our souls will not die. Instead, we will live forever with God.

Hebrews 11:1
Mark 9:23
John 3:16

FAITHFULNESS.

God's never-ending love for us. The Bible says, "God's love can always be trusted, and his faithfulness lasts as long as the heavens." "No one is as loving and faithful" as God. His faithfulness gives us strength. It protects us from evil. If we tell God about our sins, He will be faithful and forgive us. God's faithfulness is so great that it reaches to the skies.

Psalm 89:2 CEV
Psalm 89:8 CEV
2 Thessalonians 3:3
1 John 1:9
Psalm 108:4 NIV

FALL OF MAN.

When Adam and Eve made a huge mistake by disobeying God. Adam and Eve were the first people on earth. God made them, and they had everything they needed—no worries. God gave them just one rule to obey. They could not eat fruit from one special tree in the garden. Adam and Eve knew only good things, and if they ate the fruit, they would know the difference between good and evil. The fall of man—the big mistake—came when a talking snake got Eve to taste the fruit. Eve gave some to Adam. After they ate it, they knew all about good and evil. That snake was Satan. He tricked Adam and Eve into disobeying God. God sent Adam and Eve out of the garden forever. Since then, all humans know good from evil. They have a choice to obey or disobey God. When you disobey, you sin. There is not one person on earth who has not disobeyed.

Genesis 3
Romans 3:23

FALSE PROPHET.

A liar. A false prophet says that a message is from God when it's not. If a person says God gave him or her a message, and that message leads you away from God or what His Word says, that person is a false prophet. The Bible says that many false prophets are in the world. We need to watch out for them.

1 John 4:1
Matthew 24:4, 24

FALSE WITNESS.

A lie. "Do not tell lies about others." That is one of God's Ten Commandments. When you are a false witness, you are saying something that is untrue.

Exodus 20:16 CEV

FAMILY.

A group of people related to one another. Who are your family members? Your parents? Brothers and sisters? Aunts? Uncles? Grandparents? Cousins? If you believe in Jesus, you have another family: the family of believers. As members of Jesus' family, you should do good to all people, especially those who believe in Him.

Galatians 6:10

FAMINE.

No food for a long time. A famine happens when there is no food supply. When the Israelites were in the Desert of Sin, they were starving until God made manna appear on the ground. There were several famines in Bible times. Some were caused when there wasn't enough rain. Others were caused by hailstorms, insects, and enemies.

Exodus 16:4
Exodus 9:23
Exodus 10:15
Deuteronomy 28:49–51

FAST.

Not eating or drinking for a while. Fasting was very common in Bible times. People still fast today. It is one way to be close to God. Leaders in Bible times ordered people to fast. Jesus fasted. He taught that when you fast, you should do it in secret. In other words, it should be a quiet time shared between you and God. You should not fast if you are sick or if it causes you to lose too much weight.

Ezra 8:21
Luke 4:1–4
Matthew 6:16–18

FATHER.

A name for God. You have an earthly father and a heavenly Father. Your earthly father is your dad. He is the head of your household. Your heavenly Father is God. He is your dad's heavenly Father, too. In fact, God is the Father of us all.

When Jesus taught people to pray, His prayer began: "Our Father who is in heaven." The next time you pray, try using Jesus' words to begin your prayer. Say, "Dear Father," instead of "Dear God."

Deuteronomy 26:7
Ephesians 4:6
Matthew 6:9 NASB

FEAR.

Being afraid. Everyone feels afraid sometimes. When you feel afraid, there's help. The Bible says if you pray to God and trust Him, He will give you peace. When you feel afraid, you can count on Jesus. He will make you strong. The Bible reminds us that we should fear God. That means we should have respect for Him and His commandments.

Philippians 4:6–7
Philippians 4:13
Ecclesiastes 12:13

FEAST.

A big party or festival. Feasts marked great events in Jewish history. In Bible times, the Jews celebrated several major festivals. One of the most well-known is the feast of unleavened bread.

Exodus 12:17

Men enjoy a feast in the modern middle east.

FELLOWSHIP.

Get-togethers with other people who believe in Jesus Christ. Shortly after Jesus ascended into heaven, believers ate together and prayed. Today, people have fellowship in their churches and Sunday schools. Just like the disciples of long ago, people today come together to learn about Jesus and worship God.

Acts 2:42

FIG.

The pear-shaped fruit of the fig tree. In Bible times, a fig tree was a symbol that a person was rich. Figs were dried or pressed into cakes.

1 Kings 4:25
1 Samuel 25:18

FIRE.

Something burning. Fire in the Bible often showed the power of God. He spoke to Moses through a fiery bush. A chariot and horses made of fire came down from heaven and took Elijah away.

Exodus 3
2 Kings 2:11

FIRMAMENT.

The sky. *Firmament* is an Old Testament word for the heavens, or the sky above the earth.

Genesis 1:6–8 KJV

FIRSTBORN.

The oldest kid in a family. In Bible times the firstborn son had a special position in the family.

a b c d e F g h i j k l m n o p q r s t u v w x y z

The firstborn son would become the leader of the family when the father died. In Old Testament times, a young man named Esau did a very dumb thing. He was the oldest boy in his family, and he sold his birthright to his younger brother, Jacob. All he got for it was a single bowl of stew!

Genesis 49:3
Genesis 25:29–34

FIRSTFRUITS. —————
The first and best of a person's crop or livestock. In Bible times, people gave their best to God. It was a sacrifice—something that they loved or wanted to keep. Often, a sacrifice was the best animal that a person owned. The very best was known as the "first of the firstfruits."

Exodus 23:19 KJV

FLEECE. —————
Wool that grows on a sheep. Gideon used a fleece to test God. He wanted to make sure that the real God was telling him what to do.

Judges 6:37–40

FLESH. —————
A word that stands for the human body and the sinful desires we have as humans. God created our bodies. He gave Jesus a human body so He could live among the people on earth. The Bible says, "The Word became flesh." It means that God became a living, breathing human being in the body of Jesus Christ.

Have you heard the saying "flesh and blood"? You will find it in the Bible. Flesh and blood means all of the people born into your family. In the spiritual sense, "the flesh" is the part of us that wants to do wrong.

Ezekiel 37:6
John 1:14
2 Samuel 19:12
1 John 2:16

FLOCK. —————
A group of sheep or birds. On the night Jesus was born, shepherds were watching their flocks of sheep. A flock is also a group of people who believe in Jesus. Jesus called his followers "sheep" and Himself the Shepherd. The apostle Paul told his helpers to watch over the flock—those who believe in Jesus. He said that "wolves"—evil people—would come along and try to hurt the flock.

Genesis 4:4
Luke 2:8
John 10:16
Acts 20:28–29

FLOOD, THE. —————
God's do-over in the time of Noah. After Adam and Eve sinned in the Garden of Eden, people got bad really fast. God decided to wipe out the whole earth with a gigantic flood. Only Noah, seven members of his family, and pairs of certain animals survived in a giant boat Noah built (the ark). When the flood went away—about a year later—the people and animals were to start over and refill the earth with life. God

told Noah He would never flood the earth again. God sealed that promise with a rainbow.

Genesis 6–9
Genesis 9:13–17

FOAL. —————
A colt or young donkey. Jesus rode into Jerusalem on a donkey colt. We remember that day as Palm Sunday.

Mark 11:1–11

FOOLISH. —————
Using poor judgment. Foolish is the opposite of wise. The Old Testament book called Proverbs says a lot about being foolish and wise. For example: "Foolish talk will get you into a lot of trouble"; "Children with good sense make their parents happy, but foolish children make them sad"; "Anyone with good sense is eager to learn more, but fools are hungry for foolishness."

Proverbs 18:6 CEV
Proverbs 10:1 CEV
Proverbs 15:14 CEV

Peter doesn't want Jesus to act like a servant—but finally allows the Lord to wash his feet (John 13).

FOOT-WASHING. —————
Washing the feet of guests in your home. In Bible times, people

Furnace

washed their visitors' feet. Feet got really dirty on the dry, dusty lands of the Bible. Foot-washing was a way of saying, "Welcome to our home." Servants usually did the foot-washing. Jesus washed His disciples' feet to teach them a lesson. He taught them not to think they are better than anyone else.

john 13:1–17

FORBEARANCE.
Patience and self-control. Forbearance, or patience, helps us improve our faith in God. The apostle Peter said, "Do your best to improve your faith. You can do this by adding goodness, understanding, self-control, patience, devotion to God, concern for others, and love."

2 Peter 1:5–7 CEV

FORERUNNER.
Someone who goes ahead to get things ready. Imagine that you are in church for a family member's baptism. Your grandma leaves right after church to get things ready for a baptism party. She is the forerunner. She goes to get things ready. John the Baptist was a forerunner for Jesus. He told people that the powerful one named Jesus was coming.

Matthew 3:11–12

FORGIVENESS.
Overlooking the wrong another person has done. Forgiveness is hard sometimes, especially if someone has done a very bad

thing. Jesus said if we forgive others for the bad things they do, God will forgive us for the bad things we do. Everyone does bad stuff. That's why Jesus came to earth. He took the punishment for our sins. When you pray, ask God to forgive you. Then ask Him to help you to forgive others.

Matthew 6:14–15
Romans 3:23
Acts 10:43
Matthew 6:12

Jesus forgives a woman caught in sin (John 8:1–11).

FOUNDATION.
The strong base that a building sits on. In the beginning of time, God laid the foundations of the earth. His foundations are so strong that they can never be moved. The apostle Paul said that Jesus is the foundation for all believers. You can read what Jesus said about wise and foolish builders in Luke 6:46–49.

Psalm 102:25
Psalm 104:5
1 Corinthians 3:11

FOUNTAIN.
A source of fresh, flowing water, like a spring. Fountain also means God's blessings upon His people.

Deuteronomy 8:7 KJV
Jeremiah 2:13 KJV

FRANKINCENSE.
Something that smells good when it's burned. Frankincense is the yellowish gum of a tree. It was a gift that the wise men brought to the baby Jesus.

Matthew 2:1–2, 11

FRUITFULNESS.
Making a lot of something. When something is fruitful, it increases in its amount. When God created animals, He blessed them and told them to be fruitful and multiply—to live everywhere on earth. The apostle Paul said that we should be fruitful in our good works and in increasing our knowledge of God. That means we should do many good things and keep on learning about God.

Genesis 1:20–23
Colossians 1:9–11

FURNACE.
In Bible times, an oven used for cooking or making bricks. A furnace was also called "a smoking firepot." Shadrach, Meshach, and Abednego were thrown into a fiery furnace and lived! Read about it in Daniel 3.

Genesis 15:17 NIV

55

G

b
c
d
e
f
g
h
i
j
k
l
m
n
o
p
q
r
s
t
u
v
w
x
y
z

GABRIEL. —————

A very important angel. Gabriel brought messages from God. He's appeared only a few times. The prophet Daniel saw him twice. Daniel had dreams that he couldn't understand. So Gabriel helped him understand his dreams. Gabriel appeared to Zechariah, too. He told him that his son would grow up to be John the Baptist. He also appeared to Mary, Jesus' mom. He said that her baby was Jesus, the Son of God.

> Daniel 8:15–17
> Daniel 9:21–24
> Luke 1:11–19
> Luke 1:26–45

GAD. —————

Jacob's seventh son. Gad's descendants were called the Gadites. They were a fierce tribe that lived east of the Jordan River.

> Genesis 30:10–11
> Joshua 13:24–28

GALATIANS, LETTER TO THE. —————

A New Testament book. Galatians is Paul's letter to the churches at Galatia. Galatia was a region in the Roman Empire. The people who lived there were called Galatians. In his letter, Paul tells how he became an apostle. He also says that we will live forever in heaven because of our faith in God. Paul told the Galatians to stay away from evil things like wild parties and worshipping false gods. He said we should have a Godlike spirit. We should be loving, happy, peaceful, patient, kind, good, faithful, gentle, and self-controlled.

> Galatians 1:13–24
> Galatians 3–4
> Galatians 5:19–23

GALILEE. —————

A region in northern Israel. The prophet Isaiah said that the Prince of Peace, Jesus, would bring glory to Galilee. And that is where Jesus spent most of His life. Many of His miracles happened there. After He rose from the dead, Jesus went to Galilee. There, His disciples saw Him alive again. The Sea of Galilee is in this region, too. Some of Jesus' disciples were fishermen who worked on the sea. One day, a terrible storm came over the sea. Jesus and His disciples were out in a boat. Jesus told the storm to stop. And it obeyed Him! (Find out more by reading Mark 4:35–41).

> Isaiah 9:1
> Matthew 15:29
> Matthew 28:16–20
> Matthew 4:18–19

GALL. —————

A bitter, poisonous herb. Gall was used as a drug to kill pain. When Jesus was on the cross, He was offered a drink containing gall.

> Matthew 27:34

GALLOWS. —————

A tower on which criminals are hanged. The gallows played an important role in the life of Haman, an evil man who planned to kill all the Jews. When his plan was discovered, he was hanged on the gallows. What's especially interesting is that Haman died on a gallows he himself had ordered built for the Jewish man Mordecai!

> Esther 3:5–6
> Esther 7:9–10

GARDEN OF EDEN. —————

Adam's and Eve's first home. God created this place for Adam and Eve to live in. A river flowed through the garden. It split into four other rivers: the Pishon and Gihon (which no longer exist) and the Tigris and Euphrates. The garden had many trees full of tasty fruit. But there was one tree Adam and Eve could not eat from— the "tree of the knowledge of good and evil." God commanded

Adam and Eve not to eat its fruit. Adam and Eve had everything they needed in this place. But they had to move out. They broke God's rule and ate fruit from the forbidden tree, bringing sin and death into the world. God made them leave the garden forever. (Read all about it in Genesis 3.)

Genesis 2:9
Genesis 2:16–17
Romans 5:12

Healthy plants and peaceful animals filled the Garden of Eden.

a
b
c
d
e
f
G
h
i
j
k
l
m
n
o
p
q
r
s
t
u
v
w
x
y
z

GATH. ————

Hometown of the giant Goliath. Gath was a city of the Philistines that was captured by David.

1 Chronicles 18:1

GAZA. ————

A Philistine city near the Mediterranean Sea. Samson died in Gaza after he destroyed the temple of the false god Dagon. Gaza still exists. You might see or read about it in the news.

Judges 16:21–30

GEHAZI. ————

Elisha's servant. Gehazi got sick with leprosy because he was dishonest and greedy. Leprosy was a terrible skin disease.

2 Kings 5

GENEALOGY. ————

A record of a person's family line (see Genesis 5:1 and 1 Chronicles 1:8). Jesus' genealogy is found in the books of Matthew (1:1–16) and Luke (3:23–38). Genealogy records were important to the Jewish people. They were proof of who was next in line to be a tribe leader, king, or priest. They also proved who had the right to take a person's belongings when he or she died.

GENERAL EPISTLES. ————

Letters to all Christians. Many books of the New Testament are letters called epistles. For example, Galatians was Paul's epistle to specific churches in Galatia. Some letters, or epistles, are addressed to all Christians. The general epistles are Hebrews; James; 1 and 2 Peter; 1, 2, and 3 John; and Jude. The general epistles are sometimes called the catholic (meaning "universal") epistles.

GENERATION. ————

A group of people who are around the same age. Your grandparents make up one generation. Your parents make up another genera-tion. You and your siblings are a generation, too. The Old Testament is about many generations of people. Take a look at Genesis 5. It lists some of the generations that followed Adam, the first man on earth.

Here are five generations: A baby, its mother, grandmother, great-grandmother, and great-great-grandmother.

GENESIS, BOOK OF. ————

The first book in the Bible. In the beginning, before there was earth or sky or anything else, there was only God. Can you imagine? From nothing, God created everything! Genesis tells about God's creations. In this interesting book, you'll learn about the first people on earth and

a
b
c
d
e
f
G
h
i
j
k
l
m
n
o
p
q
r
s
t
u
v
w
x
y
z

Noah and the great flood. You'll read about the Tower of Babel, where God changed the people's language so they couldn't understand each other. Genesis tells about several important Bible characters, too: Abraham, Isaac, Jacob, and Joseph.

Genesis 1
Genesis 2–3
Genesis 6–9
Genesis 11:1–9
Genesis 11–21
Genesis 25–50

GENTILES.

People who are not of the Jewish race. In Bible times, Jews looked down on Gentiles. Gentiles were thought of as unclean. In other words, "not good enough." In fact, it was against the law for a Jew to even visit a Gentile. Jesus changed all that. He died and then rose from the dead so that everyone could believe in Him and be forgiven for their sins. When the Gentiles heard that Jesus died for their sins, too, they were very glad.

Acts 10:28
Galatians 3:28
Acts 13:46–48

GETHSEMANE.

A garden outside of Jerusalem. The Garden of Gethsemane is a famous place near the Mount of Olives. It is where Jesus prayed the night He was arrested. Earlier that evening, Jesus ate supper with His disciples. Then they went to the Mount of Olives. Jesus told them He was about to be arrested

and killed. He went into the Garden of Gethsemane to pray. Jesus was very sad. He said to God, "My Father, if it is possible, don't make me suffer by having me drink from this cup. But do what you want, and not what I want." "Having me drink from this cup" means "having me do this difficult thing." A short time later, Jesus was arrested and taken away.

Matthew 26:30
Mark 14:33–34
Matthew 26:39 CEV
John 18:1–12

GIANT.

A very, very tall person. The most famous giant in the Bible is Goliath. He was more than nine feet tall and very mean. A boy named David killed him, using just a slingshot and a stone. Other giants found in the Bible are the Anakims, the Emims, and the Zamzummims.

1 Samuel 17:4, 44
1 Samuel 17:48–50
Deuteronomy 2:10–11
Deuteronomy 2:20

GIDEON.

A faithful hero. Gideon was a leader in Israel. God called him to fight the powerful Midianite army. The Midianites were punishing the Israelites for doing bad things. But God wanted it to stop. One night, Gideon and his servants sneaked into the enemy's territory. The Midianites had built an altar to the false god Baal. So Gideon destroyed the altar to Baal and built

an altar to God. That made the Midianites mad. They came after Gideon with a huge army, "thick as locusts." Gideon's army had only 300 men. With God's help, Gideon's tiny army defeated the Midianites! It was a huge victory that was remembered for many years.

Hebrews 11:32–34
Judges 6:14–16
Judges 6:1
Judges 6:25–27
Judges 7:12 NIV
Judges 7:16–25

Not quite as tall as the Bible's Goliath, Robert Wadlow measures 8 feet, 8½ inches in this photo.

GILEAD.

A hill east of the Jordan River. Gilead overlooked the plain where Gideon organized his army to fight the Midianites.

Judges 7:2–5

GILGAL.

Site of an important monument, not far from Jericho. Gilgal is where the Hebrews built a monument out of stones. It was to be a reminder of how God dried up the river so that Joshua and the Israelites could cross the Jordan on dry ground.

Joshua 4:19–24

GLEANING.

Gathering leftover grain. The Bible tells about pickers who went into fields to harvest grain. Poor people were allowed to follow them and collect the leftovers. This was called gleaning. In the Bible, there is a story about a woman named Ruth. She gleaned barley and wheat from a field that belonged to a man named Boaz.

Leviticus 19:9–10
Ruth 2

GLORY.

Excellence! Glory is the excellence of God and His goodness. The Bible tells about the glory of the Lord. Sometimes it can be seen moving. Another example: On the night Jesus was born, the glory of the Lord showed up all around the shepherds in the field. The shepherds were afraid. Then, an angel of the Lord appeared. The angel said to them, "Do not be afraid. I bring you good news of great joy that will be for all the people. Today in the town of David a Savior has

been born to you; he is Christ the Lord."

Exodus 33:18–19
Ezekiel 11:23
Luke 2:8–11 NIV

GLUTTONY.

Eating or drinking too much of anything. If you ate your whole birthday cake, that would be gluttony. In Bible times, kings and other leaders had feasts with all sorts of wonderful food. A person who ate too much was called a glutton. The Bible warns about overeating. Proverbs 23:1–3 says that we shouldn't stuff ourselves with food. Eating too much is greedy.

Deuteronomy 21:20

GOAD.

A sharp, pointed stick used to lead oxen. Shamgar, a judge of Israel, used a goad as a weapon against the Philistines.

1 Samuel 13:21
Judges 3:31

GOD.

The creator and ruler of the universe. God is the most extreme superhero. He can do anything and everything. God is our heavenly Father. He knows all our weaknesses, thoughts, and words. God also knows our actions and our needs. He is so great that He is everywhere at the same time. He is more powerful than anything else. He is forgiving, wise, and truthful. God loves us so much that He sent

His Son Jesus to earth to save us from our sins. God promised that if we believe in Jesus, our souls will live forever with Him. You can know God by having faith in Jesus and by doing what God wants you to do. The Bible tells us all about God and what we need to do to please Him.

Isaiah 40:28
Isaiah 40:18
Jeremiah 32:17
Matthew 6:9
Psalm 103:14
Psalm 44:21
Psalm 139:2,4
Matthew 6:32
Jeremiah 23:23–24
Revelation 19:6
Psalm 136
Colossians 2:2–3
Titus 1:2
John 3:16
John 14:1, 6
Mark 3:35

GODDESS.

A female false god or idol. In Bible times, Egypt, Greece, and Rome worshipped goddesses. The First Commandment warns that worshipping gods and goddesses is wrong. Idol worship makes God angry.

Exodus 20:3

GODLINESS.

Behavior that pleases God. Jesus wanted to please His heavenly Father. We should try to please Him, too. You can learn to be godly by setting a good Christian example for others and by studying the Bible. Godliness takes hard work. It's a lot like exercise and staying

in shape. Living to please God isn't always easy—especially since Satan will work just as hard to get you to do bad things.

john 8:29
Galatians 1:10
1 Timothy 4:12–13
1 Timothy 4:7–9

GOLD.

An expensive metal used to make coins, jewelry, and many other things. Solomon's temple had a lot of gold in it. The three wise men brought gold to the baby Jesus. People often want expensive things. But the apostle Peter said that our faith in Jesus is worth more than gold. Things can be destroyed. The gift of eternal life cannot. Faith in Jesus allows us to live forever with God. And that's worth far more than gold.

1 Kings 7:48–50
Matthew 2:11
1 Peter 1:7
1 Peter 1:18

GOLDEN CALF.

An idol Aaron made. In Bible times, people created false gods and worshipped them. This made the real God angry. There is a well-known Bible story about Moses' brother, Aaron, making a false god. He was waiting with the Israelites while Moses was in the mountains with God. When Moses was gone too long, the people lost faith in Moses and in God. They asked Aaron to make a god to lead them. Aaron made a golden calf out of the Israelites' earrings. The people bowed down and worshipped the statue. When God saw it, He was very angry. You can read the whole story of Aaron and the golden calf in Exodus 32.

GOLGOTHA.

The place where Jesus was crucified. Golgotha is a hill that is just outside the walls of ancient Jerusalem. It is sometimes called Calvary or "The place of a skull." On this hill, the greatest event of all time took place. This is where Jesus died on the cross. Before He was crucified at Golgotha, Jesus promised that He would not stay dead. He said that after a few days, He would rise again. It happened! Jesus came back to life again, and we celebrate this event every year at Easter.

john 19:16–17
Luke 23:33
Mark 15:22 KJV
Matthew 16:21
john 20

GOLIATH.

A giant more than nine feet tall. Goliath was a Philistine warrior from the city of Gath. He fought in the Philistine army in a great war with the Israelites. Every day, Goliath dared the Israelites to choose a soldier to fight him one-on-one. Goliath looked scary. "He wore a bronze helmet and had bronze armor to protect his chest and legs. The chest armor alone weighed about one hundred twenty-five pounds. He carried a bronze sword strapped on his back, and his spear was

Israelites party around an idol—the Golden Calf in this classic painting. God was not pleased!

a b c d e f G h i j k l m n o p q r s t u v w x y z

Gigantic, armored Goliath is no match for teenager David, who has God on his side.

so big that the iron spearhead alone weighed more than fifteen pounds." The Israelite soldiers were too afraid to fight Goliath. Then a brave young shepherd boy decided to give it a try. His name was David, and he trusted God. With just a slingshot and a stone, David killed the giant warrior. You can read the story of David and Goliath in 1 Samuel 17.

1 Samuel 17:5–7 CEV

GOMER.

The prophet Hosea's wife. Gomer did not understand how blessed she was to have a loving husband and kids. She left them to live on her own. Gomer's life took a turn for the worse. She did bad things and was sold as a slave. Hosea still loved her and wanted her back. So God told him to go find Gomer and buy her back out of her slavery. What Hosea did was a picture of what God did for his "wife," the people of Israel.

GOODNESS.

Acting in a clean, well-mannered way. Is your language clean, and do you try to do what's right? Followers of Jesus Christ should try to act as He would, to be full of His goodness. The earth is full of God's goodness. True goodness is a gift from God.

Ephesians 5:1
Galatians 5:22
Psalm 33:5
Psalm 31:19

GOSHEN.

An area of Egypt where the Israelites lived. Goshen is in the Nile delta where the Nile River empties into the Mediterranean Sea. The Israelites lived there for over 400 years. Moses led them out of the land of Goshen and to the Promised Land.

Genesis 45:10

GOSPEL.

Christ's good news. Have you heard the good news? Jesus died so you can live forever! This "good news" is called the gospel. God sent His Son, Jesus, into the world to live among the people. While He was here, Jesus taught about God. Jesus knew that His earthly life would be short. He knew He would die on a cross and three days later rise up from the dead. That's exactly what happened. Jesus suffered the pain of death so all believers would be forgiven for their sins. He promised that whoever believes in Him will not die, but will live forever with God. So spread the good news! Tell your friends about Jesus. Ask them to believe.

Mark 1:15
Luke 24:3–8
John 3:16

GOSPELS, THE.

The first four books of the New Testament. The four Gospels are the books of Matthew, Mark, Luke, and John. Each one tells about the life and ministry of Jesus. The books are different because they are told from each author's point of view. If you read all four, you will have a good idea of what Jesus is like. If you want to learn about Jesus, the Gospels are the best place to start.

GOSSIP.

To talk about people behind their backs. Gossiping is telling stories about people. It is spreading rumors and repeating so-called secrets. The Bible warns about saying things that you know you shouldn't. The book of Proverbs says, "Gossip is no good! It causes hard feelings and comes between friends."

Proverbs 11:13
1 Timothy 5:13
Proverbs 16:28 CEV

GOVERNMENT.

Those who have power over the people. In the United States, this includes leaders like the president, members of Congress,

a
b
c
d
e
f
G
h
i
j
k
l
m
n
o
p
q
r
s
t
u
v
w
x
y
z

a
b
c
d
e
f
G
h
i
j
k
l
m
n
o
p
q
r
s
t
u
v
w
x
y
z

senators, and state and local leaders. Christians should have respect for their governments. They should pay taxes. Everyone should pray for their leaders. If a government forces you to do something that is clearly against God's commands, you have the right to say "no."

Romans 13:1
Romans 13:6–7
1 Timothy 2:2
Acts 5:28–29

GRACE. ─────────

God's favor that we don't deserve. Our sins offend God. But grace is given to those who believe in Jesus. There is no way humans can be perfect like God. Everyone sins. After Adam and Eve disobeyed God, humans were punished for their sins. In the Old Testament, people had to sacrifice animals to get right with God. Jesus changed that. He died on the cross. He took the blame for the bad things we do. If we believe in Jesus, by the grace of God we are saved. That means, after we die, our souls will live forever with God. Grace is a gift from God. Although Jesus took our punishment, God still wants us to obey His rules and live good Christian lives.

Titus 2:11
1 John 1:8
Romans 4:25
Ephesians 2:4–9
Romans 6:1–2

GRAVEN IMAGE. ─────────

A statue or picture of a false god. False gods are also called idols. People who do not know the real God, or who have wandered away from Him, sometimes worship idols. They make graven images of made-up gods and pray to them. (Read Exodus 32.) God hates idol worship. His second commandment warns against it.

Exodus 20:4–6

GREED. ─────────

Wanting a lot more stuff. When your mind is set on getting a bunch of stuff, Satan will work on you. He will try to get you to put your faith in things instead of God. Jesus warned against greed. He said a good Christian life is not built on things. It is built on setting your mind on God.

1 Timothy 6:7–10
Luke 12:15
1 Peter 5:2

GREEKS. ─────────

People from Greece, a small country in southeastern Europe. It is a very old nation. Athens is its biggest city. The apostle Paul visited Athens. He found many false gods there. He preached and argued with the Greek people about the danger of worshipping idols.

Acts 17:16–17

GUILE. ─────────

Sneaky behavior. Guile is trickery. God does not like it. Often guile includes lying. The Bible says the Lord blesses those who don't practice sneaky behavior. Jesus used a man named Nathanael as an example of honesty and truthfulness. Nathanael had no guile.

Psalm 34:13
Psalm 32:2
John 1:47

GUILT. ─────────

Feeling sorry when you do something wrong. When you hear that little voice in your head that says, "I shouldn't have done that," that's guilt. Doing what you know is wrong is sin. Christians should try their very best not to do what is wrong. When you feel guilty, remember Jesus took the punishment for your sins when He died on the cross. Pray to God, and tell Him what you did wrong. Ask His forgiveness. God will always forgive Christians when they admit they've done wrong.

2 Samuel 24:10
1 Peter 3:18
1 John 1:9

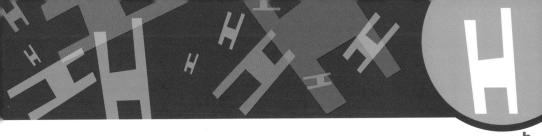

HABAKKUK, BOOK OF. ————

An Old Testament book named for the prophet who wrote it. Habakkuk wondered why the Babylonians got away with worshipping idols. They did other bad things, too. God explained it was part of His great plan. Habakkuk's book shows that God always hears our prayers. He might not answer the way we expect Him to. But He listens.

Habakkuk 1:2–4
Habakkuk 1:1
Habakkuk 1:12

HADES. ————

Another name for hell. Hades is a Greek word. It means "unseen underworld." It also means "place of the dead." The Bible says Hades will be thrown into the lake of fire as part of "the second death."

Revelation 20:14 NIV

HAGAR. ————

A slave owned by Abraham's wife, Sarah. After her son Ishmael was born, Hagar and Sarah did not get along. So Abraham sent Hagar and her little boy away. All they had with them was bread and water. When the water ran out, Ishmael started to cry. God heard him. He showed Hagar a well where she could get more water. After that, God stayed with Hagar and Ishmael and took care of them. (Read all about it in Genesis 21:15–20.)

Genesis 16:1
Genesis 21:14

HAGGAI, BOOK OF. ————

An Old Testament book named for the prophet who wrote it. For years, the Babylonians and Persians held the Jews as slaves. When the Israelites finally returned to their homeland, God spoke to them through Haggai. He told them to finish rebuilding the temple in Jerusalem. He reminded them to stay faithful to Him in bad times.

Haggai 1:8, 14–15
Haggai 2:19

HAIR. ————

The fluffy stuff on your head. Jesus said that God knows everything about everybody. He even knows how many hairs you have on your head. Would you want to count all those hairs?

Matthew 10:30

HAM. ————

Noah's youngest son. Ham had four sons. They had kids and their kids had kids. And, after a while, the peoples of Canaan, Africa, Egypt, and Arabia could all say they came from Ham.

Genesis 5:32
Genesis 10:6

HAMAN. ————

A shifty aide to the Persian king. Haman planned to kill a good man named Mordecai and all of Mordecai's people—the Jews. Queen Esther, who just happened to be Mordecai's cousin, stopped Haman. In the end, Haman was hanged on the gallows he'd had built for Mordecai.

Esther 3:1
Esther 9:25

b
c
d
e
f
g
h
i
j
k
l
m
n
o
p
q
r
s
t
u
v
w
x
y
z

Talk about a twist! Haman honors his greatest enemy, Mordecai (on horse), at the king's command. (See the whole story in Esther 6:1–12.)

HANDBREADTH.

An ancient way of measuring things. A handbreadth was between three and four inches. It was about the width of the palm of a person's hand. Does the width of your palm equal a handbreadth?

Exodus 25:25

HANDKERCHIEF.

A small, square piece of cloth. A handkerchief is used to wipe a person's face or hands and, often, the nose! In Bible times, a handkerchief was used to cover a dead person's face.

Acts 19:12
John 20:7

HANGING.

A way to put criminals to death. In a hanging, a rope is put around a person's neck and the person is dropped through the floor of a gallows. Haman was hanged after he plotted to kill the Jews and Mordecai.

Esther 9:25

HANNAH.

Samuel's mom. Hannah asked God for a son. God said yes! Hannah promised God that her son would be faithful and serve Him. So Hannah allowed the priest Eli to raise Samuel in the tabernacle. That was where the people of Israel went to worship God. Hannah knew Eli would teach Samuel all about God. It was tough for Hannah to give up her son. But when she did, she said a beautiful prayer thanking God for His blessings.

1 Samuel 1
1 Samuel 2:1–10

HARAN.

An evil city in Mesopotamia. It was well-known as a place where people worshipped false gods called idols. Abraham lived there for a while until God told him to get out of there.

2 Kings 19:12
Genesis 12:4–5

HARDNESS OF HEART.

Stubbornness and not caring about how others feel. The pharaoh of Egypt had hardness of heart when he wouldn't free the Hebrew slaves. The Bible warns against having a hard heart. How's your heart? Is it soft or hard?

Exodus 9:35
Proverbs 28:14

HAREM.

In Bible times, it was common for a king to have a harem—many women. For example, Esther was one of the girls who belonged to the harem of the king of Persia. Later the king married her.

Esther 2:8

HARP.

A stringed musical instrument. Harps were often used for worshipping God. David played the harp. Do you have the gift of making music? Use it to praise the Lord.

Psalm 33:2
1 Samuel 16:23
Psalm 149:3

HARVEST.

Picking ripe fruits and vegetables. The word harvest has another meaning, too. Jesus said, "The harvest is plentiful, but the workers are few. Ask the Lord of the harvest, therefore, to send out workers into his harvest field." Jesus was talking to His disciples. He wanted them to go out and tell people about God. Those who were ready to hear about and believe in God were the "harvest." You can be a worker in God's big field. Get out there. Tell people that Jesus is awesome.

Luke 10:2 NIV
Mark 4:28–29

HATE.

The opposite of love. If you hate something, you don't like anything about it. Jesus taught that we shouldn't hate our enemies. Instead, we should love them. But there are some things that God hates—and we should, too. He hates "proud eyes, a lying tongue, and hands that kill those who aren't guilty. He also hates hearts that make evil plans, feet that are quick to do evil, any witness who pours out lies, and anyone who stirs up family fights."

Luke 6:27
Proverbs 6:17–19 NIRV

HEAL.

To make someone well again. God is the Great Healer. He can fix a broken body or a broken heart. Jesus raised lots of people. He even raised a twelve-year-old girl from the dead. Jesus' power came from God. God decides whether or not someone will be healed. Sometimes when people pray for healing, God says no. We don't know why that is, but we do know that God loves us. His decisions are always right.

Psalm 147:3
Matthew 4:24
Mark 5:35–43
Luke 5:17
Romans 8:38–39

Jesus heals a blind man by putting clay—dirt mixed with spit—on his eyes.

HEART.

The organ that pumps blood through our bodies. Heart also means our deepest feelings. The Hebrews believed that the heart is the center of life. They also believed that it rules our feelings. The heart even rules wisdom and skills. Have you heard someone say, "She spoke straight from her heart"? That means she spoke with truth and feeling. If God is in your heart, you will do and say good things. If evil is in your heart, it will lead to bad things. Guard your heart carefully. If you love God with all your heart, your heart will be right with God.

Deuteronomy 6:5
Genesis 42:28
Exodus 35:35 KJV
Matthew 15:18–19
Proverbs 4:23
Mark 12:30

HEATHEN.

People who don't know God. In Bible times, heathen also meant people who were not Jews.

1 Thessalonians 4:5
Ezekiel 22:15 KJV

HEAVEN.

God's home. Jesus said He was going to heaven to prepare a place for us. He promised to come back for us so we can be with Him always. Heaven is a wonderful place. It will be our great reward.

1 Kings 8:34
John 14:2–3
Matthew 5:12

HEAVENLY CITY.

Our forever home. Someday God will make an amazing city for all believers to live in. It will be called the New Jerusalem. Earth, as we know it, will be gone. Everything will be brand-new. Everyone who has ever believed in Jesus will live there. Would you like to take a peek at the heavenly city? Read Revelation 21:10–23.

Hebrews 11:16
Hebrews 12:22
Revelation 21:1–2

HEBREWS, LETTER TO THE.

A book in the New Testament. Hebrews is an epistle, or letter. It was written to a group of Jewish people. Its message is that Jesus changed the old ways of doing

a
b
c
d
e
f
g
H
i
j
k
l
m
n
o
p
q
r
s
t
u
v
w
x
y
z

things. In Old Testament times, people killed their best animals and offered them to God as sacrifices. It was their way of showing God that He was more important than anything else. The book of Hebrews says that Jesus was the last and best sacrifice. He gave up His life so we could be forgiven for our sins once and for all. Because of His sacrifice, Old Testament sacrifices are over. Now all that believers need to do is have faith in and follow Jesus, the One who saved us.

Hebrews 4–10
Hebrews 12–13

HEBRON. ────────────

A very old town in Israel. Hebron is southwest of Jerusalem and Bethlehem. In ancient days, it was called Kirjath-arba. This was the royal city where King David lived when he ruled over Judah. Abraham and Sarah lived there, too. It's where Sarah died. Many people believe the burial site of Abraham and his family still exists in Hebron. It's called the Tomb of the Patriarchs.

2 Samuel 2:3
2 Samuel 5:5
Genesis 23:2–6

HEIFER. ────────────

A young cow. In Old Testament times, heifers were killed and offered to God as sacrifices.

Genesis 15:9
1 Samuel 16:2

HELL. ────────────

Where unbelievers go when they die. Hell is the opposite of heaven. It's a terrible place. Another name for it is the Greek word *Hades* which means "unseen underworld" or "place of the dead." The Bible describes hell as a lake of fire. In hell, there is nothing but suffering. People there are shut away from God and His kindness. The only way not to go to hell is to believe in the Lord Jesus Christ. Do you believe in Him?

Revelation 19:20
2 Thessalonians 1:9
Luke 12:4–5
John 3:16

HELMET. ────────────

A protective hat. Like today's soldiers, ancient soldiers wore helmets. A helmet protects your head from getting hurt. The apostle Paul had another meaning for this word. He said our belief in Jesus is like a helmet. It protects us from evil.

1 Samuel 17:38
Ephesians 6:17

HELP MEET. ────────────

Another word for helper, companion, or mate. God created Eve as a help meet for Adam.

Genesis 2:18 KJV

Demons herd screaming souls into the fires of hell in a painting from the 1400s.

HERALD. ────────────

A messenger. A herald was sent by a leader to deliver a message or announce good news. See if you can find the answer to this question: In the Christmas carol "Hark! the Herald Angels Sing," what good news did the herald angels bring?

Daniel 3:4

HERB. ────────────

A plant used for healing or for seasoning food. Maybe your mom or someone you know cooks with herbs. The Israelites used bitter herbs with their bread at the first Passover meal.

Genesis 1:29
Exodus 12:8

HERDSMAN. ────────────

A shepherd. Herdsmen took care of sheep and other livestock. The prophet Amos was a herdsman.

Amos 7:14 KJV

HERESY.

Beliefs and teachings about God and the Bible that aren't true. The Bible says to honor your mother and father. You don't like that idea? You think it's okay with God to obey your mom and dad only when you want to? It's heresy when you twist what God said and make it into something that works for you. The Bible says there are a lot of people who teach untrue things about God. Watch out for them. Heresy is everywhere.

Exodus 20:12
2 Peter 2:1

HEROD.

A mean king. Herod the Great was king when Jesus was born. Three wise men were on their way to see baby Jesus. They decided to visit Herod first. They told him that a special baby was born in Bethlehem. The baby would grow up to be a great king. Herod hated that idea. He worried that Jesus would be greater than he. So Herod did an awful thing. He decided to kill all the Jewish baby boys in Bethlehem! He didn't know which one was Jesus, so he planned to kill them all. That way, Jesus would surely be among them. An angel of the Lord told Jesus' mom and dad to get him out of Bethlehem. The family hurried away to Egypt, and Jesus' life was saved.

Matthew 2:1-16

HEZEKIAH.

The tunneling king. Hezekiah was a king in Jerusalem. He was a godly man. He stopped his people from worshipping idols. He also took advice from God's prophet Isaiah. Hezekiah thought the Assyrian army might attack Jerusalem. Walls surrounded the city. The king worried that he and his people would be trapped inside. So Hezekiah made a plan: He dug a tunnel through solid rock. It led from Jerusalem to a spring outside. The tunnel carried water into the city. If they were trapped inside, there would be water to drink. It also left less water for the Assyrians to use.

Isaiah 38:1-8
2 Chronicles 32:30
2 Chronicles 32:2-4

HIGH PLACE.

Where false gods were worshipped. Some people didn't know the real God. So they worshipped statues of false gods called idols. The people went into high places, like hills or mountains, to worship. This made God really mad. He told His followers to destroy the high places and all the idols with them.

2 Kings 12:3
Numbers 33:52

HIGH PRIEST.

The leader of the priests. Throughout Bible history, many men served as high priests in Israel. Aaron, Moses' older brother, was the first one. When he died, his son Eleazar became the high priest. This went on from generation to generation. The high priests of Israel were all Aaron's ancestors. Jesus Christ is called the Great High Priest. He is the greatest because He is the Son of God and the One who died for our sins.

Exodus 28
Hebrews 4:14

The high priest's fancy clothes are shown (left) along with a regular priest's outfit.

a
b
c
d
e
f
g
H
i
j
k
l
m
n
o
p
q
r
s
t
u
v
w
x
y
z

HITTITES. —————
Ancient people who lived in the land that became Israel. The Hittites lived in Canaan at the time of Abraham. Abraham bought his burial tomb from Ephron, a Hittite.

Genesis 23:1–20

HOLY. —————
Set apart especially for God. God is holy. He expects His people to be holy, too. Jesus is the perfect example of holiness. He is called the Holy One of God. Nobody can be totally perfect like He is. In His whole life, Jesus never did anything wrong! You should try your best to be like Jesus.

Exodus 15:11
Romans 12:1
Mark 1:24
1 Peter 1:15–16

HOLY OF HOLIES. ——
A place deep inside the temple of God. The Holy of Holies held a very holy thing: the ark of the covenant. The ark was the gold-covered wooden chest containing the Ten Commandments. The high priest was the only one allowed in the Holy of Holies. He could enter just one time a year, on the Day of Atonement. This was a holy day when the Jewish people asked God's forgiveness for their sins. When the high priest went inside, he made a sacrifice for himself and for the sins of the people. To get to the Holy of Holies, the priest walked through the Holy Place, where lampstands, tables, and an altar of incense stood. Then he walked through the curtain or veil that separated the Holy Place from the Holy of Holies. The Holy of Holies was where the presence of the Lord gave His instructions for Israel.

1 Kings 8:1–11
Leviticus 16
Hebrews 9:2–7
Exodus 25:22

HOLY SPIRIT. —————
God's third "person." God is three persons in one: God the Father, Jesus the Son, and the Holy Spirit. The Holy Spirit's purpose is to help and support all the people who believe in God. After Jesus died and went up to heaven, He sent the Holy Spirit to be with His followers. The Holy Spirit is sometimes called the Helper. He helps us to understand what's in the Bible. He also helps us to praise God. The Comforter is another name for the Holy Spirit. He's called the Comforter because He will stay with us forever, especially in hard times (John 14:16). The Holy Spirit can also make non-believers feel guilty (John 16:8). He does it so they might believe in Jesus and be saved.

Matthew 28:19
John 14:12–27
Acts 2:1–21
1 Corinthians 2:13

HONEST. —————
Telling the truth. Being honest is playing fair in everything you do. An honest person does not lie or try to trick someone. God wants all believers to be honest. The Bible says: "Giving an honest answer is a sign of true friendship."

Proverbs 24:26 CEV

HONOR. —————
To show respect toward others. First, we should honor God. He gets our highest honor, or respect. Next, we should honor other people. One of the Ten Commandments says "honor your father and mother." That means you should show respect to your mom and dad all the time. Do you know who else you should you honor? If you said, "Everyone," you answered right. Christians should treat everyone with honor.

John 5:23
Exodus 20:12
1 Peter 2:17

HOPE. —————
To expect God to do exactly what He promises. God doesn't always give us what we ask for. But even when things seem hopeless, He wants us to have faith in Him. When God makes a promise, He will do exactly what He says. The Bible is filled with God's promises. We can hope for and expect strength in bad times. We can also hope for and expect God to give us what we need. One thing is for sure: We can hope for and expect to receive salvation. That

means if we believe in Jesus, we'll live forever with Him.

> Job 6:8
> Romans 4:18
> Isaiah 40:31
> 1 Timothy 6:17
> 1 Peter 1:3

HORNS OF THE ALTAR. —

Points that stick out from the corners of an altar. In Old Testament times, the blood of sacrificed animals was sprinkled on the horns of the altar.

> Exodus 27:1-2
> Exodus 29:12

HOSANNA. —————

A shout of praise to God. Hosanna means "save us now." This is what the crowd shouted when Jesus rode into Jerusalem on a young donkey. Today, we celebrate that day as Palm Sunday.

> Matthew 21:9

HOSEA, BOOK OF. ———

An Old Testament book named for the prophet who wrote it. Hosea preached to the northern kingdom of Israel. God told Hosea what to say to the people. He said that God would allow His people to be punished by their enemies for a while. Then God would save them from their punishment. The book of Hosea is about God's personality. He expects us to behave. When we don't, we will be punished. But then God will forgive us. He loves us, and He wants to save us from our sins.

> Hosea 4-14

HOSHEA. ——————

Joshua's birth name. When Joshua was born, he was given the name Hoshea. When Hoshea grew up, he was a soldier in the Israelite army. His commander, Moses, renamed him Joshua.

> Numbers 13:8
> Numbers 13:16

Crowds shout "Hosanna!" as they lead Jesus into Jerusalem.

HOSPITALITY. ————

Welcoming people into your home. If you invite a friend for a sleepover, you give him or her something to eat and a place to sleep. You show your friend a good time. That's hospitality! The Bible says that we should practice hospitality. Not only with our friends, but with people who are in need. Maybe you know someone at school who needs a friend. Ask your parents if you can invite that person over for some hospitality.

> Romans 12:13

HOST OF HEAVEN. ———

Beings who live with God. Imagine this: It is the first Christmas—the night Jesus was born. An angel appears to the shepherds and announces the good news. "And suddenly there was with the angel a multitude of the heavenly host praising God, and saying, Glory to God in the highest, and on earth peace, good will toward men." What an awesome night that was!

> Luke 2:13-14 KJV

HUMILITY. —————

Not having a prideful or stuck-up attitude. If you go around telling people how great you are, you are not practicing humility. Humility is when you are quiet about all the great things you can do. Everything you are and everything you own is a gift from

a b c d e f g H i j k l m n o p q r s t u v w x y z

69

a
b
c
d
e
f
g
H
i
j
k
l
m
n
o
p
q
r
s
t
u
v
w
x
y
z

God. He gets the credit for all the good stuff. Sometimes when an athlete or celebrity receives an award, you'll hear him or her thank God. That's humility. So instead of taking all the credit for yourself, spread it around.

Romans 12:3
1 Thessalonians 5:18

HUSBANDMAN.

A farmer who tills the land. Sometimes a husbandman worked on land owned by someone else. Then he was paid with a share of the crops (2 Timothy 2:6 KJV).

Genesis 9:20 KJV

HYMN.

A song of praise and thanksgiving to God. When you sing songs in church, you are singing hymns. Jesus and His disciples sang a hymn after they finished the Last Supper. Do you have a favorite hymn?

Ephesians 5:19
Mark 14:26

A butterfly lands on the flowers of a hyssop plant.

Theater masks were used by ancient Greek actors, called *hypokrites*—people who pretended to be something they weren't.

HYPOCRITE.

A person who pretends to be something he or she isn't. Jesus called the Pharisees hypocrites. The Pharisees did good deeds just to show off. They pretended to love God, but they didn't really know Him. When Christians do good deeds, they should be quiet about it. That way, God gets all the credit. And that makes Him happy.

Matthew 23:13
Matthew 6:2

HYSSOP.

A plant used to season food and make medicine. On the first Passover, hyssop was used to sprinkle blood on the doorposts of the Israelites' homes so that the angel of death would pass over. Hyssop was also used in burnt offerings. When Jesus was on the cross and thirsty, a sponge filled with vinegar was offered to Him on a hyssop branch.

Exodus 12:21–23
Numbers 19:6
John 19:28–30

I AM.

God's special name for Himself. God spoke to Moses through a burning bush. He called Himself "I Am." He said, "This is my name forever, the name by which I am to be remembered from generation to generation." God has always existed. He will exist forever. He is! Many people call Jesus "the great I Am." He used the words "I am" to describe Himself in the Gospel of John.

Exodus 3:14–15 NIV
Revelation 1:8
John 6:35; 8:12; 10:7; 10:11;
11:25; 14:6; 15:5

ICONIUM.

An ancient city in Asia Minor (modern-day Turkey). Paul and Barnabas went to Iconium on their first missionary journey. They taught the people about Jesus.

Acts 14:1

IDOL.

Anything worshipped that is not God. In Bible times, there was a lot of idol worship going on. Many people worshipped a false god named Baal. Often, idols were made from wood or metal. In Exodus 32, you can read about Aaron making a golden calf. The people bowed down and worshipped it. The first of God's Ten Commandments says: "You shall have no other gods before me." Idol worship is wrong. It makes God jealous and angry.

Romans 1:25
Numbers 25:3
Exodus 20:3 NIV
Psalm 78:58

IGNORANCE.

Not understanding or knowing about something. When the people crucified Jesus, they did not understand that He is the Son of God. Ignorance is no excuse for doing bad things. Even if you didn't mean it, you should apologize for your ignorance.

Luke 23:34
Acts 17:30–31

IMAGE OF GOD.

Something like God. When God made humans, He made them in His image. That means He created people—you, me, and everyone else—to be like Him. God wants us to be as perfect as we can be. The difference between God and us is that we sin. God doesn't. You can be more like God by learning about Jesus. Try your best to be like Him. That will please God. All Christians will be together in heaven one day. In heaven there is no sin. Someday we will be perfect like God meant us to be.

Genesis 1:27
Romans 3:10
1 John 3:5
Revelation 22:14–15
1 John 3:2

IMPARTIAL.

Not taking sides. Being impartial means being fair to everyone. Judges are impartial. They listen to both sides. Then they decide if someone is innocent or guilty. God is impartial, too. He wants everyone to follow Him and be forgiven for their sins.

Acts 10:34
2 Peter 3:9

IMPUTE.

To pass something from one person to another. When Adam and Eve sinned, they passed their sin on to us. Our sins were imputed —passed along—to Jesus. He took the blame for our sins. Jesus is excellent and good. He passes those qualities on to us. If we trust in Him, we are forgiven for our sins. Then, someday, we will live with Jesus in heaven. (Check out Romans 5:17–19.)

Romans 5:17
Isaiah 53:5–6

b
c
d
e
f
g
h
i
j
k
l
m
n
o
p
q
r
s
t
u
v
w
x
y
z

INCARNATION OF CHRIST. — Jesus as God living in a human body. God is three persons in one. He is God the Father, the Holy Spirit, and Jesus the Son. Jesus is part of God. He is perfect in every way. It was God's plan to send Jesus to earth to live as a human. This is known as the incarnation of Christ.

Luke 24:36–39
John 1:14

INCENSE. ————
A sweet perfume burned in worship ceremonies. In Old Testament times, priests burned incense on the altar in the tabernacle and the temple.

Exodus 30:7–8
2 Chronicles 29:11

INFIDEL. ————
Someone who does not believe in God. The Bible says that an infidel will be separated from God forever.

2 Thessalonians 1:8–9 KJV

INHERITANCE. ————
A gift passed from a father to his children. In Bible times, the oldest son was sometimes promised a special gift: When his father died, the son got a double portion of what his father owned. This was the son's inheritance. If a son behaved badly, his inheritance could be taken away. Reuben lost his inheritance for behaving badly. Esau traded his inheritance for a bowl of stew. All Christians are promised an inheritance. They are the adopted children of God. In heaven, they will receive all the good gifts that God has put away for them.

Deuteronomy 21:17
Genesis 25:29–34
Galatians 4:5–7
Ephesians 1:13–14

INIQUITY. ————
Sin, wickedness, or evil. Jesus taught that iniquity comes from deep inside of us. When our hearts are not right with God, we sin. Jesus rescues us from iniquity (Isaiah 53:6). He makes our hearts clean and pure. He wants us to follow Him and be happy to do what is right (Titus 2:14).

Matthew 23:28

INN. ————
A place where travelers can rest. Today, we'd call it a hotel. Mary and Joseph wanted to stay at an inn in Bethlehem. There was no room, so they rested in a nearby stable. That's where the baby Jesus was born.

Luke 2:1–7

INSPIRATION. ————
God leading people to do godly things. God inspires people in many ways. He gives wisdom to help us understand. He inspired great men to write the Bible. He spoke to prophets and sent them into the world with His messages. Sometimes God talked out loud to people. He also inspired through dreams and visions.

Job 32:8
2 Timothy 3:16
1 Samuel 19:20
Exodus 3
Daniel 1:17
Ezekiel 11:24–25

INTERCESSION. ————
Praying for family, friends, and others. Jesus set a good example for intercession. He prayed for those who crucified Him. He prayed for His disciples and all believers. He also prayed for ordinary people. Jesus' followers prayed for the sick (James 5:14–16). They prayed to grow in their understanding of God. Jesus said we should pray for our enemies (Matthew 5:44). We should pray for everyone (1 Timothy 2:1–6). Praying brings us closer to God. Who will you pray for today?

Luke 23:34
John 17:6–26

ISAAC. ————
Abraham and Sarah's son. When Isaac was born, his parents were very old. His dad was 100 years old! His mom, Sarah, was 90. Isaac's dad was a very faithful man. One day, God decided to test his faith. He asked Abraham to offer Isaac as a sacrifice to Him. God wanted to see if Abraham would kill his own son to show that God was the most

important thing in Abraham's life. Abraham was going to do what God asked. Then an angel of the Lord appeared. "Don't hurt the boy!" the angel said. Isaac's life was spared. He grew up and married a girl named Rebekah. They had two boys named Jacob and Esau.

Genesis 21:5
Genesis 17:17
Genesis 22:1–2
Genesis 22:12 CEV
Genesis 25:20
Genesis 25:23–26

ISAIAH. ————

An Old Testament prophet. Isaiah worked in the city of Jerusalem. He gave messages from God to King Uzziah and the kings who followed him. Isaiah warned that the Assyrians would destroy Jerusalem and Israel. He said some of God's people would be saved. He predicted King Hezekiah's death then told the king that God was going to give him fifteen more years to live. He also predicted Jesus' birth. Isaiah said a man would tell people to

God's angel stops Abraham from sacrificing his son Isaac. But God Himself would later sacrifice His only son, Jesus.

prepare for Jesus. That man was John the Baptist.

Isaiah 1:2–9; 11:11
2 Kings 20
Isaiah 7:14
Isaiah 40:3
Matthew 3:1–3

ISAIAH, BOOK OF. ————

An Old Testament book written by the prophet Isaiah. This book is sometimes called the "Fifth Gospel" because it predicts so many things about Jesus. Isaiah said a messenger would announce that Jesus was coming. Isaiah predicted Jesus' birth. He told what Jesus would be like. Isaiah said people would turn against Jesus. He predicted Jesus would be crucified. He even said Jesus would be buried in a rich man's tomb. Isaiah predicted that Jesus would bring salvation to the world. All of these messages came to Isaiah from God.

Isaiah 40:3
Isaiah 7:14
Isaiah 42:1–9
Isaiah 53:3
Isaiah 53:5, 10–12
Isaiah 53:9
Isaiah 49:6

ISHMAEL. ————

A son of Abraham. Ishmael's mom, Hagar, was a slave. Abraham's wife, Sarah, owned Hagar. She and Sarah did not get along. To keep Sarah happy, Abraham sent Ishmael and Hagar away. They took with them just bread and water. When the water ran out, Ishmael cried. God heard him. He showed Ishmael's mom a well where she could get more water. After that, God stayed with them. He protected them and made sure they had what they needed. (See Genesis 21:15–20.)

Genesis 16:1
Genesis 21:9–10
Genesis 21:14

ISRAEL. —————

A very important Bible name. Israel has three meanings. First, it was a new name God gave to Jacob. That was after Jacob wrestled all night with God at a place called Penuel. Second, Jacob's twelve sons, and all of their

kids, and all of their kids, and so on, became a nation called Israel after Jacob's new name. Third, a smaller nation of Israel formed in 931 BC when ten tribes split from the twelve tribes of Israel. They created their own nation with its own king named Jeroboam. Samaria was the capital city. It existed for about 200 years. Then, Israel was captured by Assyria, and foreigners took over. Do the names Israel, Syria, and Samaria sound familiar? These places still exist. You might see or read about them in the news.

Genesis 32:24–32
1 Kings 12
2 Kings 17:23–24

ITALY. —————

A boot-shaped country of southern Europe. Italy extends out into the Mediterranean Sea. The capital city of Italy is Rome. In New Testament times, this city was the center of the Roman Empire. The apostle Paul sailed to Rome as a prisoner. His journey was an exciting adventure. You can read all about it in Acts 27 and 28:1–16.

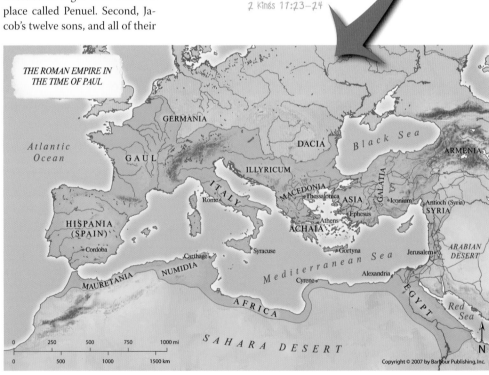

THE ROMAN EMPIRE IN THE TIME OF PAUL

Copyright © 2007 by Barbour Publishing, Inc.

Jacob wrestles with an angel, demanding God's blessing. Jacob's name was changed to *Israel*, meaning "one who struggles with God."

JACOB.

The son of Isaac and Rebekah. He saw angels on a ladder and later struggled with God. Jacob and his brother, Esau, were twins. Esau was the older of the two. As the oldest, Esau was promised a fortune after his dad died. But he sold his right to the fortune. His brother Jacob bought it with a bowl of stew! Jacob wanted his dad's blessing. That made Esau angry. He decided to kill his twin brother (see Genesis 27:1–41). When their mom found out, she sent Jacob to live with his uncle. On his way, Jacob had a dream. He saw a ladder with angels going up and down it. God spoke to Jacob. He promised him land and many descendants. (Check out Genesis 28:10–15.) Jacob grew up, got married, and had lots of kids. God changed Jacob's name to Israel. All of his descendants were known as the Israelites. His son Joseph became important in the kingdom of Egypt.

Genesis 25:24–34
Genesis 27:42–46
Genesis 32:28

JAEL.

A woman who killed an army commander. Jael drove a tent peg through the head of Sisera, a soldier who had come to her tent to rest from battle.

Judges 4:17–22

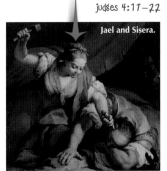

Jael and Sisera.

JAIR.

The eighth judge of Israel. Jair led the nation for twenty-two years. He had thirty sons who rode thirty donkeys.

Judges 10:3–5

JAIRUS.

A man whose daughter died and came back to life. One day, Jesus was teaching near Capernaum. Jairus, a ruler of the synagogue (a Jewish gathering place) came to Jesus and begged Him to come to his house. Jairus's little girl was dying, and he wanted Jesus to save her. When Jesus got there, the girl was already dead. Jesus held her hand and said, "My child, get up!" All at once, she came back to life. Read all about it in Luke 8:40–42, 49–56.

Luke 8:54 NIV

JAMES.

Several men in the Bible are named James. One of them was a disciple of Jesus. James lived in Capernaum and worked as a fisherman. He was fishing in the Sea of Galilee when Jesus chose him as a disciple. James's younger brother John was also chosen. Jesus called the brothers "Sons of Thunder," perhaps because they had strong tempers. James shared some important times with Jesus. He was there when God appeared to Jesus in a bright cloud. God said: "This is my Son, whom I love; with him I am well pleased." James was there when Jesus brought a dead girl back to life. He was also with Jesus the night He was arrested.

Matthew 4:21
Mark 3:17
Matthew 17:5 NIV
Luke 8:49–56
Mark 14:33

JAMES, LETTER OF. ———
A New Testament book. Jesus' half brother James is probably the author of this book. He was not the James that was Jesus' disciple. The book of James is actually a letter. It was written to the twelve tribes of Israel. James wrote about living the Christian life. He said it was not enough just to read the Bible; Christians should practice what Jesus taught. James also said a lot about how we should speak. Christians shouldn't curse. Their words should be pleasing to God.

Matthew 13:55
James 1:1
James 1:22–27
James 3:3–10

JAPHETH. ———
One of Noah's sons. Noah was more than 500 years old when Japheth was born. God saved Japheth and his family from the big flood. They lived in a giant boat called the ark until the flood was over.

Genesis 5:32
Genesis 9:18

JEALOUS. ———
Wanting what someone else has. Have you ever been jealous?

Joseph's brothers were. Joseph was his dad's favorite son. His brothers were jealous, and they treated Joseph badly. In fact, they sold him as a slave! (Check out Genesis 37:12–35.) The Bible warns Christians about being jealous. The next time you feel jealous, think of Joseph. Switch your thoughts from jealousy to kindness.

Genesis 37:4
Galatians 5:26

JEBUSITES. ———
Enemies of the Israelites. The Jebusites controlled Jerusalem before David took over the city and made it Israel's capital.

JEHOIACHIN. ———
A king of Israel. King Nebuchadnezzar came along and took over Jehoiachin's kingdom. The king and most of his people were taken away to Babylon. Jehoiachin was put in prison there for thirty-seven years.

2 Kings 24:8–16
Jeremiah 52:31–34

JEHOSHAPHAT. ———
A king of Judah. Jehoshaphat hated it when people worshipped false gods (idols). He sent teachers to help them learn about the one true God. But he got into trouble with God when he made friends with evil King Ahab of Israel.

2 Chronicles 17:3–9
2 Chronicles 19:1–3

JEHOVAH. ———
Another name for God, which usually appears in Bibles as "Lord." Jehovah means that God is and always has been. When God spoke to Moses from the burning bush, He called Himself "I Am." He meant that He has always existed and will exist forever. Jehovah comes from the Hebrew word *Yahweh*. God is known by many names in the Bible. Jehovah is an ancient holy name for Him used by the Hebrews.

Exodus 6:3 KJV
Isaiah 26:4
Exodus 3:14

JEHOVAH–JIREH. ———
A name for God that means "the Lord will provide." Abraham used this name after God saved his son Isaac from being killed as a sacrifice.

Genesis 22:14

JEHOVAH–NISSI. ———
A name for God that means "the Lord is my banner." Moses used this name after God helped him win a battle with the Amalekites.

Exodus 17:15

JEHOVAH–SHALOM. ———
A name for God that means "the Lord is peace." Jehovah–shalom is the name of an altar that Gideon built.

Judges 6:24

JEHU.

A king who had the wicked King Ahab's family destroyed. The prophet Elisha made Jehu the new king of Israel and told him he was to destroy King Ahab's family members because they had killed many of God's prophets. Jehu had all of Ahab's sons killed. He also had Ahab's wife, Queen Jezebel, killed.

2 Kings 9:1–37

JEPHTHAH.

The ninth judge of Israel. He made a big mistake. Jephthah asked God to let Israel win a nasty battle. Then he made a big promise to God. If Israel won, he would sacrifice (kill and give to God) whatever met him at the door when he got home. You'd have to think he meant an animal, but after Israel won the battle, who met him at the door? His sweet little girl!

Judges 11:30–35

JEREMIAH.

A prophet in Old Testament times. God chose Jeremiah to be a prophet even before he was born. When he grew up, Jeremiah was sad that the Israelites were behaving badly. Jeremiah warned them. He said God would punish them for their behavior. The people did not listen. They turned against Jeremiah. They wanted to kill him. Even his family turned on him. Then God did just as He promised. The Babylonians took over the land, and the people were taken away as prisoners.

Jeremiah 1:4–5
Jeremiah 9:1
Jeremiah 16:1–21
Jeremiah 11:21
Jeremiah 12:6
Jeremiah 21:6

JEREMIAH, BOOK OF.

An Old Testament book written by the prophet Jeremiah. This book is a book of warnings. God spoke to Jeremiah. He told him things that would happen. The people were misbehaving. They were worshipping false gods. Jeremiah said God would punish them because of this. He described what would happen to Jerusalem. He predicted the Babylonians would capture the people and take them away. Everything happened just as God said. In Jeremiah 31, Jeremiah wrote of God's promise of His continuing love for His people.

Jeremiah 52:1–30

JERICHO.

An ancient city with walls around it. Jericho was near the Jordan River and the Dead Sea. Joshua captured Jericho when the Israelites entered the Promised Land. His faith in God made the walls around the city fall down! In New Testament times, Jesus visited Jericho. He taught there and healed people. This was where Jesus healed Bartimaeus, a man who was blind. Jericho was also the place where Zacchaeus climbed a tree so he could see Jesus better.

Joshua 6:1–27
Hebrews 11:30
Mark 10:46–52
Luke 19:1–9

Soldiers from Israel march around Jericho, waiting for God to perform a miracle—knocking the walls down flat.

JEROBOAM.

A king with a shriveled hand. Jeroboam was the first king to lead the northern kingdom of Israel. He was a bad man who allowed idol worship in his cities. When a godly man spoke out against the idols (false gods), an amazing thing happened. King Jeroboam stretched out his hand. He demanded that the man be taken away. But God punished the king. He made his hand shrivel up so he couldn't use it anymore. There was another king of Israel named Jeroboam, who ruled about 150 years later. The second Jeroboam was just as bad as the first.

1 Kings 11:29–31
1 Kings 12:26–30
1 Kings 13:4

JERUSALEM.

A famous city, both in Bible times and today. Jerusalem is a very ancient city. It is the most important city to the Jewish people. Jerusalem is mentioned many times in the Old Testament. It existed when the first book of the Bible, Genesis, was written. Back then it was called Salem. It was later called Jebus. The name Jerusalem does not appear until the sixth book of the Bible, Joshua. It was the site of the temple of God. Many wars happened in and around Jerusalem. This is true even today. Jesus cried because Jerusalem was a sinful city. Jesus rode into Jerusalem on a young donkey. He was crucified just outside the city walls. Jerusalem still exists today, and it is often in the news. Someday God will create a perfect city where there will be no sin. Its name will be "the New Jerusalem."

Genesis 14:18
Judges 19:10
Joshua 10:1
1 Kings 3:1
1 Kings 6:1–38
Luke 19:41–42
Matthew 21:1–11
Luke 23:33
Revelation 21:2

JERUSALEM COUNCIL.

A group of wise church leaders. The Jerusalem Council decided how Gentiles would fit as members of the early Christian church. Gentiles were not Jews. They did not obey Jewish laws. Still, many Gentiles believed in Jesus. Members of the council discussed whether Gentiles needed to be circumcised to join the church. They decided it was enough for Gentiles to be saved by God's grace alone. (Read all about it in Acts 15:6–19.)

Acts 15:6

JESSE.

The father of Israel's greatest king. God chose Jesse's youngest son, David, to replace the foolish King Saul. As father of David, Jesse is a direct ancestor of Jesus.

Isaiah 11

JESUS CHRIST.

Son of God, Savior of the world. Jesus is more powerful than any superhero you could ever imagine. Every day, He saves people from sin. Without Him, no one would ever enter heaven.

Jesus was born in Bethlehem. His mother was Mary. His father is God. Since Mary's husband was Joseph, Joseph acted as Jesus' father on earth. When Jesus was born, Herod was king. He was jealous of Jesus. Herod believed Jesus would grow up to be a greater king than he. So Herod plotted to kill Jesus. An angel warned Mary and Joseph. They ran away with Jesus, and His life was spared.

When Jesus grew up, He taught crowds of people about God. He chose twelve men—apostles—to help Him. Jesus taught about what God expects from us. He healed the sick and did all kinds of miracles. The people were amazed at what He could do. Some believed

The gold-topped Dome of the Rock, a Muslim church, is part of the modern Jerusalem skyline.

Jesus was the Son of God. Others did not.

The Jewish leaders were jealous of Jesus. They wanted Him killed. They arrested Him and said He lied about being God's Son. They killed Jesus by crucifying Him on a cross; then Jesus' body was put in a tomb. Everyone knew He was dead. But three days later, Jesus came back to life! His body was gone from the tomb. Many people saw Him alive again. After one last meeting with His disciples, Jesus went up to heaven on a cloud.

Why is Jesus so awesome? Because God sacrificed Jesus, His own Son, to save us from sin. When Jesus died, He took all of our sins with Him. When He came back to life, He proved that He is the Son of God. If we believe in what Jesus did, God will forgive us for the bad things we do. Jesus promised to come back someday. Everyone who believes in Him will have a place in heaven.

> Luke 2:4–7, 21
> Matthew 2:13–14
> Matthew 10:1–4
> Matthew 26:3–4
> Mark 14:55–65
> john 19
> Matthew 28:1–10
> Luke 24:36–51
> Mark 10:45
> Acts 16:31

JETHRO.

Moses' father-in-law. Jethro, the father of Moses' wife, Zipporah, gave Moses advice. He said that Moses was working too hard and

getting worn out. He said Moses should ask people to help him.

> Exodus 18:11–23

JEWS.

God's special people. The Old Testament is mostly the history of the Jewish people—the Israelites. The men who wrote the Bible were Jews (Luke might have been a Gentile). In Genesis, the first book of the Bible, we learn about Jacob. God changed Jacob's name to Israel. He said Jacob would have many children and grandchildren and great-grandchildren—and on and on until his family became a large nation. Those people are the Jews. Throughout history, the Jews have been at war with other nations. In Old Testament times, they were held prisoner in Egypt for more than 400 years. Jesus was a Jew. In fact, He was King of the Jews. Many Jews did not believe that Jesus was the Son of God. Some still do not believe to this day.

> john 18:37
> john 12:37–50

JEZEBEL.

King Ahab's wicked wife. Queen Jezebel was bad, bad, bad! She got the Israelites to worship Baal —a false god. Her husband was wicked, too. He made altars to the false gods. Jezebel killed some of God's prophets. Then another of His prophets, Elijah, predicted Jezebel would be killed. That made her hopping

mad. She planned to kill Elijah. But he got away. A new king came into power. His name was Jehu. He had Jezebel and her whole family murdered. No one from her family ever ruled Israel again.

> 1 Kings 16:32–33
> 1 Kings 18:4
> 1 Kings 19:1–2
> 2 Kings 9:30–31

JEZREEL.

Where Ahab and Jezebel lived. Jezreel was a city with walls. King Ahab's palace was there. Many battles took place in Jezreel. This is the place where Ahab's family was killed by King Jehu's army. Some believe the last battle in the world will happen near here. It will be a battle between good and evil. Evil will lose. Then Satan will be thrown into a lake of fire.

> 1 Kings 21:1
> 2 Kings 10:1–11
> Revelation 20:10

JOAB.

Commander of King David's army. He carried out David's plan to have Uriah the Hittite killed in battle. Then David took Uriah's beautiful wife, Bathsheba.

> 2 Samuel 8:15–16
> 2 Samuel 11:14–11

JOASH.

A boy king, also known as Jehoash. Joash became king when he was seven years old! The wicked Queen Athaliah wanted him killed. So Joash's aunt hid him.

a
b
c
d
e
f
g
h
i
J
k
l
m
n
o
p
q
r
s
t
u
v
w
x
y
z

As a man, Joash obeyed God for a while. Then he started worshipping false gods. He ended up being murdered by his own officers.

2 Kings 11:21
2 Kings 11:1–3
2 Chronicles 24:2
2 Chronicles 24:17–19
2 Kings 12:20

JOB.

A man famous for suffering. Job was a very good man with a big family and lots of stuff—sheep, camels, cows, and servants. When Satan said Job served God only for the blessings, God let Satan take away Job's things. First, Job lost his children, animals, and servants. Then he lost his health. But Job refused to "curse God and die," as his wife suggested. The old phrase "the patience of Job" isn't really true, because Job spent a lot of time complaining to God. In the end, though, Job learned that God knows best, even when we suffer. And God gave Job back all the things he'd lost—and more.

Job 1:1
Job 2:9
Job 42

JOCHEBED.

Mother of Moses. Jochebed saved Moses' life when he was a baby. The king of Egypt wanted all the Jewish baby boys killed. So Moses' mom hid him in a basket in the Nile River. That's where the princess of Egypt found him, and later she adopted him. (Check out Exodus 1:22–2:10.)

Exodus 6:20

JOEL.

One of God's prophets. Joel wrote the Old Testament book that has his name. He foretold the coming of God's Holy Spirit. He said God's people would be saved from sin. Joel predicted a big swarm of locusts would come. It would be God's way of telling His people to behave.

Joel 2:28–29
Joel 2:31–33
Joel 1:1–13

JOHN.

Jesus' closest friend. John was one of Jesus' disciples and an apostle. He lived in Capernaum and fished in the Sea of Galilee. His dad was Zebedee. His brother was James, another disciple. John was very loyal to Jesus. In fact, he was willing to die for Him. He might have had a temper, since Jesus called John and his brother James "Sons of Thunder." John described himself as the disciple whom Jesus loved. He was eager to share the things Jesus taught. After Jesus went back to heaven, John wrote one of the four Gospels. He also wrote three letters and the book of Revelation.

Matthew 4:21–22
Mark 3:17
Mark 10:35–39
John 19:26

JOHN, GOSPEL OF.

The fourth book of the New Testament. The book of John was written by the apostle John. He was one of Jesus' twelve apostles. When you read John's book, you can tell that he was close to Jesus. He often wrote using Jesus' own words. John told about Jesus' life. He wrote about many of His miracles. John said that Jesus fed 5,000 people with just a few loaves of bread and some fish. He also told about Jesus walking on water. There is another amazing story in John's book. He wrote about Jesus bringing a dead friend back to life. The friend's name was Lazarus. He had been dead for four days!

John 6:5–21
John 11:38–44

JOHN, FIRST, SECOND, AND THIRD LETTERS OF.

Three letters written by Jesus' disciple John. You will find these letters toward the back of the New Testament. In his letters, John warned of false teachings about Jesus. He told Christians not to believe everything they heard. John also said we should love one another. He reminded Christians to follow God's commands.

2 John 1:5–10

John the Baptist tells Herod the king shouldn't have married his own sister-in-law (Mark 6:16–18).

JOHN THE BAPTIST.

A prophet who prepared the way for Jesus. The son of Zacharias and Elizabeth, John was also related to Jesus. The Old Testament prophet Isaiah made predictions about John. "Someone is shouting: 'Clear a path in the desert! Make a straight road for the LORD our God.' " Years later, those predictions came true. John the Baptist began preaching in the desert. He led the way for Jesus.

John was a bit of a character. He wore clothes made of camel hair. He ate grasshoppers and wild honey. Crowds of people came to him to be baptized in the Jordan River. In fact, John baptized Jesus. He didn't want to do it, though. He didn't think he was worthy to baptize such a great man.

John criticized King Herod for his sinful behavior, so the king threw him into prison. Then he had John killed. Jesus' disciples buried John the Baptist's body. Then they told Jesus what hap-pened. Jesus was very sad. (Check out Matthew 14:1–13.) Jesus loved John. He said, "I tell you that no one ever born on this earth is greater than John the Baptist."

Isaiah 40:3 CEV
Matthew 3:13–15
Matthew 3:1–3
Luke 3:19–20
Matthew 11:11 CEV

JONAH.

A prophet who was swallowed by a big fish. God told Jonah to go to Nineveh and preach to the people there. The Ninevites were wicked, and God wanted them to change their ways. But Jonah didn't want to go. Instead, he ran away.

Jonah got aboard a boat headed toward Spain. A huge storm came up. The sailors were afraid that God was punishing someone on board. Jonah admitted that he was running from God, so the sailors threw him overboard. That's when the big fish swallowed him! Poor Jonah. He sat in the fish's belly for three days and nights. All the while, he prayed to God. Finally, the fish spit Jonah out onto the shore.

After that, Jonah obeyed the Lord God. He went to Nineveh and preached to the people. The Ninevites changed their ways, and God was pleased.

Jonah might have written the Old Testament book that tells his story. Read it to find out more about his great adventure.

Jonah 1:1–2
Jonah 1:3
Jonah 1:8–15
Jonah 1:17
Jonah 2:10
Jonah 3

Jonah becomes lunch for a giant fish.

a b c d e f g h i J k l m n o p q r s t u v w x y z

Jonathan

JONATHAN.

King Saul's oldest son. Jonathan was David's best friend. The men remained friends even when King Saul was trying to kill David. Jonathan and his dad both died in a battle with the Philistines. When David found out, he was very sad. He sang a song in memory of his friend.

1 Samuel 14:49
1 Samuel 19–20
1 Samuel 31:1–6
2 Samuel 1:17–27

The Jordan River snakes through modern-day Israel.

JOPPA.

A city on the coast of the Mediterranean Sea. This is where Peter learned that Gentiles could be Christians. Today, Joppa is part of the city of Tel Aviv, Israel.

Acts 11:4–18

JORDAN RIVER.

Where Jesus was baptized. The Jordan River starts in Syria and flows about 200 miles south through the Sea of Galilee to the northern end of the Dead Sea. It is the largest and most important river in Palestine, stretching all the way from the Sea of Galilee to the Dead Sea—that's about 65 miles! The river and the land around it are mentioned a lot in the Bible—about 200 times. This is where the Israelites crossed into the Promised Land. It is also where John the Baptist preached and baptized people. The river is best known as the place where John baptized Jesus.

Joshua 3:15–17
Matthew 3:13–17

JOSEPH.

The name shared by several men in the Bible. If someone says, "Tell me about Joseph," you can ask, "Which one?" There were four important Josephs in the Bible. One was married to Jesus' mom, Mary. He was Jesus' adopted dad, because Jesus' birth father was God. Another Joseph was sold as a slave. His own brothers sold him! Maybe you have read about him. He was the boy with the colorful coat. Later, he was an important leader in the Egyptian pharaoh's kingdom. The third Joseph was a man from Arimathea. Jesus was buried in this Joseph's tomb. Another Joseph almost became the twelfth disciple to replace the wicked Judas Iscariot. But the job went to another man named Matthias.

Matthew 1:20–25
Genesis 37:3–4
Matthew 27:57–61
Acts 1:23–26

Mary kisses young Jesus, as Joseph works wood in his carpentry shop.

JOSHUA.

The man who followed Moses as leader of the Israelites. Joshua led God's people into the Promised Land. There was a city called Jericho in the Promised Land. Joshua and his army had to capture it. They needed to kick the people out because they were on the Israelites' land. Thick walls surrounded Jericho. The walls were impossible to knock down. But God gave Joshua a plan. Joshua and his army marched around the city for six days. They blew trumpets. Everyone thought they were crazy. Then, on the seventh day, Joshua commanded: "Shout praises to the Lord!" The army shouted loud and strong. And the walls came tumbling down. (You can read more about the walls of Jericho in Joshua 6:1–20.)

Joshua 1:1–6

JOSIAH.

A kid king. Can you imagine becoming a king at the age of eight? It happened to Josiah. He became king of Judah when he was just eight years old. Josiah ruled for thirty-one years. He loved God and did what was right. (Check out 2 Kings 22:1–2.) He did great things. First, he worked hard to get people to obey God's laws. Then he commanded that the temple of the Lord be rebuilt. It had been destroyed in a battle. He also stopped people from worshipping false gods. Josiah was an ancestor of Jesus Christ.

2 Kings 22:3–9
2 Kings 23:4–24
Matthew 1:1–11

Joshua asks God to make the sun stand still in a battle at Aijalon (Joshua 10).

JOY.

Great happiness! What makes you feel really happy? Imagine it now, and remember how you felt. Joyful feelings are wonderful. They make you want to sing. In fact, you should sing for joy because God is great. He is so great that the trees of the forest will sing joyful songs. Even the mountains will sing for joy. Joy

was there when Jesus was born. It was there, too, when He rose from the dead. The Bible says we should always be joyful.

Psalm 81:1
Psalm 96:11–13
Psalm 98:8–9
Luke 2:10
Matthew 28:8
1 Thessalonians 5:16

JUBILEE.

A year of celebrating. Jubilee was a festival that was held every fifty years. Think of it as an ancient cousin to our Earth Day. For one whole year, the land was at rest. No crops were grown on it. And any land that had been taken to pay a debt was given back to its owner. Slaves in the fields were set free. (Find out more about it in Leviticus 25:8–55.)

JUDAH.

The southern Jewish kingdom. When King Solomon died, the Israelites split into two kingdoms. One was the northern kingdom, called Israel. The southern kingdom of Judah had its capital at Jerusalem. The people of Judah worshipped idols. They did not love God. And that made God angry. He let the Babylonian army destroy Jerusalem. That army took the people away and made them slaves. Years later, some of the people came back. Their goal was to rebuild Jerusalem.

1 Kings 14:21
2 Chronicles 36:20–23

JUDAS.

Brother of James. He was the disciple known as Thaddaeus. Don't confuse him with the disciple who betrayed Jesus. His name was Judas Iscariot. (See Luke 6:13–16.)

Matthew 10:3

JUDAS ISCARIOT.

The disciple who betrayed Jesus. He seemed like a trustworthy man. In fact, he was keeper of the money for Jesus and His disciples. But Judas was the one who turned Jesus in. He gave Him over to be killed. The high priests and elders were sneaky. They were looking for a way to arrest Jesus. So Judas agreed to help. He was paid with thirty silver coins. After Jesus was arrested, Judas felt guilty. He tried to give the money back. But it was too late. Judas decided to kill himself. The place where he died is called the Field of Blood. (Check out Matthew 27:1–10.) It exists, to this day, not far from Jerusalem.

John 13:29
Matthew 26:14–15

Judas Iscariot kisses Jesus—a sign to those who wanted to arrest the Lord.

a b c d e f g h i J k l m n o p q r s t u v w x y z

JUDE.

Jesus' half brother. At first, Jude did not believe that his brother, Jesus, was the Son of God. He didn't believe it until Jesus rose from the dead. Then he became a disciple. Jude wrote a book in the New Testament. It is a short book named Jude. This book is an epistle, or letter. In it, Jude warned about false teachers. Some people were not telling the truth about Jesus. So Jude told believers to be careful whom they listened to.

Matthew 13:55
John 7:5
Acts 1:14

JUDEA.

A region in southern Israel. Long ago, the Israelites were taken away to Babylonia. They lived there as slaves until they were set free. When they returned to their homeland, they lived in Judea. Some important places in Judea were Bethlehem, Jerusalem, and Jericho.

Ezra 5:8
Matthew 2:1
Matthew 3:5

JUDGES, BOOK OF.

The seventh book of the Old Testament. Judges were military leaders. The book of Judges tells about some of them. How many times have you heard, "Don't do that again?" That's what God told His people. But they kept on sinning. When that happened, God punished them. He sent enemy armies and allowed wars to happen. This was God's judgment. When a war got really bad, the people stopped sinning. They cried out to God for help, and He answered their prayers by sending "judges" to help them fight. The people didn't learn their lesson, though. Over and over they sinned. God judged them, and they sinned again.

Judges 4:1

JUDGMENT.

When God accuses us of sin. When you do something wrong, your parents correct you. They do it because they love you. God corrects His children, too. We are all God's children, and He judges the things we do. God decides whether or not to punish us. The Bible says, "When the Lord punishes you, don't make light of it, and when he corrects you, don't be discouraged. The Lord corrects the people he loves and disciplines those he calls his own."

Hebrews 12:5–6 CEV

JUDGMENT, LAST.

The day when God separates the saved from the lost. At the end of time, Jesus will return. He will gather all His people and take them away to heaven. Everyone who does not believe will be judged. It will be a terrible day for nonbelievers. It will be a wonderful day for those who believe. On Judgment Day, God's children will begin to live with Him forever. No one knows when Jesus will come. So the Bible says to be prepared. If you believe in Jesus, you don't have to worry. He will save a place for you in heaven.

Romans 2:5–8
1 Thessalonians 5:1–11

JUSTICE.

Treating someone fairly. When you make a decision about someone, are you always fair? Justice means treating everyone equally. God is always fair, or just. God wants us to treat others with justice. Keep that in mind the next time you play sports or other games. Justice is an important part of being a good sport.

1 Timothy 5:21
Deuteronomy 32:4
Zechariah 7:9–10

JUSTIFICATION.

Being made right with God. You can't be right with God by accomplishing great things or by doing good work. There is just one way to be justified, or right, with God. You can only be justified by believing in Jesus Christ. When you are right with God, you are at peace with Him. Then you can hope to live with Him in heaven.

Romans 4:25
Titus 3:5–7

KADESH-BARNEA.

A wilderness area between Egypt and Canaan. The Israelites probably spent much of forty years in Kadesh-barnea. They camped there waiting for God to let them into the Promised Land.

Deuteronomy 9:23

KEY.

A tool used to unlock a door. In Bible times, keys were long rods with metal pins. The book of Revelation says that Jesus holds the keys to heaven and hell.

Judges 3:25
Revelation 1:18

KID.

A young goat. Kids were used as offerings to God. They were also killed and cooked for people to eat at special occasions.

Judges 13:19
Genesis 27:9

A young goat—or kid.

KIDRON.

A valley near Jerusalem. In Old Testament times, idols (statues of false gods) were burned in this valley. Jesus probably crossed Kidron on the night of His arrest.

1 Kings 15:13
John 18:1

KINDRED.

Your relatives. Kindred are members of your family: parents, brothers, sisters, grandparents, aunts, uncles, and cousins. In Bible times, kindred were sometimes called tribes.

Numbers 32:28

KING.

The big leader. A king makes the rules for everyone in his kingdom. The first king of Israel was Saul. He was appointed by God. Other well-known Bible kings were King David, King Solomon, King Nebuchadnezzar, and King Herod. Many kings were evil. They led their people to sin. They encouraged them to worship false gods called idols. Only a few kings were good, godly men. The king of all believers is Jesus Christ. He is called the King of kings. His kingdom will last forever.

1 Samuel 10:1
Revelation 19:16

KINGDOM OF GOD.

The rule of God in Christians' hearts. When you pray and try to please God, you experience some of His kingdom. Learning about God and His love helps prepare you for living with Him someday. One day, when you get to heaven, you will get to see the whole kingdom of God.

Luke 17:20–21
Matthew 6:33

KINGS, FIRST AND SECOND BOOKS OF.

The eleventh and twelfth books of the Old Testament. These two books together cover about 400 years of history. First Kings tells about wise King Solomon and the building of his temple. It explains that the kingdom was divided into two nations—Judah and Israel. Near the end of the book, you will meet God's prophet Elijah. In Second Kings, you will find out that Elijah was carried off on a chariot made from fire. You will also meet his friend, the prophet Elisha. Second Kings explains that the Babylonians attacked Jerusalem and destroyed Solomon's temple.

1 Kings 6–7
2 Kings 2:11
2 Kings 25:8–11

b c d e f g h i j k l m n o p q r s t u v w x y z

Kinsman-Redeemer. —

A family member who pays off a relative's debt. Imagine owing your brother ten dollars. You have no money to pay him, so your dad helps you out. He pays your debt for you. Your dad is acting as a kinsman–redeemer. Jesus is our kinsman–redeemer. We could never pay God enough for all the bad things we've done. So Jesus paid that debt for us. He died on the cross for our sins.

Ruth 2:20 NIV

Kiss. —

A sign of affection. When you give your parents kisses, you show that you love them. But Judas Iscariot used a kiss to betray Jesus. He kissed His cheek. It was a signal to the soldiers to identify Jesus so he could be arrested.

Genesis 27:26
Matthew 26:48–49

Kneel. —

To get down on your knees. At night when you say your prayers, do you kneel by your bed? Kneeling is a sign of great respect. When you kneel and pray, you show God just how great you think He is.

Luke 22:41

Knife. —

A sharp tool used for cutting. In Bible times, knives were made from flint, bronze, or iron.

Jeremiah 36:23

Knowledge. —

The things you know. What you learn in school adds to the knowledge stored up in your brain. What you know about God adds to your faith. God-knowledge is the most important kind. Knowing about God helps you to live a good, godly life. You can find out more about God by reading your Bible, praying, and learning from your church and Sunday school. God wants you to grow up knowing Him. Throughout your life, remember to add to your knowledge about Him. He is so awesome. If you studied about God your whole life, you would still never know all that He can do.

Philippians 3:8

Jacob kisses Rachel—the only romantic kiss described in the Bible (Genesis 29:11).

a b g d e f g h i j K l m n o p q r s t u v w x y z

LABAN.

Uncle of Jacob. Jacob's brother, Esau, was mad at him. Their mom, Rebekah, was scared that Esau would hurt Jacob. So she told Jacob to run away and stay with her brother Laban. (Check out Genesis 27:41–45.) Laban was a dad to two girls. Their names were Rachel and Leah. Jacob fell in love with Rachel. He worked for Laban for seven years so that he could marry her. But Laban fooled Jacob into marrying Leah! Jacob worked for another seven years so that Rachel could be his wife. (Read more about it in Genesis 29:18–30.)

LAKE OF FIRE.

Another name for hell. It is also called the "second death." This is the last place anyone is sent to be punished. It is a very bad place full of pain and suffering. The devil will be in the lake of fire. Who else gets sent there? Anyone whose name isn't written in God's Book of Life. But people who believe in the Lord Jesus Christ will not go there. Jesus died to give us a way out. Do you believe in Jesus?

Revelation 20:14
Revelation 20:10
Revelation 20:15
Luke 12:4–5
John 3:16

LAMB.

A young sheep. The meat of lambs was used for food. Their wool was used to make clothing. In Bible times, lambs were used for religious sacrifices. A lamb is a symbol for the sacrifice Jesus had to make. The book of Isaiah says that Jesus will bring peace to all of God's creatures. "Leopards will lie down with young goats, and wolves will rest with lambs."

2 Samuel 12:4
Proverbs 27:26
Exodus 12:5–7
Isaiah 53:7
Isaiah 11:6 CEV

LAMB OF GOD.

A name used for Christ. In Bible times, lambs were often used for sacrifices. This name fits Jesus because His death was a sacrifice for our sins. The prophet Isaiah said we were like sheep that had wandered off. He also compared our Savior's death to the death of a lamb. "He was silent like a lamb being led to the butcher, as quiet as a sheep having its wool cut off." When John the Baptist saw Jesus, he said, "Here is the Lamb of God who takes away the sin of the world!" We should praise and honor Jesus as the Lamb of God.

Isaiah 53:7 CEV
John 1:29 CEV
Revelation 5:12–13

LAMENTATIONS, BOOK OF.

The twenty-fifth book in the Old Testament. Lamentations is short, written in the form of a poem. Nonbelievers from Babylon destroyed Jerusalem. In Lamentations, the prophet Jeremiah tells how sad this made him. He explains how awful it was to live there during the attack. In what was once a great city, jewels from the temple lay in the streets while the people starved.

Lamentations 4:1–5

LANDMARK.

A pile of stones used to mark property lines. It was against the law to move a stone or take one away.

Deuteronomy 19:14

LAODICEA.

A big city in Asia Minor—in modern-day Turkey. The book of Revelation says the Lord spoke to John. He told John to write down a message for seven churches. One of them was the church in Laodicea. Jesus scolded the people in this church because they were lukewarm in their faith. They thought they were all that because they were rich. But Jesus said those who don't put their

a
b
c
d
e
f
g
h
i
j
k
L
m
n
o
p
q
r
s
t
u
v
w
x
y
z

trust in God are poor. (Read more about it in Revelation 3:14–22.)

Revelation 1:1–11

LAW OF MOSES. ———
The rules—including the Ten Commandments—in the first five books of the Bible. The Lord gave these laws to Moses on Mount Sinai. Some of them have to do with ceremonies and procedures. But others are moral laws. They tell us what is right and wrong. These laws are here to stay. When Jesus gave the Sermon on the Mount, he talked about the Law of Moses. He said that nothing about the Law would ever change. Not even the dot of an *i* or the cross of a *t*.

Deuteronomy 5:1–2
Romans 7:7–12
Matthew 5:17–20

LAWYER. ———
A person who taught the law in Bible times. These teachers were also called scribes.

Luke 11:53
Nehemiah 8:13

LAYING ON OF HANDS. —
A way to bless others. Jacob laid his hands on his grandchildren to predict the good things they would do. Church leaders laid hands on Paul and Barnabas to show that they had been called to serve God. When Jesus laid His hands on people, many of them were healed. Laying on of hands

was done during the sacrifice of an animal, too. By laying his hands on a goat, a priest gave the sins of the people to the goat.

Genesis 48:14–18
Acts 13:2–3
Luke 4:40
Leviticus 16:21

LAZARUS. ———
Mary's and Martha's brother. When Jesus heard that Lazarus was sick, He said, "His sickness won't end in death. It will bring glory to God and his Son." After Lazarus died, Jesus brought him back to life. The people who saw this put their faith in Jesus. But this made others mad. The Jewish leaders had a meeting to talk about what to do. They worried that others would follow Jesus if He kept doing such amazing things. The leaders made plans to kill Jesus. (Check the story out in John 11:41–53.) They planned to kill Lazarus, too. They blamed him for making so many people put their faith in Jesus.

John 11:4 CEV
John 12:10–11

LEAH. ———
Jacob's surprise wife. Leah was the oldest daughter of Laban, who was Jacob's uncle. Jacob loved Laban's younger daughter, Rachel. But in Bible times, the oldest was supposed to be the first to marry. Laban tricked Jacob into marrying Leah. When

Jacob found out that he'd married the wrong sister, he was angry. Laban let Jacob marry Rachel a week later. (See Genesis 29:15–30.) Leah had seven kids. Her sons grew up to start six of the twelve tribes of Israel. Leah was a loyal wife to Jacob. When he left Laban to go to Canaan, Leah and their kids went with him.

Genesis 30:21
Genesis 35:23
Genesis 31:17–18

LEAVEN. ———
An ingredient in bread. Like yeast, leaven makes bread puff up. Jesus used this word to warn the disciples not to listen to those not teaching the truth. He meant that bad teaching would work its way through a person's life.

Matthew 16:11–12

LEBANON. ———
A land north of Israel. Lebanon is a harsh region with lots of mountains. It is also known for its cedar trees. These trees smell nice and are a deep red color. They are also very tall and strong. When Solomon was king, he built a temple in Jerusalem. It was made out of cedars from Lebanon.

1 Kings 5:6–10

LEGION. ———
A huge number. The Romans used this word to describe a group in their army. One legion was a few thousand soldiers, both on foot

and riding on horses. This word can also be used for any really big number. In the Bible, Jesus used the word legion to describe the number of angels that God could send to help Him.

Matthew 26:47
Matthew 26:53

LEPROSY.

Skin diseases. People with leprosy were called lepers. In Bible times, people were afraid of them. Lepers had to follow special rules. One was that they must live apart from others. They also had to shout, "Unclean!" wherever they went. This was done so people could stay away from them. But Jesus was not afraid of lepers. He was kind to those who were sick. Once, ten lepers asked for His help. Jesus healed them all! Jesus gave His disciples the power to heal. He told them to cure the sick people who had leprosy.

Leviticus 13:45–46
Luke 17:11–14
Matthew 10:1
Matthew 10:8

LEVI.

A name shared by Jacob's son and a tax collector. There were a few Levis in the Bible. One was the third son of Jacob and Leah. He was the first of the Levites, one of the great tribes of Israel. Levi had three sons: Kohath, Gershon, and Merari. They were ancestors of the three main groups of Levites. Another Levi was also known as Matthew. His job was collecting taxes. He became a disciple of Jesus and wrote the Gospel of Matthew.

Genesis 35:23
Genesis 46:11
Matthew 9:9
Luke 5:27

LEVIATHAN.

A sea monster. Some think Leviathan was really a crocodile. Others guess it could have been a kind of dinosaur. This word was also used to describe an enemy of Israel in the Bible.

Job 41:1
Isaiah 27:1

LEVITES.

Members of Levi's tribe. The Levites were one of the twelve tribes of Israel. Moses and Aaron were Levites. The Lord told Moses, "I have chosen these Levites from all Israel, and they will belong to me in a special way." Their job was caring for the tabernacle and the temple. They also helped the priests.

Numbers 3:11 CEV
Numbers 3:5–10

LEVITICUS, BOOK OF.

The third book in the Old Testament. Leviticus has many rules that tell how to worship and make offerings. It also lists which animals were okay and not okay to eat. The main idea of the book is holiness. God is holy, and He wants His people to be holy, too. The first half of this book is about sacrifices. It tells how people could be holy by making the right sacrifice to God. The second half is about the things people could do to deal with sin. The Lord gave these rules to Moses.

Leviticus 1:1

LIAR.

Someone who doesn't tell the truth. The devil is the father of lies. When you tell a lie to another person, you are also lying to God.

John 8:44

LIBERALITY.

A giving spirit. A person with a giving spirit helps those who need it. Being kind and caring proves your faith. The Bible tells us to help people whenever we can, especially if they follow the Lord. The book of Luke says that if you give to others, you'll get back the same or more.

Galatians 6:10
Luke 6:38

LICE.

Gnats or small bugs that bite. Lice were the third plague sent by God on Egypt. He was forcing the pharaoh into letting the Israelites leave his country.

Exodus 8:16–18

a b c d e f g h i j k L m n o p q r s t u v w x y z

LIGHT.

The opposite of darkness. The first thing God did when He created the world was to make light. Have you ever been afraid of the dark? Think about how safe you felt when you turned on the light. In the Bible, this word is used to describe things that are true and good. The Word of God is like a lamp that lights your way wherever you go. Jesus called people who believe in God "the light of the world." He said, "Make your light shine, so that others will see the good that you do and will praise your Father in heaven."

Genesis 1:3–5
Psalm 119:105
Matthew 5:14 KJV
Matthew 5:16 CEV

LIONS' DEN.

A home for a bunch of lions. There is a famous Bible story about Daniel and a lions' den. Daniel worked as an official for King Darius. Daniel did his job so well that he made the other officials look bad. They talked Darius into making a law that said no one could pray to any god or human other than the king. Anyone who broke the law would be thrown into a pit of lions. Daniel prayed to God anyway. He was thrown into a lions' den! But not one lion hurt Daniel. He came out of their den without a scratch! Daniel was kept safe by God. (See Daniel 6:1–23.)

Locust swarms can destroy all the green plants they see.

LOCUST.

An insect with wings, like a grasshopper. Big groups of locusts, called swarms, move from place to place and eat plants. The Lord sent swarms of locusts to Egypt. "The ground was black with locusts, and they ate everything left on the trees and in the fields. Nothing green remained in Egypt—not a tree or a plant." He did this to force the pharaoh to free the people of Israel. Back then, the Hebrews could eat locusts and grasshoppers.

Exodus 10:1–6
Exodus 10:15 CEV
Leviticus 11:22

LOGOS.

A Greek word that means both "the Word" and "reason." Jesus came into the world as the Logos. John 1:1–14 says that the Word of God became human and lived here with us. That means Jesus! He was the only Son of the Father, God. All of God's kindness and truth came down to us in Him.

John 1:14

LOINS.

The middle part of your body, just below your stomach. Jewish people wrapped their loose-fitting clothes around their loins so it was easier to move when they worked or traveled.

2 Kings 4:29 KJV

LONGSUFFERING.

Patient and forgiving. It is in God's nature to be longsuffering. He told Moses, "I am merciful and very patient with my people. I show great love, and I can be trusted." The Lord acts this way because He wants us to be sorry for our sins and to ask for forgiveness.

Exodus 34:6 CEV
2 Peter 3:9

LORD.

A name for God and Jesus. It is also a name used for people in charge, such as kings. Lord is an English word used in Bibles for a few different Hebrew words. One is Yahweh. This was a very holy name that the Hebrews used for God. It might mean "I am the one who is" or "I am the one who brings into being." To show respect for God, the Hebrews did not say the word Yahweh out loud. In some English Bibles, Yahweh has been replaced with Lord. In other Bibles, the word Jehovah is used.

Exodus 3:15–16 CEV, footnote

LORD'S DAY. ————————

Sunday. This is the first day of the week. The Lord's Day is also the day that most Christians worship God in church. People of the Jewish faith worship on Saturday, the last day of the week. They call this the Sabbath. This is their day of rest. After Jesus rose from the dead on the first day, Christians made Sunday their normal day for worship. Sundays have been the Lord's Day for a very long time. In the year AD 321, the Roman emperor made it a Christian holiday.

Revelation 1:10
Acts 20:7

LORD'S PRAYER. ————————

A prayer that teaches us how to pray. Jesus taught this prayer to His disciples when they said, "Lord, teach us to pray." The prayer begins with coming to God with respect and awe. By saying the words "Give us this day our daily bread," we ask God to take care of the needs of our bodies, such as food. Then we ask God to forgive us just as we have forgiven others. We also ask God to protect us. Isn't it amazing that God can do all these things for us if we pray to Him? Read the whole prayer in Matthew 6:9–13.

Luke 11:1

LORD'S SUPPER. ————————

Jesus' last meal before the crucifixion. Jesus used this meal to talk about His death, which He knew would come soon. He used the food as symbols. Jesus blessed the bread and broke it. The bread stood for His body. Then He picked up a cup of wine and gave thanks to God. He gave it to the disciples. He told them to drink it. The wine stood for His blood. Jesus said that His blood would be poured out, like the wine, so that our sins would be forgiven. (Check out Matthew 26:26–28.) As Christians, we remember the Lord's Supper when we take communion. The Bible tells us that we should do this until the Lord returns.

Luke 22:15–16
1 Corinthians 11:25–26

LOT. ————————

Abraham's nephew. Lot went with his uncle Abraham to Canaan. Abraham let him be the first to choose where to live in Canaan. Lot picked the Jordan Valley. It was green and had lots of water. Lot took his family to live near the city of Sodom. Later, the Lord decided to destroy Sodom because the people there were bad. But He sent an angel to save Lot's family. The angel told them to run and never look back. Lot escaped, but his wife didn't. She looked back and was turned into a statue of salt. (Find out more about it in Genesis 19:15–26.)

Genesis 12:5
Genesis 13:10–11

LOTS. ————————

Making a decision by throwing small stones out of a jar. In Bible times, the casting of lots was done to find out the will of God.

Proverbs 16:33

LUCIFER. ————————

Another name for Satan. Jesus said, "I saw Satan fall from heaven like a flash of lightning." God created Satan to be a good guy. But he turned on God and became really bad. Then God kicked him out of heaven. Lucifer is also called the devil. No matter what you call him, he is out to do evil. But don't worry. Jesus gave us the power to stand against him.

Luke 10:18 CEV
Isaiah 14:12–14
Luke 10:19

LUKE. ————————

A Christian doctor and author of two New Testament books. Luke wrote the third and longest gospel and the book of Acts. Luke was born a Gentile, which means

a
b
c
d
e
f
g
h
i
j
k
L
m
n
o
p
q
r
s
t
u
v
w
x
y
z

a
b
c
d
e
f
g
h
i
j
k
L
m
n
o
p
q
r
s
t
u
v
w
x
y
z

his family was not Jewish. He also went with Paul on some of his trips to preach the Word of God. Luke was a very loyal and brave friend. He was the last to stay with Paul before he died. The book of Luke is about Jesus. The book of Acts covers about thirty-five years. It shows how Christianity spread from Jerusalem to Rome.

Colossians 4:14
Acts 16:10
2 Timothy 4:11

LUKE, GOSPEL OF.

The third book of the New Testament. Luke was the author of this book. He was a doctor who came from a family of Gentiles. In his book, Luke showed that Jesus was the Savior of all people, both Gentiles and Jews. He wrote about how Jesus talked to all kinds of people. He spent time with people whom others ignored. He ate with sinners. He blessed the poor. And He healed the sick, too. Luke was a friend of the apostle Paul. He also wrote the New Testament book called Acts.

Luke 15:2
Luke 6:20
Luke 17:11–19

LUKEWARM.

Not hot or cold. Do you ever answer a question with "Whatever"? If you don't care one way or the other, you are being lukewarm. In the Bible, some church members were scolded for being lukewarm in their faith.

Revelation 3:16

LYDIA.

A businesswoman of the Bible. Lydia lived in the city of Thyatira where she sold purple cloth. After Lydia heard Paul preach in Philippi, she and her household were baptized and became Christians. She asked Paul and his friends to stay at her home. (Read more about Lydia in Acts 16:14–15.)

One legend says that Luke, author of the third Gospel, was also a painter. This painting, by Raphael, is from around 1500.

MACEDONIA.

A region north of Greece. The apostle Paul set up churches there (see Acts 16, 17, 20). He went to Macedonia after he had a vision of a man begging him to come and help.

Acts 16:9

MAD.

Crazy or nuts. In the first book of Samuel, you can read about David acting like he was crazy. He did this to get away from King Achish in the town of Gath.

1 Samuel 21:13–15

MAGDALA.

A city in Galilee. It is on the coast of the Sea of Galilee near Capernaum and is the place where Jesus went after feeding four thousand people. It was probably the home of Mary Magdalene.

Matthew 15:39
Matthew 27:55–56

MAGIC.

Messing around with the world of demons. In the Bible, magic wasn't just tricks with playing cards or rabbits in hats. God told Moses that the people of Israel must not go to magicians or sorcerers for miracles. Sorcery is the use of power from evil or dead spirits to find things out. The Lord said, "And don't try to use any kind of magic or witchcraft to tell fortunes or to cast spells or to talk with spirits of the dead."

Leviticus 19:31
Exodus 7:11
Deuteronomy 18:10–11 CEV

MAGNIFICAT.

The song of the Virgin Mary. She sang this when she learned she would give birth to Jesus. In the song, Mary praised God for caring for her and blessing her. She sang about all the good things God does, like feeding the hungry and showing mercy to those who worship Him. She also praised Him for keeping His promise to bless Abraham and his descendants.

Luke 1:46–55

MAJESTY.

The power and right of a king. There are many verses in the Bible that praise the power of God. One example is in the book of Psalms: "The LORD reigns, he is robed in majesty; the LORD is robed in majesty and is armed with strength." Majesty is also used as a name for a king or other high official. In the book of Genesis, Joseph called the king "Your Majesty" when he spoke to him.

Psalm 93:1 NIV
Genesis 41:16 CEV

MAJOR PROPHETS.

The longer books written by prophets in the Old Testament. There are four. They are Isaiah, Jeremiah, Ezekiel, and Daniel. In the Bible, their books come before the shorter books written by prophets. The book of Lamentations comes after the book of Jeremiah because he wrote both. God sent the prophets to deliver His messages. Many times, their job was to warn people not to be sinful.

MALACHI.

A prophet in the Old Testament. He wrote the short book in the Bible that has his name—the last book in the Old Testament. His name means "my messenger." Malachi wrote about the wrong way to worship. He scolded the people of Israel who sacrificed animals that were blind or sick. He also spoke against those who did not give tithes and offerings to God.

Malachi 1:1
Malachi 1:8
Malachi 3:8–10

a
b
c
d
e
f
g
h
i
j
k
l
M
n
o
p
q
r
s
t
u
v
w
x
y
z

MALCHUS. ———

A man who lost his ear—then got it back. Malchus was a servant of the high priest who came to arrest Jesus. Peter swung a sword at Malchus and cut off his ear. Jesus told Peter to put away his sword and healed Malchus's ear. Jesus knew being arrested was part of God's plan. (Check out this story in Luke 22:47–51 and John 18:1–11.)

John 18:10

MALEFACTOR. ———

A person who does something wrong. When Christ was crucified, a malefactor—or criminal—was crucified on each side of Him. Read more about it in Luke 23:26–43.

MAMMON. ———

Money or wealth. Christ warned that money and belongings are false gods. We should not worship them. He said that if we "put God's work first," then all our needs will be met.

Matthew 6:24
Matthew 6:33 CEV

MAN. ———

Humans created by God in His image. This is you, me, and everyone of us. The Bible tells us that God created each of us to bring honor to Him. God gave us the power to rule all that He made on earth. Our sin put us apart from God. But we can be saved thanks to Jesus. God loves us and forgives our sins. He treats each of us the same. But we must have faith in Jesus to be accepted by Him.

Genesis 1:26
Isaiah 43:7
Psalm 8:4–6
Romans 3:22–24

MANASSEH. ———

A name shared by Joseph's son and Hezekiah's son. There were five men by this name in the Bible. One of them was the first son of Joseph. His relatives became one of the tribes of Israel. The tribe of Manasseh lived on both sides of the Jordan River. The other Manasseh became the king of Judah after his dad. He was a wicked ruler. He helped idol worship spread through the land. He was captured and taken to Babylonia. Later, he asked God to forgive him. Then he was able to go home and rule again. (Check it out in 2 Chronicles 33:10–13.) His son Amon was king after him.

Genesis 46:20
Genesis 48:5–6
Joshua 16:1–4
2 Chronicles 33:20

MANGER. ———

A feeding trough for farm animals. A manger was used as a bed for baby Jesus after He was born.

Luke 2:7

MANNA. ———

A miracle food. God gave the Israelites manna when they were in the wilderness. In Hebrew, the word *manna* means "what is it?" So what is manna? In the Bible, it's called "bread from heaven". It's described as tiny white seeds that "tasted like something baked with sweet olive oil." The people would grind or crush the seeds into flour. Then they would "boil it and make it into thin wafers."

Exodus 16:4
Numbers 11:8 CEV
Numbers 11:9 CEV

MARANATHA. ———

An Aramaic phrase that means "Come, O Lord." It shows hope that Jesus will come a second time.

1 Corinthians 16:22

MARK. ———

A cousin of Barnabas. Mark went with Barnabas and Paul on the first mission trip. Mark went as far as Perga. Then he went back to Jerusalem. Paul wouldn't let Mark go with them on the next trip. Because of this, Barnabas and Paul went their own ways. Mark's mom was a Christian woman named Mary. People who followed the Lord went to her home to pray. Mark wrote the New Testament book of Mark. It is one of the four Gospels.

Colossians 4:10
Acts 12:25
Acts 13:3–13
Acts 15:36–41
Acts 12:12

MARK, GOSPEL OF.

The second book of the New Testament. It was most likely the first to be written. It is a short book with just sixteen chapters. Mark shows Jesus as a man of action. In Mark's book, he lets us know Jesus had no time to waste. He had a big job to do for God! Mark makes it clear that Jesus was the Son of God. But he also writes about Jesus acting like a human. Just like us, Jesus could get angry, sad, and sleepy.

> Mark 15:39
> Mark 11:15–17
> Mark 4:38
> Mark 14:34

MARRIAGE.

A man and a woman joined as husband and wife. Have you ever been to a wedding? That's just the start of a marriage. God performed the first wedding in the Garden of Eden. Jesus said no one should break up a couple that God has joined in marriage. Paul described how husbands and wives should love each other. He said that this love is like Christ's love for the church.

> Genesis 2:18–24
> Matthew 19:4–6
> Ephesians 5:22–28

MARTHA.

The sister of Mary and Lazarus. The book of John tells the story of her brother's death. It made Martha very sad, and she asked Jesus for help. Read more about it in John 11:1–44.

MARY.

A name shared by many women in the Bible. The most well-known are Jesus' mom and Mary Magdalene. Jesus' mom is often called the Virgin Mary. She was engaged to Joseph. An angel told her she would give birth to Jesus. After He was born, Mary and Joseph took Him to Egypt. They had to get away from a mean king named Herod. The other Mary, Mary Magdalene, saw Jesus being crucified. Later, when she saw His empty tomb, she told the disciples. This Mary was one of the first to see Jesus after He'd risen from death. A third Mary was the sister of Martha and Lazarus. She listened to Jesus when He was in their home. She also poured perfume on His feet and wiped them with her hair.

> Luke 1:26–35
> Matthew 2:13–18
> Matthew 27:55–61
> John 20:1–2
> Mark 16:9
> Luke 10:38–39
> John 12:1–3

MATTHEW.

A tax collector who became one of Jesus' twelve disciples. He wrote the Bible book that has his name. It is the first of the Gospels and the first book in the New Testament. How could Matthew write a book about Jesus? Because he was a tax collector! In Bible times, many people didn't know how to read or write. But those who collected taxes had to be good at keeping records. That made Matthew a good choice for a writer. Some people called Mathew "Levi."

> Matthew 9:9
> Mark 2:13–17
> Luke 5:27–32

MATTHEW, GOSPEL OF.

The first book of the New Testament. Matthew wrote this book. He wanted to show the Jews that Jesus was the One the Jews had been waiting for. This book tells us that Jesus was a relative of Abraham and David. Matthew said these people were related to Jesus through Joseph, His dad on earth. A big part of this Gospel tells us of the teachings of Jesus. Matthew 5–7 is all about what He told His disciples in the Sermon on the Mount. There are also many verses about the kingdom of God or the kingdom of heaven.

> Matthew 1:1–2
> Matthew 1:6
> Matthew 5:3; 6:33; 8:11; 12:28; 13:43–46; 19:23; 25:34

MATTHIAS.

The man who took Judas Iscariot's job as an apostle. The others chose him by the casting of lots. Casting lots was like drawing straws.

> Acts 1:15–26

a
b
c
d
e
f
g
h
i
j
k
l
M
n
o
p
q
r
s
t
u
v
w
x
y
z

MEDES.

Relatives of Noah's son Japheth. They were also called Medians. The Medes were from the ancient land of Media. It was east of the Tigris River and south of the Caspian Sea. After the king of Assyria took over part of Israel, he sent some of its people there. Later, the Medes were part of the Persian Empire. King Cyrus had an army of Medes and Persians. They captured the city of Babylon.

2 Kings 17:6
Ezra 6:1–5
Isaiah 21:1–2

MEDIATOR.

A person who ends a fight by working with both sides. Have you ever helped two friends make up after a fight? If So you were acting as a mediator. Jesus is a mediator, too. He works at bringing God and His people together. He died so that we could have peace with God and each other.

Ephesians 2:13–16
1 Timothy 2:5

MEDITATION.

Careful and deep thought. Have you ever sat and thought about something for a long time? After you did, what you thought about most likely made more sense to you. If we think about what God has told us, His words will make sense, too. Thinking about God

can make us happy. Giving deep thought to the Word of God helps us to obey Him.

Psalm 49:3
Psalm 63:5–6
Joshua 1:8

MEDIUM.

A person who speaks to the spirit world. The prophet Isaiah warned that it was wrong to talk to the dead. He said we should listen only to the Lord.

Isaiah 8:19–20

MEEK.

Kind, gentle, and humble. Being meek is a good thing! The Bible says, "the meek will inherit the land and enjoy great peace." The Bible also says God loves us. He chose us as His own special people. We should be meek and patient. We should forgive others and remember that "love is more important than anything else."

Psalm 37:11 NIV
Colossians 3:12–14 CEV

MELCHIZEDEK.

An ancient king and priest. Abraham gave Melchizedek a tenth of all he had. We do not know about Melchizedek's parents or his death. In the book of Hebrews, it says that his priesthood was endless. You can read more about him in Hebrews 7. In the book of Psalms, King David said that Jesus will be a

priest forever, just like this King Melchizedek.

Genesis 14:18–20
Hebrews 7:3
Hebrews 7:16
Psalm 110:4

MERCY.

Pity or kindness for others. Have you ever forgiven a kid at school who hurt you? If you did, you showed mercy. God told Moses, "I am the LORD, and I show mercy and kindness to anyone I choose." God showed us great mercy by raising Jesus from the dead. In doing this, He gave us new life and hope. Paul called God "the Father of mercies and God of all comfort." In the book of Luke, Jesus told a story about a good man. He showed kindness to a hurt traveler and took care of him. To be a real neighbor to others, we should show them mercy like the Good Samaritan.

Exodus 33:19 CEV
1 Peter 1:3
2 Corinthians 1:3 NKJV
Luke 10:27–37

MERCY SEAT.

The lid of the ark of the covenant. It was made out of wood and covered with gold. On top, two carved angels faced each other. The Lord told Moses, "I will meet you there between the two creatures and tell you what my people must do and what they must not do." Once a year, the high priest sprinkled blood from a sacrificed bull and goat on the mercy seat. This was done for the high priest's sins and the sins of the people.

Exodus 25:17–21
Exodus 25:22 CEV
Leviticus 16:11–16

MESHACH.

One of Daniel's friends. The king threw him into a hot oven or furnace because he would not worship an idol. But God saved him from the fire. (See Daniel 3.)

Daniel 1:7

MESSENGER.

A person who delivers a message. John the Baptist was a messenger for God. He made the people ready to welcome Jesus.

Matthew 11:10–11

MESSIAH.

The name given by the Jews to a future leader. He is also called the Chosen Leader. In Old Testament times, the person chosen to be king had oil poured on his head. This was called "anointing"—a word that relates to the title Christ. "The Hebrew word 'Messiah' means the same as the Greek word 'Christ.' " In the Bible, the woman at the well said, "I know that the Messiah will come. He is the one we call Christ." Jesus replied that He was that one. Jesus was the Messiah the Jews had waited for. But He didn't save them in the way

A statue of the Philistine god Dagon falls and breaks in front of the ark of the covenant.

they expected. They thought He would save them from others who treated them badly. Instead, He saved all believers from sin.

Daniel 9:25–26 CEV
1 Samuel 10:1
John 1:41 CEV
John 4:25–26
Romans 6:1–9

METHUSELAH.

A son of Enoch, and the grandpa of Noah. He lived to be 969 years old! That's the oldest age written down in the Bible.

Genesis 5:21
Genesis 5:27

MICAH.

A prophet of the Old Testament. There are several Micah's in the Old Testament. But this one wrote the seventh-to-last book in the Old Testament. God spoke to him when Jotham, Ahaz, and Hezekiah were the kings of Judah. That was about 700 years before Jesus was born. Micah was a stern prophet. He judged

the bad things going on in Samaria and Judah. Micah spoke out against those who used their power to steal and cheat.

Micah 1:1–16
Micah 2:1–5

MICHAEL.

A name shared by an archangel and the son of a king. There are eleven Michaels in the Bible. One of them was the son of Jehoshaphat, the king of Judah. This Michael's older brother, Jehoram, became king when his father died. He is known for having his brothers killed! (Check it out in 2 Chronicles 21:2–4.) Another Michael was an angel called "the great prince." He guarded the nation of Israel.

Daniel 12:1
Daniel 10:21 CEV

MIDIANITES.

Traders who roamed around the land of Midian. Midian is southeast of the Dead Sea, in the Arabian Desert. Joseph's brothers sold him to a group from this tribe. The Midianites took Joseph to Egypt, where they sold him as a slave. (Check out Genesis 37:28–36.) The Midianites and Moabites attacked Israel. They failed to conquer Israel, though. Later, this tribe most likely became part of the Moabites or the Arabs.

Numbers 22

MIDWIFE.
A woman who helps others give birth to babies. The king of Egypt once told Jewish midwives to kill any male babies that were born. But they didn't obey him. (Check out Exodus 1:15–17.)

MIGHTY MEN.
Brave and loyal soldiers of Israel. These were the superheroes of Bible times. Some "mighty men of valor" supported Joshua in battle. During King David's time, there were three mighty men. In some versions of the Bible, they are called "fighting men" or "warriors." They did many brave deeds. They even risked their lives for King David. The second-best group of soldiers was called the thirty warriors. They fought for David, too, and they are listed by name in 2 Samuel 23:24–39. The Bible tells us of other very brave fighting men in 2 Samuel 23:18–23.

Joshua 10:7
2 Samuel 23:8–11

MILL.
A tool that grinds grain into flour. A mill has two stones that crush the grain between them.

Matthew 24:41

MIND.
The part of our bodies that thinks. In the Bible, the word *heart* often means "mind." Those who reject God have "useless minds." It is wrong to let our minds only think of ourselves. If our minds are ruled by what we want, we can't obey God's laws. But if the Holy Spirit rules our minds, we will have life and peace. (Check out Romans 8:5–7.) Jesus said, "Love the Lord your God with all your heart, soul, and mind". Paul told the Christians in Rome, "Let God change the way you think." If they did, they would know how to do good things to please God.

Psalm 19:14 NIV
Romans 1:28 CEV
Matthew 22:37 CEV
Romans 12:2 CEV
Romans 12:2

MINISTER.
A person who serves others. It can be used the same way as the word *servant*. It can also mean "to serve" or help someone. This word can be used for many kinds of people. In Bible times, "servant" was used for leaders like Moses. It was also used for people in the royal court and rulers. "Minister" was used for priests like Aaron and his sons. It

is still used for religious leaders today. In a church, the minister is the servant of the people. All Christians are told to "preach the word" as part of their "ministry" or service to God.

Joshua 1:1–2 CEV
1 Kings 10:5
Romans 13:4–6
Numbers 3:2–3 KJV
2 Timothy 4:2–5 NIV

MINOR PROPHETS.
The shorter books written by prophets in the Old Testament. There are twelve minor prophets. They are Hosea, Joel, Amos, Obadiah, Jonah, Micah, Nahum, Habakkuk, Zephaniah, Haggai, Zechariah, and Malachi. In the Bible, their books come after the longer books written by prophets. God sent the prophets to give us His message. Many times, their job was to warn us not to be sinful.

MIRACLE.
An act of God that seems to go against the laws of nature. In the New Testament, miracles have different names: "signs," "wonders," "mighty works," and "powers." Most miracles in the Bible took place in one of five periods of time. The first period was the Exodus. The next was during the lives of Elijah and Elisha. The third period was during the Exile. The fourth was Jesus' time. His miracles were signs that He had God's power. He healed the sick. He gave life to the dead. He

calmed the wind and sea. Jesus used miracles to teach lessons. The fifth period of miracles was the time of the apostles' work. Their miracles proved they were disciples of Jesus.

Exodus 7, 9, 10, 14
1 Kings 18:30 – 39
2 Kings 4:2 – 7
Daniel 3:9 – 27
Matthew 15:33 – 39
Matthew 8:14 – 17
Matthew 9:23 – 25
Luke 8:22 – 25
Matthew 21:18 – 22
Acts 3:6 – 9

Jesus performs a miracle by changing five loaves of bread and two small fish into a meal for more than 5,000 people.

MIRIAM.

The sister of Aaron and Moses. Have you ever looked out for a younger brother or sister? That's just what Miriam did. The king of Egypt had ordered all Hebrew boy babies to be killed. When Moses' mom gave birth to him, she hid him by the Nile River. Miriam watched over him. The king's daughter found the baby and felt sorry for him. Miriam offered to find a Hebrew woman to take care of him. Who do you think she brought? Her mom! (Find out more about it in Exodus 2:1–10.) After God saved the people of Israel from the Egyptian army, Miriam sang. In her song, she praised and thanked God. When she died, she was buried in the wilderness at Kadesh.

1 Chronicles 6:3
Exodus 1:16
Exodus 15:20 – 21
Numbers 20:1

MISSIONS.

Making disciples of all people in all places. This is what Jesus asks His believers to do: to travel to all nations and preach to the people there; to baptize the ones who believe; and to teach what Jesus taught us about God. People can't have faith in God if they've never heard of Him. They must hear about Him from those God sends. Thanks to the Holy Spirit, believers have the power to spread the Word. Missions go back as far as the Old Testament. Abraham was called to be a blessing to all nations. God told Jonah to preach to the unbelievers in Nineveh.

Matthew 28:19 – 20
Romans 10:14 – 15
Acts 1:8
Jonah 1:1 – 2

MITE.

The coin with the least value in New Testament times. It was worth less than a penny. Jesus praised a poor widow's offering of two mites because she gave all she had to live on.

Mark 12:42 – 44

MOABITES.

Bad people who came from a son of Lot. The Moabites worshipped the god Chemosh. The Bible tells us about some fights between the Israelites and the Moabites. But a Moabite woman named Ruth married a man of Israel and became the great-grandmother of King David.

Numbers 21:29

MODERATION.

Not overdoing something. Did you ever eat a small piece of cake, even though you wanted a really big piece? If So you acted with moderation. This means that you showed self-control. Paul explained moderation as a way of being gentle. He said that we should act with "moderation" in front of others. The Bible tells us, "Moderation is better than muscle."

Philippians 4:5 KJV
Proverbs 16:32 MSG

a
b
c
d
e
f
g
h
i
j
k
l
M
n
o
p
q
r
s
t
u
v
w
x
y
z

MONEY CHANGERS. ——

The bankers of Bible times. They collected foreign money from worshippers and exchanged it for money that could be used as an offering in the temple. They charged a big fee to do this. Jesus drove them out of the temple. He called them robbers.

Matthew 21:12–13

MONOGAMY. ——

One man married to just one woman. This began with Adam and Eve. Some men in the Old Testament, like Jacob, had more than one wife. And these men usually had many problems in their families.

Genesis 2:21–24
Genesis 29:16–28

MONOTHEISM. ——

The belief in one, and only one, God. Some religions worship many gods. This is called polytheism. But as Christians, we believe there is only one true God. The Bible tells us our Lord is the only true God. "So love the Lord your God with all your heart, soul, and strength." We should learn God's laws and teach them to others. God wants us to be loyal to Him. He does not want His people to make or bow down to false gods. In the Ten Commandments, God said, "Do not worship any god except me."

Deuteronomy 6:5 CEV
Deuteronomy 6:6–7
Exodus 20:4–5
Exodus 20:3 CEV

MOON. ——

The big, bright ball in the night sky. In the Bible, the moon is called the "lesser light." Some pagans worshipped the moon. God told the Hebrews not to do this.

Genesis 1:16
Deuteronomy 4:19

MORDECAI. ——

A Jew who helped Esther to become queen. Esther was Mordecai's cousin. He raised Esther as his own after her mom and dad died. When King Xerxes was looking for a new queen, Esther was brought into his harem. The king liked her so much that he made her his queen. Later, Mordecai saved the king's life when he found out two guards planned to kill him. But another bad man named Haman worked for the king. Haman hated Mordecai because he refused to kneel down and honor him. So he planned to kill all the Jews. Mordecai told Esther about this plan, and she told the king. Haman was hanged from the very tower he built to hang Mordecai.

Esther 2:7
Esther 2:17
Esther 2:19–23
Esther 3:5–6
Esther 7:10

MORIAH. ——

A hilly part of Jerusalem. God told Abraham to sacrifice his son Isaac on a mountain there. Just as Abraham was about to kill his son, an angel stopped him. God gave Abraham a ram to sacrifice in place of his son. Abraham named the place The Lord Will Provide. "And to this day it is said, 'On the mountain of the LORD it will be provided.' "

Genesis 22:2
Genesis 22:13
Genesis 22:14 NIV

MORNING STAR. ——

Another name for Jesus. He called Himself "the bright Morning Star." Peter wrote, "You must keep on paying attention until daylight comes and the morning star rises in your hearts." By "morning star," he meant Jesus. We should always "look up" and live godly lives until Jesus comes back.

Revelation 22:16 NIV
2 Peter 1:19 CEV

MORTALITY. ——

The fact that we'll all die someday. Everybody! But while our bodies will die, death is the start of eternal life for those who believe in Jesus. That's the good news! Eternal life means that our souls will live forever with God.

1 Corinthians 15:21–23

MOSES. ——

The prophet of Israel who wrote the first five books of the Bible. Moses lived to be 120 years old! He spent the first forty years of his life in Egypt. During that time,

the king ordered all Hebrew boy babies to be killed. When Moses' mom gave birth to him, she hid him. She put him in a basket along the Nile River. The king's daughter found the baby and adopted him. (Read more about it in Exodus 2:1–10.) Years later, after killing an Egyptian who hit a Hebrew slave, Moses ran away into the desert.

Moses spent the next forty years in Midian. He married Zipporah and had two sons. God called Moses to go back on Egypt to get His people out of slavery. The Lord sent ten plagues to Egypt. This forced the pharaoh to let the Hebrews go. Moses led the people into the Sinai Peninsula.

Moses spent the last forty years of his life in the wilderness. That's where God gave him the Ten Commandments. He also built the tabernacle, following God's instructions. While they were in the wilderness, in Kadesh, the Israelites had no water. All the people whined. God spoke to Moses and Aaron. He told Moses to speak to the rock and then water would come out of it. Moses hit the rock two times with his staff and water gushed from it. But God was angry. Aaron and Moses had not trusted Him; instead of just speaking to the rock, Moses had struck it! They did not honor God in front of the others. So God said they would not be the ones to lead His people into the Promised Land.

Deuteronomy 34:7
Exodus 1:16
Exodus 2:12–15
Exodus 18:2–4
Exodus 3:11–4:20
Exodus 20:1–24
Exodus 35–40
Numbers 20:2–11
Numbers 20:12–13

The Red Sea splits in two before Moses and the people of Israel (Exodus 14).

MOST HIGH.

A name for God that means "His majesty." It is often used to show God's royal power. Psalm 47:2 says: "How awesome is the LORD Most High, the great King over all the earth!" (NIV). This name was used in both the Old and New Testaments. In the book of Numbers, the Lord spoke to Balaam. Then Balaam said, "My knowledge comes from God Most High, the LORD All-Powerful." Sometimes those who didn't believe used this name. Acts tells the story of a girl who had an evil spirit in her. She followed Paul and his friends for days. She kept yelling about them, "These men are servants of the Most High God!"

Acts 7:48–49
Numbers 24:15–16 CEV
Acts 16:17 CEV

MOTE.

A speck or tiny bit of something. Jesus used this word when He talked about judging others. Jesus said you shouldn't point out a speck in another person's eye when you have a log in your own eye. That funny story meant it's wrong to point out small problems in others while ignoring huge problems of your own.

Matthew 7:3–5 KJV

MOUNT ARARAT.

Where Noah's ark landed. Mount Ararat is in Turkey. It is higher than any other mountain in its range. Its peak is topped with snow all year long. The ancient Persians called Ararat "Noah's

a
b
c
d
e
f
g
h
i
j
k
l
M
n
o
p
q
r
s
t
u
v
w
x
y
z

101

a
b
c
d
e
f
g
h
i
j
k
l
M
n
o
p
q
r
s
t
u
v
w
x
y
z

mountain." No one knows the exact spot where the ark landed. A few groups of people looked for it on Mount Urartu. That is in eastern Armenia. Wouldn't it be awesome if they found it someday?

Genesis 8:4

MOUNT CARMEL. ——

A mountain in northern Israel. In 1 Kings, the prophet Elijah told King Ahab that he had disobeyed the Lord. Ahab worshipped the pagan god Baal. Elijah told him to bring the prophets of Baal to Mount Carmel. Once there, Elijah told them his plan to prove whether his Lord or Baal was the one true God. He said, "The prophets of Baal will pray to their god, and I will pray to the LORD. The one who answers by starting the fire is God." What do you think happened? The Lord sent a scorching fire right away! When the crowd saw this, they bowed down and yelled, "The LORD is God!" (Check out 1 Kings 18:17–39.)

1 Kings 18:24 CEV
1 Kings 18:39 CEV

MOUNT NEBO. ——

Where Moses died after seeing the Promised Land. He was also buried there. Mount Nebo is in the Abarim Mountain range in Moab. Nebo was a Babylonian god. So Mount Nebo might have been a center of Nebo worship.

Deuteronomy 34:1–6
Deuteronomy 32:49

MOUNT OF OLIVES. ——

A hill beyond the Kidron Valley east of Jerusalem. Lots of stories in the Bible took place at the Mount of Olives. Many of them are about Jesus. Jesus often went to the Mount of Olives. He had a big talk with His disciples there. This is where Judas betrayed Jesus the night before He was crucified. It's also where Jesus talked to the disciples after He rose from the dead. The branches of olive trees from this place were used to make booths or tents for a special feast.

Luke 22:39
Matthew 24:3–26:2
Matthew 26:30, 41
Acts 1:1–12
Nehemiah 8:15

MOUNT SINAI. ——

A mountain where God gave Moses the Ten Commandments. In some Bibles, it is known as Mount Horeb. Its peak is more than a mile above sea level! It is in the wilderness of the Sinai Peninsula. This big peninsula is shaped like a triangle. It is south of the Mediterranean Sea and north of the Red Sea. The southern part of Sinai has mountains. This is where Moses saw the burning bush and God called him to save His people. The northern part of Sinai is a desert. The people of Israel camped here after they left Egypt.

Exodus 3:1–10
Exodus 19:1–2

MOURN. ——

To show grief or sadness. Have you ever cried when someone you loved died? If So you were mourning. In Bible times, the usual time of mourning was seven days. It was changed to thirty days when Moses and Aaron died. Jesus mourned the death of His friend Lazarus. In the Bible, it says that there is a time for everything. There is even a time to mourn.

Deuteronomy 34:8
Numbers 20:29
John 11:33–36
Ecclesiastes 3:1, 4

MURDER. ——

Taking the life of another human being. It is wrong to kill. One of the Ten Commandments says, "Do not murder".

Exodus 20:13 CEV

MYRRH. ——

A gummy material with a strong smell. Myrrh was one of the gifts for the baby Jesus. In Bible times, myrrh was used to add a good smell to incense and oil.

Matthew 2:11
Exodus 30:23–25

MYSTERY. ——

A secret thing we do not know. Jesus used stories to explain the secrets of God's kingdom. In the Bible, Paul wrote that he knew the mystery of Jesus. He said God's Spirit told it to His apostles and prophets. We know the good news about Jesus because God told us His secret. The secret is that Christ Jesus lives inside of us.

Luke 8:10
Ephesians 3:4–5
Romans 16:25–26
Colossians 1:26–27

NAAMAN.

A Syrian soldier healed of leprosy. Naaman had a skin disease. He went to Samaria to see if the prophet Elisha could cure it. Elisha told him to take a bath in the Jordan River. That made Naaman angry! What was wrong with taking a bath at home? But he finally obeyed Elisha—and he was cured. So Naaman praised the God of Israel. (Find out more in 2 Kings 5:1–15.)

NABAL.

A rich but foolish man. Nabal refused to give food to David and his army. But his beautiful wife, Abigail, gave food to them in secret. Nabal died about ten days later, and David married Abigail. (Read more about it in 1 Samuel 25:2–40.)

NABOTH.

An Israelite who was killed by Queen Jezebel. This was done so King Ahab could take over Naboth's land. The Lord was very angry with them for doing this.

1 Kings 21:1–24

NADAB.

A name shared by the oldest son of Aaron and a king. There were four Nadabs in the Bible. One of them was burned to death by the Lord. Aaron's son Nadab, along with his brother Abihu, were killed for disobeying God. Another Nadab was an evil king of Israel.

Leviticus 10:1–2
1 Kings 15:25–31

NAHUM.

A prophet of Judah. He wrote the sixth-to-last book in the Old Testament. Nahum wrote that the city of Nineveh was doomed and would be attacked. He said God was angry with the people of Assyria for doing bad things. Nahum most likely made this prediction when Hezekiah was king. Nahum showed God as the ultimate ruler. God has the last word in the fight between good and evil.

NAIN.

A village where Jesus raised a widow's son from the dead. It is southeast of Nazareth and near the Sea of Galilee.

Luke 7:11–17

NAME.

What a person or thing is called. Adam named the animals and his wife, Eve. People and places in the Bible often had names that were symbols. One example is when the Lord told Hosea to name his son Jezreel. This means "God scatters." It is first used as a threat. It means God will punish Israel. Its people will be scattered all over! Later, it is a good symbol. God promises to bless Israel with lots of people.

Genesis 2:20
Genesis 3:20
Hosea 1:4

NAOMI.

The mother-in-law of Ruth. During a famine, Naomi and her family moved from Bethlehem to Moab. While there, Naomi's husband died. Her sons married Moabite women, Orpah and Ruth. Then, about ten years later, Naomi's sons died. Naomi, Orpah, and Ruth were all alone. Naomi decided to go back home to Bethlehem, and Ruth went with her. Then Naomi planned Ruth's marriage to Boaz. You can read all about Naomi in Ruth 1–4.

NAPHTALI.

Jacob's sixth son. His descendants formed the tribe of Naphtali. They lived in northern Israel, an area with many mountains.

Genesis 30:7–8
Numbers 1:42
Joshua 19:32–39

a
b
c
d
e
f
g
h
i
j
k
l
m
N
o
p
q
r
s
t
u
v
w
x
y
z

NATHAN.

A name shared by a son of David and a brave prophet. Several Nathans are in the Bible. One of them was the son of King David and Bathsheba. He was a brother of Solomon, too. The Lord sent another Nathan, a prophet, to tell David a story. He scolded King David for disobeying the Lord. This prophet also wrote about what David and Solomon did when they were kings.

1 Chronicles 3:5
2 Samuel 12:1–15
1 Chronicles 29:29
2 Chronicles 9:29

NATION.

A country—or all the people who live in a country. In the Bible, nation can also mean a group of people who have the same ancestors.

Acts 26:4

NATURE.

A word that can mean the physical world and the basic way people are. God made all of nature and gave people control of it. When Adam and Eve disobeyed God, He cursed nature. From then on, humans had to work hard to grow food. Nature can also describe what a person is really like. The apostle Paul wrote, "When the Gentiles, which have not the law, do by nature the things contained in the law,

these, having not the law, are a law unto themselves."

Genesis 3:12–19
Genesis 1:1, 26–31
Romans 2:14 KJV

NAZARETH.

Jesus' boyhood hometown. It's a village in Galilee near the Plain of Esdraelon. Mount Carmel is fifteen miles to the northwest. Nazareth was where Jesus lived as a boy. This is why some people call Him "Jesus of Nazareth." This is where Mary was when the angel told her she was going to give birth to Jesus. Mary, Joseph, and Jesus went back there after they had run away to Egypt. The people of Nazareth were not very nice to Jesus. He said things that made them mad. One time, they tried to throw Him off a cliff!

Mark 1:24
Luke 1:26–38
Matthew 2:20–23
Luke 4:16–30

NAZARITE.

A person who is set apart to God. Nazarites took special vows. They did this by choice or because a parent made the choice for them. They had to stay away from strong drinks and could not cut their hair. The vow often lasted one to three months. But sometimes this vow was for life! Can you imagine never cutting your hair as long as you live? Samson and John the Baptist were Nazarites their whole lives. The apostle Paul took

a few Nazarite vows. You can read all about the law of the Nazarite in Numbers 6:1–21.

Judges 13:4–7
Luke 1:15
Acts 18:18
Acts 21:22–24

NEBUCHADNEZZAR.

The strong king of Babylonia. His father began the Chaldean Empire. Nebuchadnezzar was in charge of the army. When his father died, he became king. Babylon was a huge city under his rule. King Nebuchadnezzar attacked Jerusalem. His soldiers took things made of gold, silver, and bronze from the temple. Then they burned the building! The king had many people of Judah captured and taken away. Others left because they were scared. (Check out 2 Kings 25:1–26.) Why did God let this happen? He was angry at the people of Judah. They were sinning and ignoring the prophets.

2 Chronicles 36:15–20

Nebuchadnezzar goes crazy over his pride (Daniel 4).

NEHEMIAH.

The governor of Jerusalem. During the exile to Babylon, he was the cupbearer for the king of Persia. He served the king his wine and tasted it to make sure it wasn't poisoned. Later, he asked the king if he could go home to Jerusalem. He wanted to help rebuild the city and its wall. He wrote a book in the Old Testament. It is named after him. His book is about the rebuilding after the exile. It also tells of the religious changes he started with Ezra the priest. They helped the people become closer to God and follow His law.

> Nehemiah 1:11
> Nehemiah 2:3–6
> Nehemiah 8–13

NEIGHBOR.

A fellow human—not just somebody next door! Jesus said it was very important for us to love our neighbors as ourselves. Paul said that if we loved our neighbors, we would be keeping God's law. We should tell the truth and never lie to them. The Pharisees thought the word *neighbor* only meant the people in their own nation. But Jesus taught us that all people are our neighbors. His story about the Good Samaritan shows that we should help others, even if they don't live next door.

> Matthew 22:39
> Romans 13:9–10
> Ephesians 4:25
> Luke 10:25–31

NERO.

An emperor of Rome. His title was Caesar. Although his name "Nero" is not in the Bible, he was the Caesar whom Paul talks about in Acts 25:11. While Paul was in jail in Rome, he asked this Caesar for help. Nero blamed Christians for a big fire that destroyed most of Rome.

NET.

A mesh or woven fabric used to catch birds or fish. When Jesus saw fishermen with nets, He told them to come with Him and learn how to catch people instead of fish.

> Matthew 4:18–20

NEW BIRTH.

The start of the new life we will live as believers. Have you ever heard stories about the day you were born? That was the day you entered the world. But to enter the kingdom of God, you must be born of the Spirit, or saved. "Humans give life to their children. Yet only God's Spirit can change you into a child of God." We are saved thanks to our faith and God's grace. It is His gift. It isn't something we can brag about or receive by doing good works. Only the Holy Spirit can give new life.

> John 3:5–8
> John 3:6 CEV
> Ephesians 2:8–9
> John 3:8

NEW COVENANT.

God's final promise or agreement with His people. The prophet Jeremiah predicted this new agreement. Jesus' Passover meal with His disciples was a symbol of it. Jesus called the cup the "new covenant in my blood." Christ is the one who makes this new and better agreement possible. "Christ died to rescue those who had sinned and broken the old agreement. Now he brings his chosen ones a new agreement with its guarantee of God's eternal blessings!"

> Jeremiah 31:31–34
> Luke 22:20 NIV
> Hebrews 9:15 CEV

NEW TESTAMENT.

The second part of the Bible. This section of the Bible is made up of twenty-seven books. It begins with the four Gospels written by Matthew, Mark, Luke, and John. They tell about the life and ministry of Jesus. These are followed by the book of Acts. Next are the twenty-one epistles, which are letters. Paul wrote most of them. John, Peter, James, and Jude wrote the rest. The New Testament ends with the book of Revelation. This book, and the New Testament, end with God's promise of a new heaven and a new earth.

NICODEMUS.

A Pharisee who knew Jesus was the Messiah. Have you ever been the only one in a big group to believe the truth? That's how it was with Nicodemus. The other Pharisees did not believe Jesus was the Son of God. But Nicodemus did. He talked with Jesus about the new birth. Jesus told him a person must be saved—born of the Spirit—before he or she can get into God's kingdom. He warned the Jewish leaders not to judge Jesus before hearing what He had to say. Later, Nicodemus helped prepare Jesus' body to be buried.

John 3:1–7
John 7:50–51
John 19:39–42

NILE RIVER.

The great river of Egypt. It is more than four thousand miles long! It begins in Africa, goes across Egypt, and ends at the Mediterranean Sea. In Bible times, the people of Egypt counted on the Nile for water. The drying up of the Nile was a symbol for God's judgment on Egypt. When Moses was a baby, his mom hid him at the edge of this river.

Isaiah 23:10
Zechariah 10:11
Exodus 2:1–3

NIMROD.

A great-grandson of Noah. He was a strong hunter and warrior. When he was king, he ruled in Babylonia. He also built cities such as Nineveh. (Check out Genesis 10:8–12.)

NINEVEH.

The capital city of Assyria. Genesis tells us that Nineveh was originally built by Nimrod. Nineveh is in northern Iraq on the Tigris River. God sent the prophet Jonah there. He wanted Jonah to preach His message of doom. At that time, Nineveh was a large and rich city. The people there listened to Jonah. They stopped doing evil things. This pleased God. He did not destroy the city as He had planned. The ancient ruins of this city can still be seen today.

Genesis 10:8–12
Jonah 3

NOAH.

The old man who built the ark. Noah was chosen by God to save life on earth. He built a big wooden boat to escape the great flood. Noah was the son of Lamech and the father of Shem, Ham, and Japheth. After he built the ark, the 600-year-old Noah went inside with his family and some animals. God told him which ones to bring. Then God sent rain that lasted for forty days and nights. The water flooded the earth! When the flood ended, Noah's family and the animals left the ark. Then Noah built an altar to worship God, who made a covenant, or promise, with Noah. God promised never to punish the earth like that again. Noah died at the very old age of 950. Read all about Noah and his ark in Genesis 6:9–9:29.

Genesis 7:6–9
Genesis 7:1–3
Genesis 8:20
Genesis 9:1–11
Genesis 9:29

NUMBERS, BOOK OF.

The fourth book of the Old Testament, written by Moses. After the people of Israel left Egypt, they were in the wilderness of Sinai. They were there for forty years before going to Canaan. The book of Numbers is about the many things that went on at that time. It tells of the "numbering" of the people in two official counts. During this time, the people failed to trust God. They also feared the people of Canaan. The Israelites rebelled a few times. They whined about the wilderness, too. The last chapters tell how the people of Israel got ready to enter the Land of Promise.

Numbers 1, 26
Numbers 13
Numbers 15–36

Noah releases a dove from the ark to see if the water has dried from the earth.

OATH.

A solemn promise. King David let Jonathan's son, Mephibosheth, live because of his promise to Jonathan. Oaths were often used to prove that something was true. A person taking an oath would raise his or her hand in promise.

2 Samuel 21:7
Genesis 14:22–24

OBADIAH.

A name shared by a prophet and a king's servant. There were lots of men named Obadiah in the Bible. One was a prophet of Judah. He wrote the shortest book of the Old Testament. It's named after him. Another Obadiah was a servant of King Ahab. Ahab's wife, Jezebel, wanted to kill the prophets. Obadiah hid some of them so they could escape.

1 Kings 18:3–16

OBEY.

To listen to someone in charge and do what he or she says. Do you always obey your mom and dad? When you obey your parents, God is pleased. The fifth commandment says: Obey your father and mother, and you will have a long and happy life. Jesus obeyed His parents. He obeyed God, too. Jesus told people that they should obey all of God's rules. The Bible says to obey people in charge. That means people like teachers, police officers, and other trusted adults. Listen to them, and do what is right. Ask your parents which grown-ups you should trust.

Colossians 3:20
Ephesians 6:2–3
Luke 2:51
Matthew 19:17
Titus 3:1

OFFENSE.

An insult or bad action toward someone else. It is an offense if you say or do things that make others feel sad or angry. The Bible teaches that we should make up with those we hurt. Jesus said you must end a fight with a brother who is mad at you before you make an offering to God.

Matthew 5:23–24

OFFERING.

Something given to God. An offering can be a gift of money made during worship. You can also offer your time to God by doing good things for others. Giving an offering is one way of thanking God. You can make an offering to show God that you are sorry for your sins. Jesus offered His own life to make up for the sins of all people.

Hebrews 7:27

OFFSPRING.

Children or other descendants. We are all God's offspring. He created us! Through His mom, Mary, Jesus is the offspring of King David. Are you someone's offspring?

Acts 17:29
Matthew 1:1

OIL.

A thick liquid with many uses. The oil that comes from olives was used as fuel in lamps. It was also used to prepare food and as medicine.

Matthew 25:3
1 Kings 17:12
Luke 10:34

OLD TESTAMENT.

The first part of the Bible. This section of the Bible is made up of thirty-nine books. Much of the Old Testament is history. It is about God and His people. The very first book is called Genesis. It tells how God created the heavens and the earth. Moses is the author of the first five books of the Bible. These books are called the Pentateuch. They tell about God's laws. Some of the

b c d e f g h i j k l m n o p q r s t u v w x y z

a
b
c
d
e
f
g
h
i
j
k
l
m
n
O
p
q
r
s
t
u
v
w
x
y
z

Old Testament books are poetic, like the book of Psalms. Others were written by prophets.

Genesis 1

OLIVE.

The fruit of an olive tree. Olives were used for food and for oil. The branch of an olive tree is a symbol of peace.

Genesis 8:11

OMNIPOTENCE.

God's great power. There are no limits to God's power. He controls nature. He also controls what happens to all nations.

Amos 4:13
Amos 1–2

OMNIPRESENCE.

God's great presence. God is in all places at all times. No one can hide from Him. God's Spirit is with us in all we do.

Jeremiah 23:23–24
John 14:3, 18

OMNISCIENCE.

God's great knowledge. God is very wise and He knows everything. Christ is the key to understanding all of God's wisdom and knowledge.

Colossians 2:2–3

OMRI.

An evil king of Israel. Omri built Samaria as the capital city of the northern kingdom. He was a bad king who led his people into idol worship.

1 Kings 16:26

ONESIMUS.

A slave. Onesimus fled from his master, Philemon. He ran away to Rome. While there, he met Paul. Paul helped him become a Christian. Then Onesimus went back to his master with a letter. In the letter, Paul asked Philemon to show mercy and love. Paul said that Onesimus should be treated "no longer as a slave, but better than a slave, as a dear brother." Read all about Onesimus in Philemon 1.

Philemon 1:16 NIV

ORDAIN.

To choose someone for a special job in the church. Paul and Barnabas ordained people for the churches they formed. Paul told Titus to pick leaders to serve in other churches. Jesus ordained people, too: "Then he chose twelve of them to be his apostles, so that they could be with him. He also wanted to send them out to preach."

Acts 14:23
Titus 1:5
Mark 3:14 CEV

ORDINANCES.

God's rules for living. Ordinances are also special Christian celebrations. They remind us what Jesus did to save us. Baptism is an ordinance. It reminds us that Jesus is greater than sin and death. The Lord's Supper is another one. When we take communion, we remember Jesus' last meal with His disciples. It reminds us that Jesus gave His blood and body so we could be forgiven.

Psalm 19:9
Romans 6:3–6
1 Corinthians 11:23–26

ORPHAN.

Someone whose parents have died. Being kind to orphans was a law. Jesus promised: "I will not leave you as orphans; I will come to you."

Deuteronomy 24:17
John 14:18 NIV

OTHNIEL.

The first judge of Israel. In Bible times, judges were military leaders. Before Othniel was a leader, the people of Israel were doing bad things. The Lord was angry. He allowed the king of Mesopotamia to rule them for eight years. When the people cried out to the Lord, He sent Othniel to save them. He fought the Mesopotamian king and won! After that, Israel was at peace for forty years. (See Judges 3:7–11.)

OX.

A strong cowlike animal. Oxen were used for farm chores, such as plowing. They were used for food and sacrifices, too.

1 Kings 19:19 NIV
Leviticus 17:3–4

PALACE.

Where a king lives. Solomon's palace on Mount Zion was very beautiful. It even had an ivory throne!

1 Kings 7:1–12
1 Kings 10:18

PALESTINE.

The Holy Land. The name Palestine came from a Greek word that means "land of the Philistines." (Remember the giant Goliath? He was a Philistine.) Three great world religions came out of Palestine. They are Judaism, Christianity, and Islam.

PALM.

A kind of tropical tree. The palm tree got its name because its leaves look like human hands. The most common kind of palm in the Bible is the date palm. It grows to be sixty to eighty feet tall.

Exodus 15:27

PANTHEISM.

The belief that God is the universe rather than its creator. Have you heard someone say "the universe" when they mean God? That's pantheism, and it's popular today. Don't let it fool you. God and His universe aren't the same. God is greater than the universe. He created it. Jews and Christians don't agree with the idea of pantheism. They believe that God the Creator is greater than anything He has created.

Genesis 1:1
Psalm 8:1

PARABLE.

A story that teaches a lesson. A parable is like a fable. It is a comparison—it uses one thing to teach about something else. Parables teach lessons about life. Jesus used parables all the time. They were like secret codes. Jesus' followers could understand His parables. But unbelievers could not. See if you can find and read these parables in your Bible:

- The Wise and Foolish Builders
  Matthew 7:24–27
- The Lost Sheep
  Luke 15:3–7
- The Prodigal Son
  Luke 15:11–32
- The Sower
  Matthew 13:3–23

PARADISE.

Heaven. Paradise is someplace perfect. When God put Adam and Eve in the Garden of Eden, the garden was paradise. It was perfect in every way. Of course, that nasty old serpent named Satan came along and ruined it all. Not only for Adam and Eve, but also for everybody else. What is your idea of paradise? Whatever you can imagine, it is not as wonderful as the paradise that God has created for His people. His paradise is heaven. It is the most awesome place! If you believe in Jesus, someday you will live in paradise.

Genesis 2–3
Luke 23:43

PARALYTIC.

A person who cannot move certain parts of his or her body. That means they are paralyzed in some way. Jesus healed many paralytics. One day, Jesus was in the middle of a big crowd. He and the people were all inside a house when some men went up on the roof. They made a hole in it. Then they put a paralyzed man on a mat. They lowered him down through the hole. He ended up right by Jesus! Jesus healed the man and forgave him for his sins.

Matthew 4:24
Mark 2:1–12

b
c
d
e
f
g
h
i
j
k
l
m
n
o
p
q
r
s
t
u
v
w
x
y
z

109

a b c d e f g h i j k l m n o **p** q r s t u v w x y z

PARCHMENT. ———

The skin of sheep or goats, fixed up so people could write on it. Parchment was used like paper. When Paul was in prison, he asked Timothy to bring him parchments.

2 Timothy 4:13

PARDON. ———

Forgiveness. Imagine that your sister does something mean to you. Then she comes to you and says, "I'm sorry." She is asking for your pardon. In other words, she wants you to forgive her. God wants us to be forgiving. The Lord's Prayer says: "Forgive us for doing wrong, as we forgive others." Every day, we humans do things that don't please God. But if we come to Him in prayer and are truly sorry, He will forgive us. God pardons us because He loves us.

Matthew 6:12 CEV
Micah 7:18
Numbers 14:19

PARTIALITY. ———

Special treatment for someone. Some kids will only hang out with certain other kids. They have their own favorites, and that's not right. Jesus gave this command: Love one another. God's love and wisdom are for everyone, not just a few. He does not show partiality.

John 13:34
James 3:17

PASSOVER. ———

An important Jewish holiday. Passover is when Jews remember the Israelites' exodus from Egypt. The Israelites were slaves in Egypt for many years. God sent plagues to Egypt because the pharaoh would not let the Israelites go. The last plague was the death of the firstborn (the oldest child) of every Egyptian family. God wanted to protect the Israelites from this plague. He told them to paint the blood of a lamb over the doors of their houses. He said when He came to take the firstborn, He would "pass over" the homes that had blood over the doors. After all the Egyptian firstborn died, Pharaoh let the Israelites go.

Exodus 12:13

PASTOR. ———

Someone who leads a church. Pastors have many tasks. One of them is to teach. When you go to church, your pastor gives a sermon. If you listen carefully, you will learn about the Bible, Jesus, God, and the Holy Spirit. Another thing a pastor does is to lead people to believe in God and all that Jesus taught. In Old Testament times, God's people turned away from Him for a while. Speaking through the prophet Jeremiah, God said that pastors would come to bring the people back to Him.

Ephesians 4:10–11
Jeremiah 3:15

PASTORAL EPISTLES. ———

Letters about how a church should work. In the Bible, the pastoral epistles were Paul's letters: 1 and 2 Timothy and Titus.

PATIENCE. ———

Waiting without getting annoyed. Imagine that you are going to a movie. You've wanted to see this movie for weeks. But when you get to the theater, there's a very long line. You worry that by the time you get into the theater, the movie will have already started. If you wait calmly without getting upset, that's patience! God helps us to be patient. Jesus is the perfect example of patience. When He was arrested and suffering, He never lost his cool.

Romans 15:5 CEV
2 Thessalonians 3:5

PATMOS. ———

A small island in the Aegean Sea. In New Testament times, the Romans used Patmos as a prison. The apostle John was sent there. Patmos is where he wrote the book of Revelation. Patmos Island still exists. Today it has a population of about 3,000.

Revelation 1:9

PATRIARCH. ———

The male head of a family. The oldest man in your family is your patriarch. It might be your dad, grandfather, or great-grandfather. In Old Testament times, a patriarch ruled a family group called a tribe. When a patriarch died, his son took over as the ruler. Abraham, Isaac, and Jacob are examples of patriarchs.

PAUL.

Acts 7:8–9

A Jesus-hater who repented and became a Christian missionary. Paul became famous after Jesus died. At first, he was against Christianity. In fact, he wanted to kill anyone who taught about

Though the Bible doesn't say so, many people believe the apostle Paul was killed by the Roman government.

Jesus. One day, he was walking on the road to Damascus. As he went on his way, he was thinking about arresting Christians. Just then, a bright light came down from heaven. Paul fell to the ground, and Jesus' voice came from the light. He asked Paul why he was being so mean to Him. Then He told Paul to get up and go to Damascus. When Paul stood up, he discovered that he was blind! He spent three days not being able to see. Finally, God sent a man named Ananias to Paul. Ananias told Paul that Jesus had sent him. Then he healed Paul's eyes. After that, Paul believed in Jesus. (Check out Acts 9:1–19.) Paul became a missionary who taught about Jesus. He wrote many of the books in the New Testament. Before he became a Christian, Paul was known as Saul.

Acts 13:9

PEACE.

Everyone getting along. Peace is the opposite of war. God brings us peace. So do Jesus Christ and the Holy Spirit. The Bible says that Christians should work toward peace. They should try to live at peace with all people.

Philippians 4:7
John 14:27
Galatians 5:22
2 Corinthians 13:11
2 Timothy 2:22

PEARL.

A precious stone found inside the shell of some—but not every—oyster. So when you find one, it's quite a surprise! Jesus said the kingdom of heaven is like what happens when a shop owner looks for a valuable pearl. When he finds it, he sells everything he owns so he can have it. (Check out Matthew 13:45–46 CEV.)

PENIEL.

Site of Jacob's wrestling match. Peniel was east of the Jordan River and near the Jabbok River. One night, when Jacob was alone there, a man came and wrestled with him. They wrestled all night, and Jacob was winning. Then the man touched Jacob's hip, and it went out of joint. Jacob asked the man who he was. But he wouldn't say. He wanted Jacob to let him go. Jacob asked the man to bless him. Jacob said that the man was God. (Find out more in Genesis 32:22–31.)

PENTATEUCH.

The first five books of the Old Testament. How well do you know the Bible; can you name the first five books? These books are also part of the Torah or the Law of Moses. The Pentateuch includes Genesis, Exodus, Leviticus, Numbers, and Deuteronomy.

a
b
c
d
e
f
g
h
i
j
k
l
m
n
o
P
q
r
s
t
u
v
w
x
y
z

a
b
c
d
e
f
g
h
i
j
k
l
m
n
o
P
q
r
s
t
u
v
w
x
y
z

PENTECOST. ——————

Christians celebrate this day as the day the Holy Spirit came. Pentecost comes from the Greek word *pentekoste*, which means "fiftieth." The Old Testament meaning for Pentecost was a harvest festival. It was called Feast of Harvest. Pentecost was celebrated fifty days after the Passover lamb was killed. Back then, the people didn't know that their version of Pentecost was a symbol of what was to come. In New Testament times, Pentecost got a new meaning. It was the day when the Holy Spirit came down to earth to be with Jesus' followers. And guess what? It happened fifty days after Jesus— He was known as the Lamb of God—was killed. Do you see the connection with the Old Testament Pentecost? When the Holy Spirit came, believers were filled with great joy. During this time, Jesus' disciples worked many miracles. Lots of people turned from their evil ways and believed in Jesus.

Exodus 23:16
Acts 2:1–42

PEOPLE OF GOD. ———

A name shared by the nation of Israel and all Christians. In Old Testament times, the Israelites were known as God's special people. After Jesus died, everyone who accepted Him as their Lord and Savior became people of God. God's people are all over the earth. They live in many nations and speak many different languages. Are you one of God's people? You are if you believe in the Lord Jesus Christ.

Deuteronomy 7:6
1 Peter 2:9–10
Revelation 5:9
Revelation 7:9

PERDITION. ——————

Living forever in hell. Hell is a terrible place, and no one wants to live there. It is where ungodly people go when they die. People who reject Jesus Christ will live in perdition. Jesus called His disciple Judas "son of perdition." That was because Judas betrayed Him. Satan and the antichrist will also live in perdition.

2 Peter 3:7
John 17:12 KJV
Revelation 17:8, 11 KJV

The Holy Spirit comes down like a dove on the Day of Pentecost.

PERFECTION. ———————

When everything is absolutely, positively right. As hard as you try, you will never be perfect. And nothing you do can be perfect. Why? Because God is the only One who is absolutely, positively perfect. As humans, our perfection is like a sand castle. We work hard at it. For a while it is beautiful and seems just right. But then the tide comes in and washes it away. Although people cannot be perfect, we should try. We can do that by learning about Jesus and working hard to be like Him.

Philippians 3:12–15

PERSECUTION. ———————

Being picked on for what you believe in—or even what you look like. Do you know someone who is persecuted? You do if you've seen a bully picking on someone at school. Jesus was persecuted because He said He was the Son of God. His followers were persecuted for believing in Him.

Jesus said that when believers are persecuted, God will bless them. He also taught that we should pray for people who persecute us. Faith in God helps us to put up with persecution.

Matthew 5:10
Matthew 5:44
Ephesians 6:16

PERSEVERANCE. ———————

Hanging in there. Think about the players on your favorite baseball team. If they aren't winning the game, do they walk off the field? No. They hang in there. They play through to the end. That's perseverance. The New Testament tells about Jesus' followers facing hard times. People didn't believe what they said. Sometimes Jesus' followers were thrown into prison, or killed. Paul encouraged believers to hang in there. He said that persevering for God's sake is always worth it.

1 Corinthians 15:58

A mosaic of an ancient Persian soldier.

PERSIA. ———————

A great nation in Bible times. Persia was a country covering most of the same territory as modern-day Iran. The Persians conquered Babylon in 539 BC. Then they began to allow the Israelites to leave their captivity. The Persian king Artaxerxes let Nehemiah go back to Jerusalem to rebuild the city wall. Alexander the Great defeated the Persians around 330 BC.

2 Chronicles 36:20–23
Nehemiah 2:1–8

PESTILENCE. ———————

A terrible contagious disease. In Bible times, people died from pestilence. God sometimes allowed pestilence to happen as a punishment for sin.

Exodus 5:3
Ezekiel 33:27 KJV

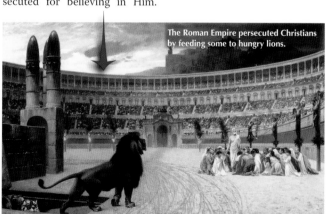
The Roman Empire persecuted Christians by feeding some to hungry lions.

a
b
c
d
e
f
g
h
i
j
k
l
m
n
o
P
q
r
s
t
u
v
w
x
y
z

a
b
c
d
e
f
g
h
i
j
k
l
m
n
o
P
q
r
s
t
u
v
w
x
y
z

PETER. ——————

One of Jesus' closest friends. Also known as Simon, Peter was one of Jesus' disciples. In the Bible, he is mostly called Peter. Before he was a disciple, Peter was a fisherman. He was daring and the kind of guy who jumped right in and got things done. Peter was the disciple who cut off a soldier's ear when he tried to arrest Jesus (John 18:10). Jesus scolded him for that and healed the soldier's ear. When Peter saw Jesus walking on water, he wanted to do it, too. And he did! (Check out Matthew 14:25–32.) Before Jesus was arrested, Peter promised that he would stay true to Him forever. But he didn't. When Jesus was taken away, Peter denied that he'd ever known Him. It wasn't that he was a bad guy. He was just being human. He was afraid that they might arrest him, too. In the end, Peter did stay true to Jesus. In fact, he was one of the first disciples who discovered that Jesus had risen from the dead.

John 20:1–10

PETER, FIRST AND SECOND LETTERS OF. ——

The twenty-first and twenty-second books of the New Testament. Peter was one of Jesus' disciples. After Jesus went back to heaven, Peter kept doing His work. He wrote letters to the churches. Two of these letters are books in the New Testament. First Peter is about persecution. (Persecution is a word that means "being picked on.") Many believers were picked on because they taught about Jesus. Peter reminded them not to get discouraged. Second Peter is about false teachers. Peter warned that some people were not telling the truth about Jesus. He told believers to watch out for them.

1 Peter 4:12–14
2 Peter 3:17

PHARAOH. ——————

The title of the king of Egypt. The Bible doesn't tell us the name of the pharaoh who lived during the time of Moses. He was known only as the king. He refused to let the Israelite slaves go free, until God got tough with him. God allowed all the firstborn children in Egypt to be killed. And that included the pharaoh's child. When that terrible thing happened, it was enough for the pharaoh to give up and free the slaves. Later, he chased them to the Red Sea.

Tradition says the apostle Peter was crucified—but he asked to be hung upside-down. He didn't feel worthy of dying the way Jesus did.

There Moses divided the waters so the Israelites could cross on dry land. But when the pharaoh and his men began to follow, the Red Sea swallowed them up and they drowned. (Read more about it in Exodus 14:5–29.)

Exodus 1:8–11
Exodus 12:29–31

PHARISEES. ——————

A powerful group of Jews. In Jesus' time, the Pharisees were like a political party today concerned with the laws of the land. The Pharisees stayed true to the oldest laws and traditions of Israel. Jesus had a problem with this group. They were so into the old laws that they didn't pay much attention to important things like justice, mercy, and love. (See Matthew 23:1–7.) They picked apart every little thing that Jesus did and tried to say that He was breaking the old laws. For example, when Jesus healed a man on the Sabbath, the Pharisees, thinking He was breaking God's law, became very angry.

Luke 6:6–11

PHILADELPHIA. ——————

A biblical city in modern-day Turkey. Did you think it was a city in Pennsylvania? The Philadelphia of the Bible was a faithful church. It is one of the seven churches written about in the book of Revelation.

Revelation 3:7–9
Revelation 1:11

PHILEMON, LETTER TO. —

A short book in the New Testament. The apostle Paul wrote it as a letter to Philemon. He was a guy who owned a slave named Onesimus. One day, Onesimus ran away. He became a believer in Christ. So Paul wrote to Philemon, asking him to take Onesimus back, not as a slave, but as a Christian brother.

Philemon 1:16, 21

PHILIP. ——————

A name shared by one of the disciples and an early church leader. Jesus invited one Philip to follow Him. Philip said yes. He brought along a friend named Nathanael. Both men became Jesus' disciples. Philip brought a group of Gentiles to see Jesus when He was in Jerusalem. Another Philip was chosen to help the twelve apostles in the church at Jerusalem. Philip was said to be honest, wise, and "full of the Holy Ghost."

John 1:43–51
John 12:20–22
Acts 6:1–7
Acts 6:3 KJV

PHILIPPIANS, LETTER TO THE. ——————

The eleventh book of the New Testament. The apostle Paul is the author of the book of Philippians. It was his epistle, or letter, to the church in Philippi. Paul told the church to follow Christ's example. He told them especially not to be conceited. He said that they should continue to grow as Christians. Paul told them to remember that Jesus promised peace and joy to all believers. Some call Philippians "Paul's letter of joy." Paul wrote: "Rejoice in the Lord always. I will say it again: Rejoice!"

Philippians 4:4 NIV

PHILISTINES. ——————

One of the Israelites' main enemies. The Philistines lived in Philistia, a region that would one day be named Palestine. The Bible tells about the Philistines in Saul's and David's time. The Philistines often fought with the Israelites. They were an evil people who worshipped false gods. Their main gods were Dagon and Baal-zebub. The Philistines' kingdom ended after the Babylonians took over the kingdom of Judah. Two famous Bible characters who were Philistines are Goliath and Delilah.

2 Samuel 5:17–25
Judges 16:23
2 Kings 1:2–3

A carving of a Philistine warrior.

PHILOSOPHY.

A search for wisdom. People who study philosophy are looking for the truth. In New Testament times, some philosophers believed in the one true God. But Athens, Greece, was a place where most people didn't believe. Their philosophy taught about false gods. When Paul went to Athens, he tried to change their philosophy. He spoke about the only true God.

Acts 17:15–34

PHYLACTERY.

Scripture holders. Phylacteries were small leather boxes. They were tied around the head or upper left arm. People wrote down scripture verses and put them inside. Jesus said people shouldn't wear them so they could easily be seen. If they did, they were acting conceited.

Matthew 23:5

PHYSICIAN.

A doctor. Just like today, there were doctors in Bible times. The Egyptians were known for studying medicine. Luke, one of the gospel writers, was a physician.

Genesis 50:2
Colossians 4:14

PILATE, PONTIUS.

The Roman governor of Judea. Pilate is the guy who supervised Jesus' trial. He didn't want to be responsible for Jesus' being crucified. So he sent Jesus to another ruler, named Herod, for sentencing. But Herod sent Him back to Pilate. Jesus' trial took place at Passover time. Each year at Passover, a criminal was let go. Pilate suggested that Jesus be the one. But the people wanted a prisoner named Barabbas to be let go. Pilate just sat back and did nothing. He didn't want people to think badly of him. He turned Jesus over to be killed. But he tried not to take the blame for it.

John 18:28–38
Luke 23:11
Matthew 27:24

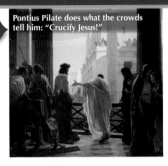

Pontius Pilate does what the crowds tell him: "Crucify Jesus!"

PILLAR OF FIRE AND PILLAR OF CLOUD.

God's super signs. When the Israelites were traveling in the wilderness, God gave them signs that He was with them. Some of these were super signs. You couldn't miss them. In the daytime, God was in a giant cloud. He guided the people on their way. He did the same thing at night. Only then, He was in a tall pillar of fire.

Numbers 14:13–14
Exodus 13:21

PITCH.

Noah's tar. Pitch was a tarlike material that Noah used when he made the ark. It was tough and sticky. Painting it on the inside and outside of the ark sealed up any cracks.

Genesis 6:14

PITY.

Concern for others. Have you ever helped an animal or person in trouble? If you did, you had pity for them. You showed them kindness and concern. James said that the Lord is merciful

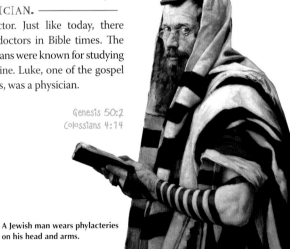

A Jewish man wears phylacteries on his head and arms.

and kind. He used the example of Job. When Job was suffering, God helped him. He had pity for Job. Part of loving God is having pity for His people in need.

James 5:11
1 John 3:17

PLAGUE.

A disaster. Plagues were awful, icky things. God sent ten plagues on Egypt because its leaders wouldn't let the Israelites go. The plagues were:

1. Water turned into blood
2. Oodles of frogs everywhere
3. Lice on everything
4. Gazillions of flies buzzing and biting
5. Sick farm animals
6. Boils and sores on humans
7. Heaps of hail
8. Swarms of locusts
9. Utter darkness for three whole days
10. Death of firstborn children

Aren't you glad that you didn't live in Egypt back then? There's a lesson to be learned in all of this: You don't want to get on God's bad side.

Exodus 7:14–25
Exodus 8:1–15
Exodus 8:16–19
Exodus 8:20–32
Exodus 9:1–7
Exodus 9:8–12
Exodus 9:13–35
Exodus 10:1–20
Exodus 10:21–29
Exodus 11:1–12:36

PLEDGE.

A promise that you will pay something back. One Old Testament law said that if a poor man used his coat as a pledge, it had to be returned to him at sunset. How come? Because he needed to use it as a blanket.

Exodus 22:26–27

PLOWSHARE.

A piece of iron used to turn over the soil. The plowshare was at the end of the plow shaft. A farmer held on to the shaft as oxen pulled the plow.

1 Samuel 13:20

PLUMB LINE.

A tool used to show a straight line up and down. Maybe you've seen a carpenter use a plumb line. Sometimes people use them to hang wallpaper. In the Bible, the word meant a test that God used to decide how honest and upright His people were.

Amos 7:1–9

An ancient plumb line.

POETIC WRITINGS.

Books written as poems. Several Bible books are written as poetry. They are Job, Psalms, Proverbs, Ecclesiastes, and the Song of Solomon. Do you like to write poetry? Try writing a poem to God. Or write a poem about Him.

POLYGAMY.

Having more than one wife. In Old Testament days, some men had more than one wife. This was not true to God's original plan of one man, one wife.

Genesis 2:24

POOR.

People who don't have much. Jesus told the Jews to help the poor. In Old Testament times, what was left over in the fields after a harvest was left for the poor. One way to show God you love Him is by helping people in need. You can contribute to a food drive or give away some of your clothes. How many other ways can you think of to help?

Luke 14:13–14
Leviticus 19:9–10

a
b
c
d
e
f
g
h
i
j
k
l
m
n
o
P
q
r
s
t
u
v
w
x
y
z

a
b
c
d
e
f
g
h
i
j
k
l
m
n
o
P
q
r
s
t
u
v
w
x
y
z

POTIPHAR.

A ruler in Egypt who was Joseph's master. Potiphar owned Joseph as a slave. He had Joseph thrown into prison because he thought Joseph was in love with his wife. (Find out more about it in Genesis 39:1–20.)

POTTAGE.

A thick vegetable soup. Pottage was so thick it was a stew. Jacob bought his brother's birthright with a bowl of pottage.

Haggai 2:12 KJV
Genesis 25:29–34 KJV

POTTER.

A person who makes pottery. Potters make pots, bowls, and other things from clay. Maybe you've used a potter's wheel in an art class. Even though people make pottery today, the craft of pottery is ancient. The book of Isaiah says that the potter has power over his clay. This was used as an example that God, the Creator, has power over His people.

Isaiah 45:9

PRAISE.

Giving thanks to God. Maybe you've heard the words praise God! They mean "Thank you, God!" When you think about it, God deserves a lot of praise. After all, He created the earth that we live on. And He created you! Just like most people, God likes to be praised. You'll find plenty of praise in the Bible, especially in the book of Psalms. When you pray, you should thank God for all the wondrous things He does. You can also praise Him by singing. Can you think of other ways to praise Him?

Psalm 50:23
Psalm 9:1
Psalm 47:6

PRAYER.

Communication with God. You can pray to God anytime. You don't have to wait in line. God is so powerful that He can talk—and listen—to everyone at once. There are lots of reasons to pray. You can ask God to help you and others. You can ask Him for things you need. You can tell God that you're sorry for the

A potter works clay, like God works on His people.

bad things you've done. You can even pray to Him when you need someone to talk to. When you pray, you should always remember to thank God and tell Him how great He is. When you are done talking, take some time to listen to what He has to say.

Ephesians 6:18
Luke 11:3
1 John 1:9

PREACH.

To tell others about Christ. Jesus told His disciples to preach His good news to everyone in the world. He wants you to do that, too. You don't have to stand up and give a sermon like a preacher does in church. You can preach the gospel just by telling your family and friends about what you've learned in this book. Be sure to remind them that Jesus came to save them from sin. If they believe that He died on the cross for them, then they will live forever with God. When you share the gospel of Christ, make sure that you always tell the truth.

Mark 16:15
1 Corinthians 15:2
Galatians 1:8

PREDESTINATION.

The belief that God knows exactly who will be saved. God already has a plan for you. He knows the whole story of your life from beginning to end—that's predestination. If you choose Him

as your Lord and Savior, He will share His greatness with you. His plan is that He works everything out for good for people who love Him. Those who love God will live with Him forever.

Romans 8:30
Romans 8:28
John 6:40

PRIDE.

Being conceited. A little pride is a good thing. When you work hard and are pleased with your work, it's fine to be proud. But a lot of pride will get you into trouble. If you go around talking about how great you are, people will notice. And they probably won't like what they see. A good example of foolish pride is in Luke 18:11–12: "The Pharisee stood up and prayed about himself: 'God, I thank you that I am not like other men—robbers, evildoers, adulterers—or even like this tax collector. I fast twice a week and give a tenth of all I get' " (NIV). In other words, he stood up and said, "Hey, God, look how great I am. You made me better than everybody else." That's foolish pride.

Proverbs 16:18

PRIEST.

In Bible times, a religious leader who made offerings to God. The first priest of Israel was Aaron. God Himself appointed him. After Aaron died, his sons filled the role of priests. The most perfect

priest of all time is Jesus. He is our high priest. Like all priests, He made an offering to God. But His offering was more awesome than any other. He paid for our sins by giving up His own life. His death gives us the opportunity to live with God in heaven someday.

Exodus 29:44
Hebrews 7:26–28

PRIESTHOOD OF BELIEVERS.

The idea that each Christian can talk directly to God. Believers today don't have to go through a priest—because Jesus is our Helper. When we pray to Jesus, we can be sure that God hears us. The priesthood of believers means that we are all ministers for God. As believers, we should serve one another in love, give our spiritual lives over to God, and talk to others about Him.

Ephesians 3:11–12
Galatians 5:13
Romans 12:1
1 Peter 2:9

PRINCIPALITY.

A rank of angels and demons. All governments have leaders with different ranks. It's the same for God's angels and Satan's demons, who have ranks, too. A principality is a rank of powerful helpers. Some serve God. Others serve Satan. God is more powerful than all principalities. In the end, He will get rid of the ones who serve Satan. Then all Christians will celebrate with God.

Romans 8:38–39
Colossians 2:10, 15

PRISCILLA. ————————
An important Christian woman from Corinth. Priscilla and her husband Aquila were Christian teachers who worked with the apostle Paul.

Acts 18:1–3

PRISON. ————————
A jail. In Bible times, prisons were dirty, dark, and awful. Sometimes they were just big underground pits. Prisoners were dropped in through a hole at the top. Then something was put over the hole so the prisoners were in complete darkness. Some of God's helpers, like Peter and Paul, were in a prison. Paul wrote several of his letters from prison.

Psalm 107:10
2 Corinthians 6:3–5
Philippians 1:12–14

PRODIGAL SON. ————————
The main character in one of Jesus' parables. Jesus told the story of a young man whose father gave him a lot of money. He took the money and went off to have a good time. He spent it all foolishly until there was nothing left. By then, he was poor and starving. Not knowing what else to do, the man decided to go home to apologize and get something to eat. When his dad saw him coming, he was filled with joy. The father put on a huge welcome-home party. But not everyone was pleased. You can read more about the prodigal son in Luke 15:11–32.

PROMISE. ————————
A pledge. When you make a promise, you should be truthful. If you say you will do something, then it is up to you to keep your promise. God always keeps His promises. That's because God is perfect and He cannot lie. There are many of God's promises in the Bible. He promised Abraham a son. He promised the land of Canaan to the Israelites. And most important, He promised eternal life to everyone who trusts in His Son, Jesus.

Hebrews 6:18
Genesis 18:10
Exodus 6:4
John 3:16

PROPHETS. ————————
Messengers of God. In the Bible, God often spoke through His prophets. He told the prophets what to say, and they passed His messages on to the people. Prophets were called God's servants, watchmen, and holy men. Another word for prophet is *seer*. God often allowed His prophets to see things in visions or dreams. What they saw always had something to do with God's will for His people. A woman who is a prophet like Miriam or Deborah is called a prophetess.

Zechariah 1:6
Ezekiel 3:17
2 Peter 1:21 NKJV
Isaiah 30:10
Exodus 15:20
Judges 4:4

PROPITIATION. ————————
A way of making things right. Jesus was a propitiation for our sins. When He died on the cross, it was a way of making things right with God for the bad things that humans do. In other words, Jesus took the blame; not only for the bad stuff people did back then, but also for the bad stuff people do right now. Why did Jesus do that for us? Because He loves us with all His heart!

1 John 2:2
Romans 3:24–25

PROVERBS, BOOK OF. ————
An Old Testament book of wisdom. Solomon and other wise men wrote the book of Proverbs. It can be fun to read. Proverbs has all sorts of neat sayings about living to please God. Proverbs are little bits of information that make you think. Here are a few to ponder: "Lazy people can learn by watching an anthill." "Eating too much honey can make you sick." "As water reflects a face, so a man's heart reflects the man." What do you think these proverbs say about pleasing God?

Proverbs 6:6 CEV
Proverbs 25:16 CEV
Proverbs 27:19 NIV

a b c d e f g h i j k l m n o **P** q r s t u v w x y z

PROVIDENCE. ———————

God guiding and caring for His people. Providence means that God is in control. He made everyone and everything, and He's in charge of it all. Jesus said that God even knows when a tiny sparrow is going to die. And did you know that God gave you the hairs on your head, and He knows how many you have? God is in charge of every single thing in heaven and here on earth. His providence shows people that He is an awesome God.

Matthew 10:29–30

PSALMS, BOOK OF. ————

A poetic book in the Old Testament. The book of Psalms is filled with hymns of praise. Many of the psalms were written to be sung and accompanied by musical instruments. "Sing joyfully to the LORD. . .Praise the LORD with the harp; make music to him on the ten-stringed lyre." Other psalms are prayers of thanksgiving. One of the most well-known is the Twenty-third Psalm: "The LORD is my shepherd; I shall not want." King David wrote that psalm and many others.

Psalm 150:4 NIV
Psalm 33:1–2 NIV
Psalm 23:1 KJV

PUBLICAN. ———————

A tax collector. Tax collectors collected money for the Roman government. Matthew was a publican. So was Zacchaeus.

Matthew 9:9–11
Luke 19:1–10

PUNISHMENT. ———————

The consequence of doing something wrong. When you misbehave, you probably get punished. That happens because your folks love you. They want you to learn to do right things and live a godly life. Like a good parent, God punishes His people. God punished Adam and Eve when they disobeyed Him. And He punished Cain for killing Abel. Do you know that Jesus took the punishment for your sins? He did! He died on the cross so that you could be forgiven and live in heaven with God someday. In the end-times, Jesus will return, and He will punish those who do not know God or believe in His gospel.

Jeremiah 23:2
Genesis 3
Genesis 4:13
Hebrews 9:28
2 Thessalonians 1:7–9

PURIFICATION. ———————

Making something clean and pure. When you get dirty, you take a bath. In Bible times, it wasn't so easy. There were laws about being clean. Everyone had to be clean to honor God. There were many reasons why people would be unclean. It might be because they had touched something icky. Or maybe it was because they had done something bad. To be clean again, people often had to participate in some sort of ceremony. After Jesus was born, His mother, Mary, offered God doves as a sacrifice. It was her way of honoring God and becoming clean in His sight.

Luke 2:21–24

PURPLE. ———————

A royal color. Kings and other high officials wore purple. Lydia was a woman who sold purple cloth. The purple dye was made from shellfish.

Judges 8:26
Acts 16:14

a
b
c
d
e
f
g
h
i
j
k
l
m
n
o
P
q
r
s
t
u
v
w
x
y
z

Q

b
c
d
e
f
g
h
i
j
k
l
m
n
o
p
q
r
s
t
u
v
w
x
y
z

QUAIL.

A kind of bird. Long ago, the Israelites were traveling through the wilderness. They were so hungry that they were starving. Then, out of nowhere, God sent quails for them to eat. It was God's special gift to them—a miracle!

Numbers 11:31–32

QUEEN.

The wife or mom of a king. Queen Esther was the wife of Persia's King Xerxes. She had a lot of power. King Solomon's mom was Queen Bathsheba. He brought her a throne so she could sit on his right side, a special place of honor.

Esther 5:2
1 Kings 2:19

QUICKEN.

To save or give life. In today's language, quicken means "to hurry up." In Bible times, it meant that God and Jesus could give eternal life. That means they could bring dead people to heaven to live with God.

John 5:21

QUIVER.

A case for arrows. In Bible times, foot soldiers carried them. God protects us just like a quiver protects arrows.

Isaiah 49:2

A decoration from the palace of Darius the Great, more than 500 years before Jesus, shows a quiver on a Persian soldier's back.

Rabbi.

A title of respect that means "master" or "teacher." Mary Magdalene called Jesus "Rabboni" when He appeared to her after rising from His tomb. *Rabboni* is the Aramaic form of Rabbi. Nicodemus also used this name for Jesus. He said, "Rabbi, we know you are a teacher who has come from God". The disciples of Jesus called Him Rabbi, too. This title was also used for John the Baptist by his followers. This word is still used in the Jewish faith today. Leaders of the congregation and those who teach Jewish law are called rabbis.

John 20:16
John 3:2 NIV
John 1:38
John 3:26

Race.

A contest to see who is faster. In New Testament times, people had races by foot, horseback, and chariot. The winner of a race usually gets a prize. In the Bible, Christians trying to be like Christ are compared to runners in a race.

1 Corinthians 9:24
Hebrews 12:1

Rachel.

The favorite wife of Jacob. She was also the younger sister of Leah. Jacob worked for Laban, the father of Leah and Rachel. Jacob loved Rachel. He asked to marry her. But in Bible times, the oldest was supposed to be the first to marry. Laban tricked Jacob into marrying Leah. When Jacob found out he'd married the wrong sister, he was angry. Laban let Jacob marry Rachel the next week. (Check out Genesis 29:15–30.) Later, she gave birth to Joseph. He was Jacob's favorite son. Rachel died giving birth to her second son, Benjamin. She was buried near Bethlehem. Her sons started two of the twelve tribes of Israel.

Genesis 29:30
Genesis 30:22–24
Genesis 35:16–20

Rahab.

A woman in Jericho who hid Joshua's spies. When the Israelites were camped nearby, Joshua sent two spies to look around Jericho. They went to stay at Rahab's house. The king found out that spies were in his city. He sent soldiers to Rahab's house to arrest them. But Rahab hid the spies on her roof. She did this because she believed in God. (Check out Joshua 2:1–13.) Later, she and her family were saved from harm when the Israelites burned the city. In the New Testament, Rahab was praised for her faith. She was also an ancestor of Jesus.

Joshua 6:22–25
Hebrews 11:31
Matthew 1:1, 5

Rainbow.

An arch of colors in the sky. A rainbow appeared after the great flood. God gave it as a sign that He would never destroy the earth with water again.

Genesis 9:9–17

Ram.

A name shared by a long beam and a male sheep. The first kind of ram is known as a battering ram, a big beam of wood used to break down the gates of walled cities. The other kind of ram was a male sheep used for food and sacrifices.

Ezekiel 4:2
Genesis 31:38
Numbers 15:6

Rameses.

A rich area of Egypt with good crops, named after a pharaoh.

b
c
d
e
f
g
h
i
j
k
l
m
n
o
p
q
r
s
t
u
v
w
x
y
z

123

a
b
c
d
e
f
g
h
i
j
k
l
m
n
o
p
q
R
s
t
u
v
w
x
y
z

This is where Jacob and his descendants settled. Rameses was also the name of a city. Hebrew slaves built it. This was where the king kept his treasure.

Genesis 47:11
Exodus 1:11

RAM'S HORN. ———————
The curved horn of a male sheep. It was blown like a trumpet. This was a signal to worshippers and warriors.

Joshua 6:4 – 13

RANSOM. ———————
A payment to buy freedom for a captive. Christ is described as a "ransom for all." He gave His life to rescue us. Jesus used this word when He talked to His disciples, too. He said that to be great, you must be the servant of others. "For even the Son of Man did not come to be served, but to serve, and to give his life as a ransom for many."

1 Timothy 2:6
Mark 10:45 NIV

RAPTURE, THE. ———————
An idea that some have about what will happen when Christ returns. Some people believe that when Christ comes back, the redeemed will be changed. He will make our bodies glorious just like His! He will also raise the dead. Our bodies will be changed into ones that can't die or decay. Then all of us will be taken up into the clouds to meet the Lord.

Philippians 3:20–21
1 Corinthians 15:51–53
1 Thessalonians 4:16–17

REAP. ———————
To harvest a crop. The Bible says you reap what you sow. This means that if you plant good things, what you harvest will also be good.

Ruth 2:3
Galatians 6:7

REBEKAH. ———————
The wife of Isaac. She was the mother of his twin boys. They were named Jacob and Esau. Jacob was his mom's favorite. But Esau was older by a few minutes. (Check it out in Genesis 25:25–28.) In Bible times, the first son was often given a blessing by his dad. This son was in charge of the family and its land after the dad died. Rebekah came up with a plan to trick Isaac into blessing Jacob instead of Esau. When her plan worked, Esau was so angry that he planned to kill Jacob! Rebekah found out and warned Jacob. She told him to run away and stay with her brother, Laban. (Find out more about it in Genesis 27:5–45.)

RECONCILIATION. ———————
Bringing together people who don't agree. Have you ever been in a fight with a friend? The Bible tells us that it is good to reconcile, or make peace, with those who are mad at us. God doesn't want you to be angry with others either. Jesus taught us that it is best to make peace with others. Otherwise, the gifts we give God mean nothing. (Check out Matthew 5:22–25.) Those who believe are at peace with God because of Jesus and His victory over sin and death. It is our job as Christians to help others make peace with God, too.

Romans 5:10
2 Corinthians 5:20

RED SEA. ———————
A body of water between Egypt and Arabia. It is also called the Sea of Reeds because of its reed-filled marshes. God split the Red Sea in two! When Moses led the Israelites out of Egypt, the king and his army came after them. God told Moses to hold his walking stick over the sea. When Moses did this, the sea split into two parts! The people of Israel walked across it on dry land with water on both sides. The Egyptian army came after them, but God told Moses to hold his arm over the sea again. The sea came back together. Water rushed at the Egyptians and washed them away. You can read the whole story in Exodus 14.

REDEEM. ———————
To buy something back. Christ is our Redeemer. He bought us back or saved us from sin and death through His death on the cross.

Matthew 20:28

REGENERATION.

New birth or spiritual change. For those who trust in Christ, regeneration is brought about by the Holy Spirit. Have you ever heard someone say, "Out with the old, in with the new"? The Bible tells us that anyone who belongs to Christ is a new person. It doesn't matter what happened in the past. That's old news! What matters is what happens now and in the future. God sent His Son to make peace between Him and us. He's not counting our sins against us, because Christ took the punishment for us.

REHOBOAM.

The son of Solomon and grandson of David. He became king of Israel after his dad. Rehoboam ruled from about 931 to 913 BC. He refused to listen to the leaders from the north. That was a big mistake! The kingdom of Israel split into two parts. The ten tribes of the north became the kingdom of Israel. The other two tribes became the kingdom of Judah. (Read more about it in 1 Kings 12:1–24.)

REJOICE.

Be joyful! If you're happy and you know it, praise the Lord! Joy can come from God's blessings. You can show your joy by singing and praising God. Many of the psalms were written as joyful praises. Psalm 118:24 says: "This is the day the LORD has made; let us rejoice and be glad in it" (NIV).

Exodus 18:9

REMISSION.

God's forgiveness of our sins. Christ died so this could happen. In the Bible, Peter said God will forgive us if we repent and get baptized in the name of Jesus Christ. Peter also tells us to have faith. "Every one of the prophets has said that all who have faith in Jesus will have their sins forgiven in his name."

Matthew 26:28
Acts 2:38
Acts 10:43 CEY

REMNANT.

A small, but good, group of God's people. They were loyal to Him even while many others sinned and worshipped idols. The prophet Isaiah said Israel would be punished for not being faithful to God. But a good group, or remnant, of His people would be saved. In some versions of the Bible, these people are called "survivors."

Isaiah 1:24–25
Isaiah 10:20–22

REPENT.

To turn from sin. This can mean a switch from rebelling against God to accepting His will. God wants all of us to repent. He warns that those who refuse to repent will be punished. Jesus called those who had sinned to repent, too. He said, "I didn't come to invite good people to turn to God. I came to invite sinners." Has a friend ever hurt your feelings and then said he was sorry? Did you forgive him? Jesus told believers to forgive a person who repents.

Acts 17:30
Revelation 2:16
Luke 5:32 CEY
Luke 17:3

REPROACH.

Shame or blame. Jesus suffered reproach for us. Some people hated and rejected Him. His life was full of sadness and pain. He even died for our sins! The Lord gave Him the punishment we deserved. Have you ever felt shame for doing something wrong? Doing the right thing brings us honor, but sin brings reproach.

Isaiah 53:3–6
Proverbs 14:34

RESTITUTION.

To pay back or return something to its owner. God's law required this. In Bible times, if a person stole one sheep, he or she had to replace it with four sheep.

Exodus 22:1

RESURRECTION.

Rising from the dead. For believers, this leads to life forever! Jesus taught His followers to believe in the resurrection. He said, "My Father wants everyone who sees the Son to have faith in him and to have eternal life. Then I will raise them to life on the last day." Paul taught that Jesus would give Christians life that lasts forever. We can believe this will happen. Jesus has already given us proof! He brought several people back to life in the Bible (see Matthew 9:24–25; Luke 7:14–15; and John 11:43–44). Jesus Himself rose to life after His death. This was foretold in the Old Testament—and Christ told His disciples that it would happen, too. This proves Jesus has the last victory over sin and death. After He rose from the dead, Jesus appeared to others many times. He came to Mary Magdalene at His empty tomb. He showed Himself to His disciples, too.

John 6:40 CEV
Romans 2:7
Mark 9:9–10
Mark 16:9

Jesus rises from the grave, and soldiers— supposed to guard His body—faint.

REUBEN. ——————
The oldest son of Jacob and Leah. He began one of the twelve tribes of Israel. His tribe settled east of the Jordan River.

Genesis 35:23
Numbers 32:1–38

REVELATION. ——————
The showing of God's will or truth. Christ shows us what God the Father is like. The Spirit of God shows us the truth through the prophets and the apostles.

John 1:18
1 Peter 1:10–12
Galatians 1:15–16

REVELATION, BOOK OF.—
The last book in the New Testament. God revealed His message to Jesus, who sent an angel to John. John wrote the message down and sent it to the seven churches of Asia. This book has several visions in it. They are:

1. Christ talking to each of the seven churches
2. Christ the Lamb with a seven-sealed scroll
3. Seven angels blowing trumpets
4. Satan and the dragon attacking the church
5. Seven bowls pouring out the anger of God
6. The judgment of Babylonia
7. God winning and His last judgment
8. The new heaven, the new earth, and the New Jerusalem

This book, and the Bible, ends with Jesus' promise that He will come back.

REVENGE. ——————
Getting even. Have you ever wanted to do something to get back at a person who harmed you? No one likes to be hurt, but we must remember that revenge is wrong. Jesus said, "But I tell you not to try to get even with a person who has done something to you." He said we must love our enemies as well as our neighbors. We should pray for anyone who mistreats us.

Matthew 5:39 CEV
Matthew 5:43–44

REVERENCE. ——————
A feeling of great respect and awe. Those who believe, show reverence to God. They also show reverence to the place where they worship, such as their church. Do you show reverence to your parents? The Bible says that you should. You should respect those in charge, such as your teachers. You should also be respectful to the other members of your family.

Psalm 89:7
Leviticus 19:30
Hebrews 12:9

REWARD. ——————
Something paid or given in return for what you've done. God rewards those who work hard to search for Him.

Hebrews 11:6

RHODA.

A servant girl. She worked in the home of Mary, the mother of John Mark. Rhoda answered the door for Peter after he was let out of prison by an angel.

Acts 12:1–16

RICHES.

Things of value. Jesus said people who worry about trying to get rich are missing the message about God's kingdom. He also warned people not to store up their things on earth. These things can get ruined or stolen. You can't count on wealth, because it is easily lost. But you can always count on God. He is rich and blesses us with all we need.

Matthew 13:22
Matthew 6:19–20
1 Timothy 6:17

RIGHTEOUS.

Being right. Righteousness is a quality of God that shows He is holy and without sin. All of God's decisions are fair and righteous. God saved us not because of the right things we have done, but because He cares for us. God knows that we need food, water, and clothes. But the Bible tells us to seek God's kingdom and do His work first. We should try to be righteous like Him. Then we will have the other things, too. (Check out Matthew 6:33.) We should not worry about tomorrow. Do you try to do good things and follow God's law? You

should! The righteous will own the land and live in it forever.

Psalm 19:9
Titus 3:5
Matthew 6:34
Psalm 37:29

ROCK.

A stone. Have you ever picked up a heavy rock? Rocks are tough, strong, and last a very long time. In the Bible, God is compared to a rock. He is a like a mountain where we can run for protection. When Jesus chose His disciples, He changed Simon's name to Peter. The Greek name Peter means "rock."

Psalm 18
John 1:42

THE ROMAN EMPIRE IN THE TIME OF PAUL

ROMAN EMPIRE.

The empire that ruled the Mediterranean world during New Testament times. Rome was a big and powerful place—and most of its people didn't believe in Jesus. A few key events in Bible history have a tie to Rome or the Romans. Caesar Augustus was the emperor of Rome when Jesus was born. Pilate was in charge of Jesus' trial. He was the Roman governor of Judea. Jesus was then crucified by Roman soldiers. (Find out more in Matthew 27:11–31.) Paul was in prison in Rome during his last days. He most likely died there, too. Rome was still a pagan city, but Christianity had started to spread. Paul wrote his letter to the Romans for the Christians who lived in Rome.

Luke 2:1–7
Philippians 1:12–13
2 Timothy 4:6–8
Romans 1:1–7

ROMANS, LETTER TO THE.

The sixth book in the New Testament, written by Paul. It is in the form of a letter. The apostle Paul wrote it to the Christians in Rome. He wrote that the gospel is God's powerful way of saving all who believe: "The good news tells how God accepts everyone who has faith, but only those who have faith." It is not enough to follow the Law of Moses. God only accepts people who have faith in Jesus. Paul also wrote that Jews and Gentiles are the same in the eyes of the Lord: "There is only one God, and he accepts Gentiles as well as Jews, simply because of their faith."

Romans 1:17 CEV
Romans 3:21–22
Romans 3:30 CEV

Root.

The base of a plant that keeps it alive. This word is used as a symbol in the Bible. "Plant your roots in Christ and let him be the foundation for your life. Be strong in your faith."

Colossians 2:7 CEV

Ruth.

A biblical example of loyalty. Ruth was the wife of one of Naomi's sons. The book of Ruth tells her story. It is a short book in the Old Testament. Ruth was from Moab. Naomi's family went to Moab because they did not have enough food in Judea. While in Moab, Naomi's sons got married. One of her sons married Ruth. Later, Naomi's husband and both sons died. Naomi wanted to go home to Judea. Ruth was very loyal. She moved with Naomi to Bethlehem. There Ruth worked in the fields owned by a man named Boaz. He was related to Naomi. Ruth and Boaz got married. This made Ruth an ancestor of David and Jesus.

Ruth 1:16–19
Ruth 4:9–22
Matthew 1:3–6

Ruth gleans in Boaz's farm fields.

a
b
c
d
e
f
g
h
i
j
k
l
m
n
o
p
q
R
s
t
u
v
w
x
y
z

SABBATH.

Saturday; the seventh day of the week. The Sabbath is the Jewish day of worship. It is a symbol of the day God rested after He created everything. Most Christians worship on the first day of the week—Sunday. Sunday is a symbol of the day Jesus rose from the dead. One of the Ten Commandments is about the Sabbath. It says that the Sabbath is a special day that should be kept holy. Jesus was criticized for not keeping the Old Testament Sabbath rules.

Genesis 2:2
1 Corinthians 16:2
Exodus 20:8
Matthew 12:1–14

SABBATH DAY'S JOURNEY.

How far Jews were allowed to travel on Saturday. The seventh day of the week was holy. On the Sabbath day, people were allowed to travel only about a half mile from their city wall.

Acts 1:12

SABEANS.

People of ancient Sheba. Sheba was where Yemen is today. The queen of Sheba was a Sabean who visited King Solomon. The Sabeans were also the people who stole Job's livestock.

1 Kings 10:1–13
Job 1:13–15

SACKCLOTH.

Cloth made from goat hair. In Bible times, people wore sackcloth when they were very sad or sorry. Jacob wore sackcloth when he thought his son Joseph was dead.

Joel 1:13
Genesis 37:34

SACRAMENT.

Special religious ceremonies. Sacraments are holy acts that can bring Christians closer to God. Baptism is a sacrament. So is communion—the Lord's Supper. When you take part in a sacrament, you show love and respect for God. The sacrament of baptism is a symbol that Christ's death washes away our sins and that we have died and risen in Him. The sacrament of communion shows how thankful we are that Christ died for us. It helps us to remember that He is here with us now, and it shows our faith and hope that Jesus will return someday.

Acts 2:38
Romans 6:3–8
1 Corinthians 10:15–17

SACRIFICE.

An offering made to show respect. In Old Testament times, people made animal sacrifices. They killed one of their best animals. Then they laid it on an altar as an offering. Good people made sacrifices to God. There were evil people who worshipped false gods. They made sacrifices to statues and other things. God warned them to stop. A sacrifice meant giving up your very best. Jesus made the most awesome sacrifice. He gave up His own perfect life for us. He died so that everyone who believes in Him will live forever with God.

Exodus 20:24
Exodus 22:20
Hebrews 9:11–15

SADDUCEES.

A group of religious leaders in Jesus' time. The Sadducees often disagreed with Jesus and His teachings. For example, they didn't believe in the resurrection of the dead.

Matthew 16:6
Mark 12:18

SAINT.

One called to serve God. Saint is a New Testament word. It means a Christian believer who is set

b
c
d
e
f
g
h
i
j
k
l
m
n
o
p
q
r
s
t
u
v
w
x
y
z

129

apart to serve God. The Old Testament had another meaning for saint. It meant a godly Jewish person. The Bible says that the saints of God's kingdom will be blessed.

Romans 1:7
Psalm 16:3
Colossians 1:12

SALOME. ——————

A woman at the cross. Salome saw Jesus being crucified. She visited His tomb after He rose from the dead. Salome might have been the mother of Jesus' disciples James and John.

Mark 15:40
Mark 16:1

SALT. ——————

A seasoning. Do you eat salty things or put salt on your food? Salt is a mineral. It is used to season and preserve food. Jesus called His followers "the salt of the earth." He probably meant that they should be pure and free from sin. Jesus warned about them losing their saltiness. If salt loses its flavor, it is good for nothing. If a believer loses his purity, he is good for nothing.

Matthew 5:13
Luke 14:34

SALUTATION. ——————

A great big hello. In Bible times, people didn't just say, "Hi." Instead, they bowed and hugged each other a bunch of times.

In Romans 16:16, Paul tells his readers to greet each other with a holy kiss. Imagine greeting your friends that way!

Luke 15:20

SALVATION. ——————

God's work of delivering humans from sin. Salvation is available to everyone in the world. But it is only possible by believing in Jesus Christ. Salvation is like the difference between your grubby play clothes and your cleanest best clothes. If you don't believe in Jesus and His death on the cross, your soul is like your grubby clothes. But once you believe that He died for your sins, the Holy Spirit comes and cleans up your soul. He makes it fresh and clean. Jesus saved you from your sins. His death made it possible for you to live in heaven with God someday. Would you like to receive salvation right now? If So pray this prayer: "Dear Jesus, I am sorry for all the bad things I have done. I believe that You died on the cross for me. Please take away my sins and save me. Thank You, Jesus. Amen." Now you have received salvation! Always remember that Jesus saved you. Try your very best to live in a way that pleases Him.

Romans 8:9
Hebrews 5:9
John 3:36

SAMARIA. ——————

In Bible times, the capital city of Israel. Samaria was the main city of the northern kingdom of Israel. Omri, a king of Israel, built the city in about 900 BC. Samaria was also the name of the whole area around the city. The Assyrians took over Samaria around 722 BC. Later, Jesus healed a man of leprosy in Samaria. He also talked with a Samaritan woman, a stranger. But Jesus knew all about her. Today Samaria is part of an area called the West Bank.

2 Kings 17:24

SAMARITAN. ——————

A person who lived in Samaria. Samaria was between Judea and Galilee. In Bible times, the Jews looked down upon the Samaritans. This was because they married outside of their race. Jesus did not look down upon them. He was their friend. He used a Samaritan as an example of a good neighbor.

Luke 9:51-52
Luke 10:29-37
John 4:1-30

SAMSON. ——————

The Bible's strongman. Before Samson was born, an angel of the Lord appeared to his mom. The angel said that Samson would serve God. He warned that Samson's hair should never be cut. When Samson grew up, he became a judge. He had faith in God. The Spirit of the Lord made him the strongest man

alive. With just his bare hands, he killed a lion. He used the jawbone of a donkey to destroy 1,000 Philistine soldiers. That made the Philistines very angry.

Samson fell in love with a woman named Delilah. The Philistines came to her and wanted to know what made Samson so strong. She found out that it was Samson's hair. So Delilah did a terrible thing. When Samson was asleep, she cut off all his hair! All at once, Samson was weak. The Philistines put him in prison. They hurt his eyes so he could not see. After a while, Samson's hair grew back. He prayed to God for strength. Samson asked God to let him destroy the Philistines as a payback for hurting his eyes.

One day, the mean Philistines brought Samson into their temple like a circus act. Samson pushed on two strong columns that held the temple up. The whole thing came crashing down, killing the Philistines and Samson, too!

Judges 13–16

SAMUEL.

The last judge of Israel. Samuel was also a prophet. When he was a little boy, his parents took him to learn from a priest named Eli. When he grew up, he became the Israelites' leader. He got them to stop worshipping false gods. He also led them into a long time of peace. When Samuel was an old man, he made Saul Israel's first king. Saul didn't work out as king. So Samuel made David the new king. When Samuel died, he was given a huge funeral. "People from all over Israel gathered to mourn for him."

1 Samuel 7:15–17
1 Samuel 3:19–20
1 Samuel 1:23–2:11
1 Samuel 10:20–24
1 Samuel 16:13
1 Samuel 25:1 CEV

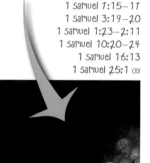

King Saul (on his knees) meets the spirit of the prophet Samuel, who has bad news: Saul will soon be dead, too! (Read more in 1 Samuel 28.)

SANCTIFICATION.

To set something aside to be made holy. In Old Testament times, certain people were sanctified. These were priests, Levites, and each family's firstborn child. If you lived back then, would you be sanctified? You would if you were the oldest kid in your family. In New Testament times, all believers were called to holiness and sanctification. Sanctified people should spread the good Word about God's power and love.

2 Thessalonians 2:13

SANCTUARY.

A holy place or a place to worship. A church is a sanctuary. It is a holy place where anyone can go to worship God. A sanctuary is a place where people feel safe under God's protection.

Leviticus 4:6
Psalm 73:17
Ezekiel 11:16

SAPPHIRA.

A woman who lied, fell down, and died! Sapphira and her husband, Ananias, belonged to the church in Jerusalem. People in the church agreed to sell their belongings and then give that money to the poor. Sapphira and Ananias agreed, too. But when they sold some land, they kept some of the money for themselves. Then they lied about it. When Ananias was caught in his lie to God, he dropped dead at

a b c d e f g h i j k l m n o p q r S t u v w x y z

131

Peter's feet. The same thing happened to Sapphira three hours later! (Read all about it in Acts 5:1–10.)

Acts 4:32–35

SAPPHIRE. ——————

A precious stone. A sapphire is a shiny blue gem. Sapphires were used in the breastplates of high priests. They will also be used in the foundation of New Jerusalem.

Exodus 28:15–18
Revelation 21:19

SARAH. ——————

Abraham's wife and Isaac's mom. Sarah was also called Sarai. She was more than 90 years old when her son, Isaac, was born. Her husband was 100 years old! God said that He would bless Sarah. She would become "a mother of nations." She did become a mother of nations! Isaac had children. His children had children. Their children had children, and on and on. Sarah was an ancestor to all the Israelites, kings, and even to Jesus. Sarah was 127 years old when she died. The burial site of Sarah and her family still exists. It is called the Tomb of the Patriarchs. You can visit it in a city called Hebron, near Jerusalem.

Genesis 11:29
Genesis 17:17
Genesis 17:16

SARDIS. ——————

An ancient city with a "dead" church. Sardis is one of the seven churches in the book of Revelation. Jesus criticized the church in Sardis, saying that the people needed to repent.

Revelation 1:11
Revelation 3:1–5

SATAN. ——————

Another name for the devil. Satan is called "the father of lies." That's because he will do anything to stop people from believing in God. He loves to get people to do bad things. For example, Adam and Eve lived in a beautiful garden. They had everything they wanted, and their life was perfect. God gave them only one rule to follow. And who got them to break that rule? Satan. (Read all about it in Genesis 3.) We all have to watch out for Satan. He's evil, and no one is safe from his tricks. The best way to keep away from him is to stay faithful to God and do what Jesus taught.

John 8:44
Ephesians 6:10–12

SAUL. ——————

A name shared by Israel's first king and a persecutor of Christians. Samuel made one Saul the king of Israel. But Saul was a big disappointment. God wasn't at all pleased with him. Saul disobeyed God. He also did many crazy things. He offered a sacrifice, which was something only priests were allowed to do. He sent his army into a war. Then he told his men they couldn't eat anything or they would be cursed. Saul was a thief and a murderer. He kept on doing bad things. Then Saul did one last evil thing. He asked a witch to predict his future. She predicted that he would die the next day. (Check out 1 Samuel 28:4–20.) And he did!

The other Saul hated Jesus and Jesus' followers. But then Jesus met him on the road to Damascus and changed Saul's mind. (Check out the story in Acts 9.) Soon, known as Paul, this Saul was a missionary and Bible writer!

1 Samuel 10:1
1 Samuel 13:9–12
1 Samuel 14:23–24

SAVIOR. ——————

Jesus Christ. A savior is someone who saves you from danger or destruction. In other words, a savior is a hero. The most awesome superhero of all time is Jesus Christ. He saved us from the worst of all things—hell. Hell is an awful place. The Bible says it is a lake of fire filled with suffering. Hell is the place where unbelievers go when they die. But Jesus came to rescue us. If you believe in the Lord Jesus Christ, then He is your Savior. If you trust that He died on the cross for your sins, then you will not go to hell.

Revelation 19:20
2 Thessalonians 1:9
Luke 12:4–5

SCARLET. ————

A deep red color. This color was used a lot in clothing worn by rich, important people. It was also a symbol of Israel's sin against God. Another name for scarlet is "crimson."

2 Samuel 1:24
Isaiah 1:18

SCEPTER. ————

A ruler's baton. A scepter was a stick carried by a king or other important leader. It was a symbol that he was in charge. Sometimes scepters were made of gold.

Ezekiel 19:11
Esther 4:11

SCOURGING. ————

A terrible beating. In Bible times, criminals were beaten with a leather strap. It had bits of sharp metal on it. Jesus was scourged before He was crucified.

Matthew 27:26 KJV

SCRIBE. ————

A secretary. Scribes wrote down the law. There were no computers back then, so they wrote everything by hand. Many scribes were also teachers of the law. Ezra was a scribe.

Jeremiah 8:8
Nehemiah 8:1

The original Bible books were printed on scrolls similar to this one.

SCROLL. ————

Rolled-up paper or some other writing material. In ancient days people wrote on pieces of leather or papyrus. Papyrus was paper made from a plant. The "paper" was rolled around a stick. You had to unroll it to read it.

Isaiah 34:4
Luke 4:17 NIV

SEA OF GALILEE. ————

A lake in the northern part of Israel. If you went to Israel today, you could visit this large body of water called a "sea." It is a freshwater lake about 14 miles long and 7 miles wide. The Sea of Galilee is a popular place for fishermen. Several of Jesus' disciples fished there. They were James, John, Peter, and Andrew. Jesus spent a lot of time near this sea. During a bad storm, He and his disciples were out in a boat on the Sea of Galilee. The disciples were very afraid as the boat was tossed about. But Jesus told the water to calm down, and it did.

Jesus also walked on water in the Sea of Galilee.

Mark 1:16–20
Matthew 8:23–27
John 6:16–20

SECOND COMING. ————

Jesus' return to earth. Before Jesus went up into heaven He said He would come back. Christians look forward to that day. He will come without any warning. So Christians should be prepared. When Jesus comes, He will raise the dead and take believers with Him into the air. The Second Coming also starts a chain of events that bring the end of life as we know it. Jesus will punish wicked people and those who won't believe in Him. He will judge the world. And He will destroy death. It will be a wonderful time for believers but an awful time for everyone else.

Matthew 24:42
1 Thessalonians 4:16
Matthew 25:32
1 Corinthians 15:25–26

SECT.

A religious or political group. The Pharisees, Sadducees, and Essenes were religious sects in Bible times. The Herodians were a political sect. Early Christians were known as "the Nazarene sect."

Acts 24:5 NIV

SEED.

You! In the Bible, the word seed can mean a parent's child. Think about it: Parents have a kid. The kid grows up—like a seed becomes a full-grown plant. Before long, the kid is a grown-up with his own kids. It's the circle of life!

Genesis 28:14 KJV

SELF-DENIAL.

Passing up something you really want. Imagine there is one pancake left at breakfast. You really want it. But you pass it up so your little sister can have it instead. That's self-denial! Jesus wanted His followers to practice self-denial. The Bible says that the Sabbath is a day of rest. It is a day when God's people should practice self-denial.

Matthew 16:24

SENNACHERIB.

An Assyrian king. He captured all the cities in Judah except Jerusalem. Then he promised to go away if King Hezekiah gave him a lot of money, which Hezekiah did. King Sennacherib died while he worshipped a false god. His own sons killed him!

2 Kings 18:13–16
2 Kings 19:36–37

SEPTUAGINT.

The Old Testament written in Greek. The Old Testament was first written in Hebrew. Between 250 and 150 BC, it was translated into the Greek language. Since then, it has been written in almost every language you can imagine.

SEPULCHER.

A tomb. In ancient days, people were buried in caves called sepulchers. Jesus was buried in a sepulcher owned by Joseph of Arimathea.

Matthew 27:51–60

Inside a sepulcher, looking out.

SERAPHIM.

Bible creatures with six wings. In some version of the Bible, they're called seraphs. Seraphim are mentioned in only one place in the Bible. They appear in a dream that Isaiah had. He saw God sitting on a throne. Seraphim were standing above Him. Each one had six wings. With two wings, they covered their faces. With two wings, they covered their feet. And with two wings, they flew. The seraphim sang praises to God. Nearby was an altar with hot coals on it. A seraph picked up one of the coals. He flew toward Isaiah. Then he touched Isaiah's lips with the hot coal. He told Isaiah that his sins were forgiven. (Read all about it in Isaiah 6:1–7.)

SERMON ON THE MOUNT.

Jesus' teachings about people's behavior. Huge crowds followed Jesus wherever He went. One day, He preached to them from a hillside near Capernaum. Jesus told the people how to find happiness. He encouraged them to speak up about God. Jesus reminded them about God's commandments. And He said they should give to the needy. He taught them the Lord's Prayer and other rules about prayer and fasting. He told them not to love money more than God. He even told them how to be free from worrying. He warned the people to be careful. He said to watch out for anyone who wants to pull them away from the one true

God. Jesus ended His sermon with a parable about obeying God's Word (Matthew 7:24–27).

Matthew 5–6
Matthew 7:15–23

SERPENT.

A snake. The serpent has been around since creation. Satan showed up as a sly serpent in the Garden of Eden. He got Eve to eat the forbidden fruit. God sent poisonous serpents to punish the Israelites by biting them. Then Moses made a brass serpent. He put it on top of a stick. When the people looked at it, they were healed of their snakebites.

Genesis 3:1–6
Numbers 21:6
Numbers 21:9

SERVANT.

A person who helps others. The word *servant* is used many times in the Bible. A servant does things to help others. Servants work for leaders who tell them what to do. Jesus said that His job was to save others and to serve God. Jesus' disciples were servants of God. If you tell others about Jesus, you are God's servant, too.

Matthew 8:9
Luke 22:27
Acts 16:17

SETH.

Adam and Eve's third son. His older brothers were Cain and Abel. When Seth was born, his dad, Adam, was 130 years old.

Adam lived to be 930! So Seth had lots of younger brothers and sisters. Seth was a distant relative of Jesus' adopted dad, Joseph.

Genesis 5:3
Genesis 5:5
Genesis 5:4
Luke 3:23–38

SEVEN.

A perfect number. The number seven shows up a lot in the Bible. It was thought to be a complete, or perfect, number. God made the heavens and earth in seven days. Noah took seven of every kind of clean animal on the ark. Seven priests carrying seven trumpets marched around the city of Jericho seven times. Peter asked Jesus how many times he should forgive someone. Jesus answered, "Seventy times seven." If you look hard enough, you can find the word *seven* written hundreds of times in the Bible.

Genesis 2:2
Genesis 7:2–3
Joshua 6:4
Matthew 18:21–22

SHADRACH.

Daniel's friend. Shadrach refused to worship false gods. So King Nebuchadnezzar had him thrown into a fiery furnace. Shadrach lived to tell about it! Read more about it in Daniel 3.

SHAME.

Feeling guilty for doing something wrong. Everyone feels shame. That's because everyone sins. Shame can be caused by laziness. It can also happen if you are full of yourself. Another cause for shame can be the people you hang around with. They might cause you to do bad things that you otherwise might not do.

Romans 3:10
Proverbs 10:5
Proverbs 11:2
Proverbs 28:1

SHEEP.

A farm animal. A sheep's fur is used to make wool cloth. Young sheep—lambs—are used for food. In Bible times, people sacrificed lambs as gifts to God. Large flocks of sheep were a sign that a person was rich. Jesus called His followers "sheep." He said that

Shadrach, Meshach, and Abednego refuse to bow down to the king's giant statue.

a
b
c
d
e
f
g
h
i
j
k
l
m
n
o
p
q
r
s
t
u
v
w
x
y
z

if just one of them got lost, He would go to find him.

2 Kings 3:4
Leviticus 9:2–4
Job 1:3
Luke 15:4–6

SHEKEL. ──────────

A Jewish measure of money. Jeremiah bought a field from his cousin for 17 shekels of silver. David paid Araunah 600 shekels of gold for his threshing floor.

Jeremiah 32:9
1 Chronicles 21:25

SHEKINAH. ──────────

God's visible glory. The Bible tells about God appearing in a cloud, fire, and a bright light. When the Israelites left Egypt, God led them. He appeared in a cloud and also in a column of fire. God talked to Moses through a burning bush. On the night Jesus was born, the glory of God showed as a very bright light. It was so bright and strange that the shepherds were afraid.

Exodus 13:20–22
Exodus 3
Luke 2:9

SHEM. ──────────

Noah's oldest son. Shem was one of the people on the ark. God saved him and his family from the big flood. Shem's children were the beginning of many nations. They and all of their children's children became the Jews, Arameans, Persians, Assyrians, and Arabians.

Genesis 5:32
Genesis 10:22

SHEPHERD. ──────────

Someone who takes care of sheep. In Bible times, rich people had huge flocks of sheep. Shepherds were needed to care for them. It was a dangerous job. Wild animals came after the sheep, and shepherds had to protect them with their slingshots. David was a shepherd boy. That's probably why he was able to kill Goliath with just his slingshot and a stone. God is like a shepherd for people. He cares for His people and protects them from harm. The Twenty-third Psalm begins, "The Lord is my shepherd." Jesus called Himself "the good shepherd." He came to protect God's people from sin and to lead them to heaven.

Genesis 24:35
John 10:7–18

SHEWBREAD. ──────────

Bread used for religious ceremonies. It was like the communion bread used in today's churches. This special bread was stored in the temple. It is also called "bread of the Presence" because it was brought out in the presence of the Lord.

Numbers 4:7 NASB

SHIELD. ──────────

A protective armor. A shield was a piece of wood covered with animal hide or metal. Soldiers carried shields in battle. They held them up to protect their bodies from weapons. God is a shield, protecting us from danger.

2 Chronicles 14:8
Psalm 3:3

SHILOH. ──────────

Where the ark of the covenant was captured. Shiloh was the Israelites' capital city. That's where the tabernacle was. And inside the tabernacle was the ark of the covenant. The ark was a holy box that held the Ten Commandments. In time, the Israelites started getting too careless with God. Although they behaved badly, they thought God would let them get away with it. He didn't. He allowed the Philistines to attack Shiloh. They came and took away the ark. If you visited the Holy Land today, you would see what is left of Shiloh. The ruins are about twenty-five miles from Jerusalem.

Exodus 40:1–33
1 Samuel 4:3–11

SIEVE. ──────────

A pan with very small holes. Maybe you've used a sieve in the kitchen. It is a utensil used for draining or sifting things. In ancient times, sieves were made from tough plants like bulrushes. They were even made from horsehair!

Amos 9:9

SIGN.

A clue that something has happened or will happen. God said the sun and moon are signs that separate the days and the seasons. He used a rainbow as a sign of His promise to Noah. Jesus told evil people to remember Jonah. The three days that Jonah was in the whale was a sign. It was a clue that Jesus would be buried for three days before He came back to life. (Check out Matthew 12:38–40.)

Genesis 1:14
Genesis 9:13

SILAS.

Paul's friend and coworker. Silas was a leader in the Jerusalem church. He traveled with Paul on his second missionary journey. Silas was with Paul at Corinth and Thessalonica. Both Paul and Silas were put into prison because they taught about Jesus.

Acts 15:40
Acts 16:16–40

SILOAM.

A pool of water in Jerusalem. The Pool of Siloam was supplied with water by an underground tunnel. The water came from a spring outside the city. Jesus healed a blind man by having him wash in the Pool of Siloam.

2 Kings 20:20
John 9:6–7

SILVER.

A valuable metal. Silver was used to make jewelry and utensils. In Bible times, it was often used in coins. They were valued by how much they weighed.

Genesis 44:2
Genesis 23:16

SIMEON.

A name shared by several Bible men. One was Jacob's son. A tribe of Israel was named after this Simeon. A second Simeon was the man who blessed the child Jesus in the temple at Jerusalem. A third Simeon was a Christian prophet at Antioch, a friend of the apostle Paul.

Genesis 35:23
Numbers 1:23
Luke 2:25–35
Acts 13:1

SIMON.

One of Jesus' disciples. Simon is also known as the apostle Peter. Simon Peter was a fisherman before he became a disciple. Peter was bold and quick-tempered. He walked on water with Jesus. He went up in the mountains with Him. There he saw Moses and Elijah. Peter was the one who cut off a soldier's ear when Jesus was arrested. Peter denied that he knew Jesus. For that, he was very sorry. He was one of the disciples who discovered that Jesus had risen from the dead. Peter's brother

was a disciple, too. He was the disciple named Andrew.

Matthew 14:25–30
Matthew 17:1–13
Luke 22:54–62
John 18:10
John 20:1–10
John 1:40–41

SIN.

The bad things that people do. Sin is being disobedient toward God. The first people ever to sin were Adam and Eve. From then on, everyone has sinned. Sin is not only about how we treat God. It is also about how we treat others and ourselves. Whenever we humans behave badly, it is sin. As hard as we try, we can never be perfect before God. The good news is that God is forgiving. If we tell Him about our sins and are truly sorry, He will forgive us. Jesus died for our sins. Without Him, no one would be good enough to get into heaven.

Romans 5:12–14
1 John 1:9
Romans 5:8

SIN OFFERING.

A sacrifice. In Bible times, people sacrificed animals to God. They would kill one of their best animals and offer it to God as a gift. They did this to show God they were sorry for doing bad things.

Leviticus 4:2–3

a b c d e f g h i j k l m n o p q r s t u v w x y z

Military commander Sisera dies from a tent peg in his head.

a
b
c
d
e
f
g
h
i
j
k
l
m
n
o
p
q
r
S
t
u
v
w
x
y
z

SISERA.

A military commander who was killed by a woman. Sisera ran away from a lost battle. He was tired from running, so he stopped for a while. He fell asleep inside a tent belonging to a woman named Jael. As Sisera slept, Jael murdered him.

Judges 4:2–22

SLANDER.

Words that hurt someone's reputation. If you go around telling people that your friend is lazy, that's slander. Your words make people think badly of your friend. Christians should not say things that slander others.

Psalm 52:2
Colossians 3:8

SLAVE.

A person who is bought and sold. Slaves are made to work for their owners. The masters told slaves what to do. Slavery was a common practice in Bible times. The apostle Paul wrote about slaves and masters. He told them how to behave.

Ephesians 6:5–9

SLIME.

Ooey, gooey stuff. In Bible times, slime was a word for tar. It held bricks together. Slime was used in building the Tower of Babel.

Genesis 11:3 KJV

SLING.

A weapon made from leather straps. Slings were used to throw stones. David killed Goliath with a slingshot. (Read more about it in 1 Samuel 17.)

Judges 20:16

SLUGGARD.

A lazy person. If you lay around all day doing nothing, you are a sluggard. A sluggard is someone who prefers not to work. Paul said those who won't work shouldn't eat.

2 Thessalonians 3:10

SMYRNA.

An ancient city north of Ephesus. One of the seven churches of Asia Minor was in Smyrna. Smyrna was a city near the Aegean Sea, in what is now western Turkey.

Revelation 1:11

SOBER.

Self-controlled, serious, or sensible. Church leaders should have a sober attitude. So should believers as they wait for Jesus to return.

1 Timothy 3:2
1 Thessalonians 5:5–6

SODOM AND GOMORRAH.—

Two wicked cities in the time of Abraham. The people of Sodom and Gomorrah did awful things. They displeased God and made Him very angry. There was a godly man named Lot who lived in Sodom. Two angels appeared to him. They told Lot to gather up his family and get out of there right away. God planned to destroy the city. So Lot took his wife and two daughters by the hand and started running. An angel said, "Run for your lives! Don't even look back. And don't stop in the valley. Run to the hills, where you will be safe." Lot's wife disobeyed. She looked back, and she turned into a block of salt! Then God destroyed Sodom and Gomorrah with a gigantic fire.

Genesis 14:1–3
Genesis 19:1
Genesis 19:12–13
Genesis 19:17 cev
Genesis 19:23–29

Lot and his two daughters escape Sodom, while Lot's wife looks back—and becomes a pillar of salt.

SOJOURNER.

Someone who lives, for a while, in a foreign country. Let's imagine your aunt lives in Japan and you live in the United States. If you went to live with her for a while, you would be a sojourner. Abraham sojourned in Egypt. Christians are sojourners on earth. That's because their forever-home is heaven. Do you know any sojourners?

Hebrews 11:9 kjv
Genesis 12:10 kjv
1 Peter 1:17 kjv

SOLDIER.

A person who serves in the military. Are there any soldiers in your family? There are if you are Christians who serve the Lord. The Bible says Christian workers are "soldiers." Read Ephesians 6:11–18. In it, Paul tells us what Christian soldiers need to do.

2 Timothy 2:3

SOLOMON.

A wise king. Solomon was David's son. He followed David as king of Israel. Solomon prayed that God would give him wisdom. He became famous for his wisdom and wealth. At God's command, Solomon built a temple at Jerusalem. But later, Solomon pulled away from God. He married wives who worshipped idols. He put heavy taxes on his people. After Solomon died, the people rebelled and the nation was divided. The rebels formed the northern kingdom of Israel, where Solomon's servant, Jeroboam, ruled. King Solomon's son, Rehoboam, ruled the southern kingdom of Judah. (Find out more about it in 1 Kings 12:1–19.)

1 Kings 3
1 Kings 4:20–34
1 Kings 5–8
1 Kings 11:1–8
1 Kings 12:4

SON OF GOD.

A special name for Jesus. Before Jesus was born, an angel appeared to His mom, Mary. The angel said Mary would give birth to the Son of God. After Jesus was baptized, God spoke from heaven. He said, "This is My beloved Son." John wrote his Gospel to encourage people to believe in the Son of God. Some other names for Jesus are Emmanuel, Messiah, and Son of Man.

Luke 1:35
John 20:31

Solomon uses his wisdom to decide who's really the mother of a live baby. Read the whole story in 1 Kings 3.

SON OF MAN.

Another name for Jesus. Son of Man is a name Jesus sometimes used for Himself. It showed that He was human, like earthly men. But He was special, because He was God's Son, too. He came to save other humans from sin. God's prophet Ezekiel was also known as the son of man. It showed that he, like Jesus, was on a special mission for God. Ezekiel helped to carry God's messages to the people.

Matthew 26:45
Ezekiel 2:1

SONG OF SONGS.

The twenty-second book of the Old Testament. Song of Songs is another name for the book called Song of Solomon. It is a book of poems about two people in love—a husband and wife. King Solomon probably wrote it

139

a
b
c
d
e
f
g
h
i
j
k
l
m
n
o
p
q
r
s
t
u
v
w
x
y
z

a
b
c
d
e
f
g
h
i
j
k
l
m
n
o
p
q
r
S
t
u
v
w
x
y
z

as a love song to his wife. Some people believe that it represents God's love for His people.

SORROW.

Sadness. Have you ever been really, really sad? That kind of sadness is called sorrow. Sometimes sorrow comes when a beloved pet or a person dies. It can also happen if someone hurts your feelings or is mean to you. Sometimes sorrow is the result of sin. Whenever you feel sorrow, call on the Lord. Faith in Him will help you to feel better.

John 11:33–35
Psalm 35:17
Genesis 3:16–17
Nehemiah 8:10

SOUL.

The part inside you that controls your feelings. When you feel deeply about something, you feel it in your soul. You feel sadness in your soul. You feel joy in your soul. You love with your soul. The Bible says to love God with all your heart, all your soul, and all your strength.

1 Samuel 1:10
Psalm 94:19
Deuteronomy 6:5

SOVEREIGNTY OF GOD.

God rules! The sovereignty of God means that God is the King (or sovereign) of the universe. He created everyone. He created the earth, sky, and everything in them. God is so great that He will rule forever. God is also called Almighty because He is more powerful than anyone or anything. He

punishes sin. But God loves us so much that He offers us life forever with Him. To be forgiven for sin and live in heaven someday, you must trust in God's Son—the Lord Jesus Christ.

Genesis 1–2
Psalm 45:6
Revelation 1:8
Acts 16:31

SOWER.

Someone who plants seeds. Jesus told a story about a sower. Read His story in Matthew 13:3–9. The story has a hidden meaning. To find out what it is, read Matthew 13:18–23.

SPAIN.

A country in southwestern Europe. In ancient times, Spain was known as Iberia and Hispania. Jonah's ship was headed to Tarshish—probably in Spain—when he was thrown overboard.

Jonah 1:3, 15

SPAN.

A measurement that equals about nine inches. The word *span* can also mean distance in space, as in the span of a mile, or in time, as in a "life span."

Exodus 28:16
Isaiah 38:12 NKJV

SPARROW.

A small bird. You probably see these little birds every day. Sparrows seem to be everywhere. They even lived in Bible times. Back then, they were sold as food

at a price that even poor people could pay.

Matthew 10:29

SPEAR.

A weapon. A spear was a long stick with a sharp metal point on the end. It was a lot bigger than a dart or an arrow. Soldiers in the Bible often fought with spears. On the cross, Jesus was wounded with a spear.

1 Samuel 13:22
1 Chronicles 12:24
John 19:34

SPIRIT.

The part of you that connects to God. John said that a spirit is like the wind. Our spirits are invisible. They are deep within us, and they make us who we are. God gives us our spirits, and when we die they return to Him. God is a spirit. His Spirit speaks to ours. We are to worship God truthfully with our spirits. Humans depend on their bodies to stay alive on earth. But when people die, their spirits live on apart from their bodies. If you trust in Jesus, your spirit will live forever with Him.

John 3:8
Ecclesiastes 12:7
Judges 13:25
John 4:24
Psalm 23:6

SPIRITUAL GIFTS.

God's special gifts to believers. The Bible lists many gifts that God's Holy Spirit can give to believers. The greatest of these is love. Some other gifts of the Spirit are preaching, serving, teaching, encouraging, giving, leading, and helping. Wisdom, knowledge, faith, and knowing right from wrong are also His gifts. Not everyone gets all of God's gifts. It is up to Him to choose who gets what.

1 Corinthians 13:13
Romans 12:6–8
1 Corinthians 12:8–11

STAFF.

A tool made from a long stick. A staff was used to guide animals and to remove fruit from trees. Old or sick people used a staff like a cane.

Isaiah 28:27
Exodus 21:19

STAR.

Specks of light in the night sky. In ancient times, people relied on the stars. Stars helped them find their way. They also were symbols of things to come. Sometimes stars were a symbol of an angel or great ruler. A bright star shone in the east when Jesus was born. The wise men followed it so they could find the baby who would become the great King.

Isaiah 47:13
Matthew 2:1–3

STATUTE.

A rule created by government. If your mom says, "Do your homework before you hang out with your friends," that's kind of like a statute. It's a rule that tells how you should behave. In Bible times, kings and other rulers made statutes. The greatest statutes are the Ten Commandments. They came straight from God. The Ten Commandments are God's rules for how we should behave.

Exodus 18:16
Exodus 20:3–17

STEADFAST.

A word meaning determined and patient. The Bible says that Christians should be steadfast in their faith. That means we should be determined to believe in God. We should be patient for Him to answer our prayers. If we are steadfast and trust God, we won't be afraid of bad news. If our minds are set on God, we will find peace.

Psalm 112:7
Isaiah 26:3

STEPHEN.

One of the first deacons of the Christian church. Stephen loved the Lord. His job as deacon was to help Jesus' twelve disciples. After Jesus died, they had a lot to do. It was their job to spread the Word and to win other people to Christ. God gave Stephen the gift of performing miracles. The Jewish leaders didn't like the control Stephen had over the people. He spoke with power and wisdom. The leaders had Stephen arrested and stoned to death. As he was dying, Stephen said: "Lord Jesus, receive my spirit. . . . Do not hold this sin against them."

Acts 6:5
Acts 6:8
Acts 6:10
Acts 7:59–60 NIV

STEWARDSHIP.

Caring for God's gifts. God owns everything. From the beginning of time, He gave humans the job of caretakers. It is our responsibility to care for the earth, animals, and other people. Stewardship is about using your time wisely. It means using your talents to make God proud. It also involves giving some of your money to the church.

Psalm 50:10–12
Genesis 1:26
Ephesians 5:16
2 Timothy 1:6
Malachi 3:10

STONING.

An ancient punishment. When a person was to be stoned, other people stood around and threw rocks at that person until he or she died. Godly men were sometimes stoned because of their faith. Stephen was one of them.

Acts 7:59

STRIFE.

Endless quarreling. Sometimes people don't get along. They quarrel and are at each other all the time. That's strife. Strife can come from being conceited. Another cause is wanting something and not caring how you get it. You can avoid strife by being unselfish and trying hard to get along with others.

Luke 22:24
1 Corinthians 3:3
Philippians 2:3

a
b
c
d
e
f
g
h
i
j
k
l
m
n
o
p
q
r
S
t
u
v
w
x
y
z

a
b
c
d
e
f
g
h
i
j
k
l
m
n
o
p
q
r
s
T
u
v
w
x
y
z

TEACHER. ——————
Someone who instructs people. You know all about teachers, right? Who is your favorite teacher of all time? Why is that person your favorite? Teachers have an awesome job. They have to find a way into your brain so they can leave a bunch of knowledge in there. A good teacher knows how to connect with students. The best teacher of all was Jesus. He connected with people in a way that made them want to learn. He didn't teach math or reading or science. Instead, Jesus taught about life. It was His job to teach people about living right for God.

Luke 6:40 NIV
Ecclesiastes 12:10 NIV
Matthew 22:36

TEMPERANCE. ——————
Self-control. Temperance means staying in control of whatever you do. If you want to eat a whole pint of ice cream but you eat just one scoop, that's temperance. The Bible says that Christians should behave with temperance. Temperance brings us closer to knowing Jesus Christ.

Galatians 5:23 KJV
2 Peter 1:5–9 KJV

TEMPLE. ——————
A place of worship. After the death of King David, the Jewish people worshipped in temples. Solomon built the first temple. It was a beautiful place. That temple was 90 feet long and 30 feet wide.

It had a porch that was 30 feet long and 15 feet wide. Some of its walls were covered with gold and decorated with precious stones. The ark of the covenant was kept in the temple. You can read more about the temple in 2 Chronicles 3–4. After about 350 years, the Israelites' enemy, the Babylonians, destroyed the temple. A second temple was built about seventy years later. Its construction was directed by a man named Zerubbabel. And a few years before Jesus was born, King Herod the Great began to build a bigger, more impressive temple on the same site. But it was destroyed by the Roman army in AD 70.

1 Kings 6:3

TEMPTATION. ——————
Being pulled toward something you know is wrong. Imagine this: You have an assignment due tomorrow. But you haven't started it yet. Your best friend calls and wants you to hang out. You want to go and have fun. . .but you have that assignment to do. The idea of hanging out is so tempting! Temptation is when something tries to draw you into doing a wrong thing. Everyone faces temptation. Even Jesus! Read about how Satan tempted Jesus in Matthew 4:1–11. The Lord's Prayer teaches us to ask God to keep us away from temptation. The Bible says God will help us when we are tempted.

Matthew 6:9–13
1 Corinthians 10:13

TEN COMMANDMENTS. —
Part of God's law. God gave the Ten Commandments to Moses. It was his job to share them with the people. All believers should try to live by God's rules. So here's a summary of what they say:

1. Worship only the one true God.
2. Don't make images of gods

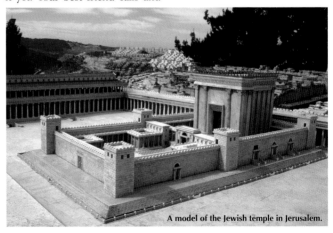
A model of the Jewish temple in Jerusalem.

or worship such false gods
3. Don't use God's name in a disrespectful way.
4. Keep the Sabbath as a day to honor God.
5. Respect your mom and dad.
6. Don't kill anyone.
7. When you get married, be faithful to your husband or wife.
8. Don't steal.
9. Don't lie.
10. Don't want anything that belongs to someone else.

How do you measure up to God's rules? Ask Him to help you follow them all.

Exodus 20:1–17

TENT.
A portable shelter, usually made of goat hair in biblical times. In ancient times, when people moved from place to place, they lived in tents. The tents were often made of thick goat hair. They were supported by poles and ropes tied to stakes. Tent-dwellers were called nomads. Sometimes they were herdsmen moving their flocks from one grazing land to another. After the Israelites left Egypt, they led a nomadic life. They lived in the wilderness in tents.

Genesis 4:20
Exodus 33:8

TESTAMENT.
An important agreement, sometimes called a covenant. A testament was an agreement promised with blood. In Old Testament times, an animal would be killed. The shedding of an animal's blood was a promise that the agreement couldn't be broken. In the New Testament, Jesus' blood was shed on the cross. His blood sealed the promise that He had come to save us from our sins.

Matthew 26:28

TESTIMONY.
Speaking the truth about what you know. Your testimony is the truth about something you have seen, heard, or done. When people give testimony in court, they swear that they are telling the truth. If you do something, or if you hear something with your own ears or see it with your own eyes, then you know it is true. Believers can share their testimony about Jesus. If you tell others about what Jesus has done for you, then you are sharing your testimony.

Acts 4:20
John 19:35

TETRARCH.
One of four governors who served in neighboring regions. In Bible times, governors of Roman provinces were sometimes called tetrarchs. Herod was a tetrarch of Galilee.

Luke 3:1

THANKSGIVING.
Saying "thank you." Thanksgiving is more than a holiday. The word *thanksgiving* means expressing your thanks, especially to God. Many psalms thank God for His goodness and blessings. Another word for thanksgiving is *praise*. When you praise God, you thank Him for being so awesome and for all He has given you. The next time you pray, don't forget to say, "Thank You, God!"

Psalm 116:12–19

THEOPHILUS.
Luke's friend. When Luke wrote his Gospel and the book of Acts, he wrote them to Theophilus. Not much is known about Theophilus. His name appears only twice in the Bible, in Luke 1:3 and Acts 1:1.

THESSALONIANS, FIRST AND SECOND LETTERS TO THE.
The thirteenth and fourteenth books of the New Testament. They were both written by Paul to the church in Thessalonica. In these letters, Paul writes about the second coming of Christ. That means the day when Jesus comes back to take all believers to heaven. Paul said we should all want to live good Christian lives because we know Jesus is coming. Nobody knows when Jesus will come back. Paul said believers have to be watchful and prepared. Like Paul, you can tell

a
b
c
d
e
f
g
h
i
j
k
l
m
n
o
p
q
r
s
T
u
v
w
x
y
z

145

your friends that Christ is coming back someday. Teach them about Jesus so they will be ready.

1 Thessalonians 5:23
1 Thessalonians 5:1–11

THIRTY PIECES OF SILVER. ———

What Judas was paid to betray Jesus. Judas Iscariot was one of the twelve disciples. He agreed to help the chief priests and elders arrest Jesus. For just thirty pieces of silver, Judas led the men to Jesus so they could capture Him. Thirty pieces of silver was about what it cost to buy a slave. Afterward, Judas was sorry. He threw his money on the temple floor. Then he killed himself.

Matthew 27:3–8

THOMAS. ———

The doubting disciple. He was also called Didymus, meaning "twin." Thomas was one of Jesus' twelve disciples. He was a guy who liked to be certain about things. Thomas wasn't so sure that Jesus had risen from the dead. Even when Jesus came back to life and was walking around and talking, Thomas thought that He might be a fake. Thomas wanted proof. He wanted to see the nail marks on Jesus' hands. He wanted to check out the place on Jesus' side where He'd been stuck with a spear. So Jesus showed him! Then Thomas believed. He said, "My Lord and my God!" Jesus reminded him that although we can't see God, we should still believe in Him. (Find out more in John 20:24–29.)

John 11:16

THORN IN THE FLESH. ———

Something that causes you to suffer. Paul wrote about his "thorn in the flesh." No one knows for sure what Paul's "thorn" was. But he prayed for the Lord to take it away from him. A thorn in the flesh doesn't have to be an injury or sickness. It might be something you are afraid of or a bad habit. Do you have a thorn in your flesh?

2 Corinthians 12:7–8

THORNS. ———

Very sharp spikes on a plant. Roses have thorns on their stems. A crown of thorns was put on Jesus' head before He was crucified. It was done to make fun of Him because He had claimed to be the King of the Jews.

Matthew 27:29

THRONE. ———

A chair fit for a king. Thrones were beautiful chairs. They were symbols that the people who sat on them had great power. Kings and queens sat on thrones. So did some priests and judges. The word *throne* is sometimes used to show the power of God: "God reigns over the nations; God is seated on his holy throne."

1 Kings 10:18
1 Kings 1:46
Psalm 47:8 NIV

"Doubting Thomas" touches the spear hole in Jesus' side.

TIGRIS.

A major river in the Middle East. The Tigris flows through Turkey and Iraq. Then it meets the Euphrates River and empties into the Persian Gulf. It might be the same river that flowed through the Garden of Eden.

Genesis 2:14

TIMOTHY.

Paul's young friend, who was like a son to him. Timothy's dad was Greek, and his mom was Jewish. Timothy was raised in the faith by his mom and grandma. His mom's name was Eunice. His grandma's name was Lois. These women had a strong faith in God. Timothy's mom and grandma were Christians, and so was Timothy. When Paul met Timothy, he wanted him to help teach others about Jesus. So the two men traveled together and taught. They were even in prison together for teaching about Jesus. Later, Paul wrote two letters to his friend Timothy. These are the New Testament books called 1 and 2 Timothy.

2 Timothy 1:5
Acts 16:1
Hebrews 13:23

TITHE.

An offering to God. A tithe is one-tenth of what a person earns. In Old Testament times, people gave a tithe of their crops. Jacob promised to give back to God a tenth of whatever God gave to

him. Jesus told people to give. He promised to bless them when they gave to God. He said: "Give, and it will be given to you. . . . For with the measure you use, it will be measured to you."

Leviticus 27:30
Genesis 28:20–22
Luke 6:38 NIV

TITUS.

Paul's helper. Titus was a Greek guy who traveled with the apostle Paul. Together they taught about Jesus. Sometimes Paul sent Titus to help some of the new Christian churches. Titus also served as a church leader in Crete, an island near Greece. While he was there, Paul wrote him a letter. That letter became the New Testament book called Titus. In his letter, Paul told Titus how to choose elders for the church. He suggested ways to deal with false teachers—people who taught untrue things about God. He also wrote about how Christians should behave when the world seems wicked.

Titus 1:4–16
Titus 3:1–11

TONGUE.

That big pink thing inside your mouth! Your tongue helps you to speak. It can say evil things or good things. Read what James said about it in James 3:5–10. *Tongue* can also mean "language." At first, everyone in the world spoke the same language, or tongue. But

God changed that. Now the world has many languages.

Genesis 11:1–9

TONGUES, SPEAKING IN.

A spiritual gift from God. On the day of Pentecost, the Holy Spirit came to Jesus' followers. His Spirit was so powerful that they cried out, praising Him. The people spoke in languages that no one understood. (Check out Acts 2:1–12.) Speaking with this sort of spiritual language is called speaking in tongues. Paul said that speaking in tongues is speaking to God, not to people.

1 Corinthians 14:2

TORAH.

The Law of Moses. The Torah includes the first five books of the Old Testament (also called the Pentateuch): Genesis, Exodus, Leviticus, Numbers, and Deuteronomy. *Torah* is a Hebrew word that means "to teach."

TOWER OF BABEL.

A place of great confusion. In ancient times, humans decided to build a really high tower. They wanted to be famous and get all kinds of glory for themselves. God didn't like that idea at all. He is the only one people should worship. The men of the area pulled together to build. They worked well together because everyone in the whole world spoke the same language.

a b c d e f g h i j k l m n o p q r s **T** u v w x y z

a
b
c
d
e
f
g
h
i
j
k
l
m
n
o
p
q
r
s
T
u
v
w
x
y
z

But God fixed them. He gave them different languages so they couldn't understand one another. Wow, were they confused! That stopped the tower building. Then God scattered the people all over the earth. That's why today we speak different languages.

Genesis 11:1–9.

The Tower of Babel.

TRADITION.

A custom or belief passed from generation to generation. Maybe your family has special traditions at Christmas: going to church on Christmas Eve, singing "Happy Birthday" to baby Jesus, eating special treats. These are all traditions, or things your family does again and again. Jesus warned the Pharisees not to let their traditions get in the way of God's commandments.

Matthew 15:2–6

TRANSFIGURATION.

A mysterious change. One day, Jesus took Peter, James, and John up a very high mountain. When they were alone, Jesus' appearance changed. His face glowed like the sun. And His clothes became like a bright, white light. This was called the transfiguration. Can you imagine seeing something like that? The disciples were scared stiff. Then something else happened. Moses and Elijah appeared. They had been dead for hundreds of years. And God's voice came booming out of a cloud! All of this made the disciples even surer that Jesus was the Son of God. Read about the transfiguration in Matthew 17:1–8.

Disciples fall on their faces as Jesus is transfigured.

TRANSGRESSION.

Bad behavior. Transgression happens when you break the rules. Maybe your school has a rule against cell phones. If you break that rule, it's a transgression. To be forgiven, you have to 'fess up and admit that what you did was wrong. It works the same way with God. Breaking any of God's rules is a transgression. A trans-gression can get you into plenty of trouble. But if you admit what you did, God will forgive you. You can thank Jesus for that. He came to earth so everyone who believes in Him will be forgiven for their transgressions.

1 Chronicles 10:13
1 John 1:9

TREE OF KNOWLEDGE OF GOOD AND EVIL.

The forbidden tree. In the Garden of Eden, God told Adam and Eve not to eat the fruit from this tree. They disobeyed Him. As punishment, God kicked them out of the garden forever.

Genesis 2:9, 17
Genesis 3

TREE OF LIFE.

The forever tree. The tree of life was in the Garden of Eden. Eating its fruit would make you live forever. But after Adam and Eve ate fruit from the tree of knowledge of good and evil, God didn't allow them anywhere near the tree of life. God took away His gift of eternal life. But Jesus came to offer us that gift again.

Genesis 3:22
John 3:16

TRIBES OF ISRAEL.

Twelve tribes formed from the sons of Jacob who was renamed Israel. The sons of Jacob were Asher, Benjamin, Dan, Gad, Issachar, Joseph, Judah, Levi, Naphtali, Reuben, Simeon, and Zebulun. After the Israelites got to the Promised Land, the twelve tribes ruled. The sons of Israel led the tribes. They were assigned their own territories in the new land. Judah was the head of the most famous tribe. He was an ancestor of King David who was an ancestor of Jesus. After a while, the twelve tribes split into two kingdoms. They didn't always get along. In fact, sometimes they fought wars with each other.

Genesis 32:28
1 Chronicles 2:1
Luke 3:23–38
1 Kings 12:21

Jesus rides a young donkey on His "triumphal entry" into Jerusalem.

John 15:26 NIV

TRIBULATION. ——————

A time of great trouble or suffering. Imagine a wicked tornado. It whips across the land, destroying everything in its path. People lose their houses and all that they own. That's a time of tribulation. The Bible says that Christians should be patient when tribulation comes along. It even says to face tribulations with joy. In the end-times, the earth will face many tribulations. They will be God's way of wrapping up His business here on earth.

Romans 12:12
2 Corinthians 7:4
Daniel 12:1

TRIBUTE. ——————

A kind of tax. In ancient times, Hebrew men paid half a shekel in taxes. This money was used to pay for the upkeep of the temple. Shekels were measured in weight. A half shekel weighed about one-fifth of an ounce.

Exodus 30:13

TRINITY. ——————

The Father, the Son, and the Holy Spirit. The word *trinity* means "three." God is three persons all wrapped up into one. He is our heavenly Father, the Father of all people and every living thing. He is also Jesus, the Son of God. When Jesus came to earth, He was really God coming here in the form of a man. The third person, or part, of God is the Holy Spirit. He is the One who makes things happen. He is the One who convicts us and guides us. The Holy Spirit gives us special talents and encourages us to use them for God. He is sometimes called the Counselor.

Ephesians 3:14–15
John 11:27
John 14:26
John 16:8
John 16:13–15

TRIUMPHAL ENTRY. ——

Jesus' famous donkey ride. On the Sunday before He was crucified, Jesus went to Jerusalem. He rode into the city on a young donkey. A large crowd followed Him. They shouted praises to Him. They even laid down palm branches for the donkey to walk on. Today we celebrate the Triumphal Entry as Palm Sunday. Read all about it in Matthew 21:1–11.

TRUMPET. ——————

A musical instrument that makes noise when you blow through it. Do you know someone who plays a trumpet? In Bible times, trumpets were made from animal horns or metal. Trumpets were used in temple ceremonies. They were also used to call people together and for sending signals. Seven priests marched around the walls of Jericho. They

a
b
c
d
e
f
g
h
i
j
k
l
m
n
o
p
q
r
s
T
u
v
w
x
y
z

149

blew on trumpets made of rams' horns. With the sound of trumpets and people shouting, the walls of Jericho tumbled down.

1 Chronicles 16:6
Numbers 10:1–3
Numbers 31:6
Joshua 6:13
Joshua 6:20

TRUST. ——————

To have confidence in something. You trust your parents to take care of you. You trust your teachers to help you learn. You should also trust God and the Bible. Everything about them is true. The Bible says that we should trust the Lord to help us. If we trust in Him, He will make things clear to us—as clear as seeing in the noonday sun. Jesus warned His disciples not to trust everyone they met. Some people cannot be trusted.

Psalm 33:21
2 Samuel 7:28
Psalm 37:5–6 CEV
Matthew 10:17–21

TRUTH. ——————

A fact—not a lie. Everything that God says is truth. The Ten Commandments are God's truth. So are all the teachings of Jesus. The Spirit of truth is God's Holy Spirit. You will be closer to the Spirit of truth if you read your Bible and learn as much as you can about Jesus. In the Gospel of John, Jesus said that He is the way and the truth and the life. That means that His truths can always be trusted. Do you believe it's true that Jesus came to save you from sin? If you do, then you will live forever with God.

John 14:16–18
John 14:6

TWELVE, THE. ——————

Jesus' twelve disciples, the guys Jesus chose. They traveled with Him and helped Him teach. The disciples were Peter, Andrew, James the son of Zebedee, John, Philip, Bartholomew, Thomas, Matthew, James the son of Alphaeus, Thaddaeus, Simon, and Judas. Jesus allowed the Twelve to get rid of evil spirits and heal sick people. There are still disciples today. Anyone who follows Jesus and spreads His Word to others is a disciple. How many disciples do you know?

John 15:16
Matthew 10:1–4
Acts 6:1–7

Many artists have painted the twelve disciples at the Last Supper—this one, by Jacopo Bassano, is from the 1500s.

a b c d e f g h i j k l m n o p q r s T u v w x y z

UNBELIEF.

Not having faith in God or the good things He does. Sometimes it's hard to believe in something you can't see. But think of God this way: He's like the air you breathe. You can't see Him, but He's always there. Do you have a hard time believing in God when something bad happens? In the book of Mark, there is a story about a man who had trouble believing because his son was sick. But the man asked for help, and Jesus healed his son. Jesus said that anything is possible for those who believe (Mark 9:23).

2 Corinthians 4:18
Mark 9:14–27

UNCLEAN.

Not pure. Your body gets dirty when you haven't had a bath. But in Bible times, being unclean was about more than a person's body. The book of Leviticus tells all about what was "clean" and "unclean" back then. People couldn't eat or touch unclean animals. Animals that ate dead animals were unclean; for example, vultures were unclean. Fish that lived at the bottom of lakes and oceans were unclean, too. People with some skin diseases were thought of as unclean. So were clothes with mildew. A person who was unclean or touched something unclean had to go through a special ritual to get clean again.

UNLEAVENED BREAD.

Bread made without yeast. Have you ever watched someone make bread? If yeast is in the recipe, the bread rises. It gets big and fat. Without yeast the bread doesn't rise. It's flat, or unleavened, bread. There is a Jewish festival called the Feast of Unleavened Bread. It celebrates the Israelites' escape from Egypt. The feast lasts seven days. It helps us remember how quickly the Israelite slaves got out of Egypt. They left in such a hurry that they had no time to put the yeast in the bread recipe. Instead, they wrapped the dough in cloth and rushed away.

Exodus 13:3
Exodus 12:33–34

UPPER ROOM.

A room upstairs or on the roof of a house. A room like this was where Jesus had His last meal with His disciples.

Mark 14:15

UR.

An old, old city in the Middle East. Abraham once lived in Ur of the Chaldeans with his father and wife. The Lord told him to leave Ur and go to Canaan. (Check out Genesis 11:27–31; 12:1–4.)

URIAH.

A name shared by a warrior and a priest. One Uriah fought in King David's army. He died in battle. Then David married Uriah's wife, Bathsheba. The other Uriah was a prophet. In some versions of the Bible, he's called Urijah. The king of Judah had him killed because Uriah said God would punish the people of Judah and Jerusalem for doing bad things.

2 Samuel 11
Jeremiah 26:20–23

b
c
d
e
f
g
h
i
j
k
l
m
n
o
p
q
r
s
t
u
v
w
x
y
z

Urim and Thummim

URIM AND THUMMIM. — Priestly objects. The true meaning of these words is a mystery. They might have been colored stones or metal. The Bible says these objects were in the breastplate of the high priest, Aaron. Maybe this meant they were a sign of the high priest's power of making known the mind of God. Or Urim and Thummim might have been cast as lots to show the will of God.

Exodus 28:30
Numbers 27:21

USURY. — A high charge made for taking out a loan. When the Lord spoke to Moses, He said that Jews could not take usury from other Jews. Nehemiah spoke out when people broke this law.

Leviticus 25:36–37
Nehemiah 5

UZ. — The land where Job lived. We don't know much else about it!

Job 1:1

UZZA. — A man from Israel. Uzza was helping to move the ark of the covenant when he died. No one was supposed to touch the ark as it was being pulled along on a cart. But the oxen pulling the cart stumbled, and Uzza grabbed on to the ark. The Lord was so angry that He struck Uzza dead!

1 Chronicles 13:7–11

UZZIAH. — A king of Judah. Uzziah built many cities. He was also a good general. But Uzziah's pride got him into trouble. He went into the temple and burned incense to the Lord. That was something only priests had the right to do. As a punishment, the Lord gave Uzziah a bad skin disease called leprosy.

2 Chronicles 26:1–21

When banks lend money, people have to pay it back with interest. That means they pay back a little more than they borrowed. Usury is when people have to pay back a lot more than they borrowed.

152

VALLEY OF DRY BONES. — One of Ezekiel's visions. Ezekiel was a prophet who had dreams sent from God. In one dream, God led Ezekiel into a valley filled with bones. Then God told Ezekiel to talk to the bones. The bones came to life and became living people! This was a symbol of God's promise. The Israelites had been sent away to a foreign land. God promised Ezekiel, "I will bring you home, and you will know that I have kept my promise."

Ezekiel 37:1–13
Ezekiel 37:14 CEV

Ezekiel's creepy vision of a valley of dry bones.

VANITY. ——
Being full of yourself. In the book of Ecclesiastes, Solomon wrote about vanity. He said that, at one time, all he did was look for ways to have fun and make money. He became rich and powerful. But then he realized that it was all vanity because it was done without God. (Find out more in Ecclesiastes 2.)

VASHTI. ——
The queen of Persia. In the third year of his rule, King Xerxes gave a big dinner for his nobles and officials. The king ordered his servants to bring Vashti to him. He wanted her to wear her crown and show his officials how beautiful she was. But she refused to come. This made the king very angry. (Check out Esther 1:1–12.) Because of this, he made Esther his queen instead.

Esther 2:17

VEIL. ——
A screen or curtain. One very important veil separated the Holy Place and the Holy of Holies in the tabernacle and temple. It was torn at Christ's death. This was a symbol that all people could be saved through Jesus Christ.

Exodus 26:31–33
Matthew 27:51
Hebrews 10:19–21

VINE. ——
A plant that grows fruit, like grapes. The Bible often compares the nation of Israel to a vine. One prophet called Israel an "empty vine." He said this because Israel had become sinful. The Israelites used their "grapes," or wealth, for things that didn't serve God. In the Gospel of John, Jesus told His disciples that He was the "true vine." He compared the disciples to His branches. What did Jesus mean? Just as a branch can't make fruit unless it stays joined to the vine, you can't be your best unless you stay joined to Jesus (John 15:1–6).

Psalm 80:8–11
Hosea 10:1 KJV
John 15:1

VINEGAR. ——
A sour liquid. In Bible times, vinegar was a sour drink made out of wine. It was offered to Jesus when He was on the cross.

Matthew 27:48

VIRGIN BIRTH. ——
How Jesus was born. Jesus' mother, the Virgin Mary, became pregnant in a very special way. An angel told Mary that the Holy Spirit would come upon her and she would have a baby. This was

153

WHEAT.

A grain used to make bread. In Bible times, the wheat harvest was a time to party!

Exodus 29:2
Exodus 34:22

Grains of wheat on the stalk.

WHIRLWIND.

A great big storm, like a tornado. The Lord took Elijah up into heaven in a whirlwind. The word *whirlwind* can also be used as a symbol. It can mean something that happens very fast or something that has terrible strength. The word is used in this way in the book of Jeremiah. It says the Lord will strike lying prophets like a whirlwind.

2 Kings 2:11
Jeremiah 23:19 NIV

WICKEDNESS.

Evil or sinful things. Wicked people do bad things on purpose! The Bible says, "The LORD protects everyone who follows Him, but the wicked follow a road that leads to ruin." The book of Job explains how God treats the wicked. They might be rich and wear fancy clothes, but their nice things will be taken from them and given to God's people. "Those sinners may go to bed rich, but they will wake up poor". Does wickedness scare you? Don't worry! Job also says, "God rescues the needy from the words of the wicked and the fist of the mighty."

Psalm 1:6 CEV
Job 27:13–19
Job 27:19 CEV
Job 5:15 CEV

WIDOW.

A woman whose husband has died. One of the laws the Lord gave to Moses was "Do not mistreat widows or orphans." The book of James says, "You must help needy orphans and widows and not let this world make you evil." The early church took care of widows by giving them food. The prophetess Anna was a widow.

Exodus 22:22 CEV
James 1:27 CEV
Acts 6:1
Luke 2:36–37

WILDERNESS.

A wild, unsettled place. John the Baptist preached in the wilderness of Judea. Moses saw the burning bush and heard God while in the wilderness of Midian. The Hebrew people wandered around the wilderness for forty years. This was God's punishment for disobeying Him. This is also where God gave Moses the Ten Commandments.

Exodus 3:1–4
Matthew 3:1
Joshua 5:6
Exodus 19:2
Exodus 20:1–24

WINE.

A strong drink made from grapes. In the Bible, many Jews drank wine. The Lord told Moses that Nazarites must not drink wine. Priests could not drink wine before going into the sacred tent. The Bible tells us that it is wrong to drink too much wine. But one of Jesus' first miracles was turning water into wine at a wedding in Cana.

Numbers 6:3
Leviticus 10:9
Proverbs 20:1
Ephesians 5:18
John 2:1–11

Making wine the old-fashioned way.

WINNOWING.

Removing chaff or straw from grains of wheat. To do this, the stalks were beaten and thrown into the air. This word can also mean God's separating believers from nonbelievers in the end-times.

Matthew 3:11–12

The wise men lead a caravan of helpers on their search for a new king—Jesus.

WISDOM.

Knowledge that comes from understanding and good sense. Respecting and obeying God is the first step to being wise. Christ is the key to God's wisdom. In the Bible, God told Solomon he could ask for anything he wanted. He asked God to make him wise. This pleased God. He said, "You could have asked to live a long time or to be rich. Or you could have asked for your enemies to be destroyed. Instead, you asked for wisdom to make right decisions." Solomon knew that wisdom is worth more than riches.

Proverbs 9:10
Colossians 2:3
1 Kings 3:11 CEV
Proverbs 8:11

WISE MEN.

The men who brought gifts to baby Jesus in Bethlehem. They are often called the Magi. These men knew about the stars. They most likely came from Persia or southern Arabia. They saw a star in the east. It was a sign telling them the king of the Jews was born! They followed this star. It led them to the place in Bethlehem where Jesus and Mary were. The wise men knelt down and worshiped Jesus. They gave Him gifts of gold, frankincense, and myrrh. Read all about it in Matthew 2:1–12.

WITNESS.

A person who hears or sees something, then tells what happened. What the witness says is called a testimony. This is often given in a court of law. In Bible times, the testimony of at least two witnesses was needed to find a person guilty of a big crime. Anyone who told lies while testifying was punished. As believers, we are called to be witnesses for Christ.

Deuteronomy 17:6
Deuteronomy 19:18–19
Acts 1:8

WOE.

Extreme grief or sadness. This word can also be used as a threat. One example is in the book of Isaiah: "Woe to the wicked! Disaster is upon them!"

Isaiah 3:11 NIV

157

a
b
c
d
e
f
g
h
i
j
k
l
m
n
o
p
q
r
s
t
u
v
W
x
y
z

WOOL.

The short, curly hair of a sheep. In Bible times, the Jewish people liked to make clothing out of wool. Have you ever worn a sweater made from wool?

Proverbs 31:13

WORD OF GOD.

The information God reveals to us. The Bible tells that God's words are still powerful today. They can reach deep into the thoughts of our hearts. Christians believe the writing in the Bible is the Word of God. Jesus is the living Word of God that will never die. He said, "The Father who sent me also speaks for me." We can believe in the Word of God. The book of Proverbs says, "Everything God says, is true— and it's a shield for all who come to him for safety."

Hebrews 4:12
John 5:37 CEV
Proverbs 30:5 CEV

WORKS.

Good deeds done to show you are a loyal believer in Christ. Works alone can't save us. We've been saved through faith and by the grace of God. But this is God's job for His people: to do good works to build His kingdom. The Bible tells us to let our light shine for others. If they see the good deeds we do, they will praise God in heaven. So get out there today and do something good for God!

Ephesians 2:8–10
Matthew 5:16

WORSHIP.

Praising and adoring God. When you go to church, you worship God. But you can also worship Him at home or anywhere else. You can worship by yourself or with others. In Bible times, the Jews worshipped in the tabernacle until they started using the temple. After they were taken to live among the Babylonians and Persians, the Jews worshipped in synagogues. The book of Psalms is full of songs and hymns to worship God. Psalm 95:6 says, "Bow down and worship the LORD our Creator!" (CEV). Have you worshipped God today? Take some time to tell Him how wonderful He is.

Deuteronomy 6:5–7
Daniel 6:10
Psalm 132:7

WRATH.

Powerful anger. Can you think of a time when you were so mad you shook with anger? If So you felt wrath. You might feel wrath if you are accused of doing something you didn't do. Your parents might feel wrath if you disobey them. God feels wrath, too. "From heaven God shows how angry he is with all the wicked and evil things that sinful people do to crush the truth." It makes God very angry when people worship idols. To avoid the wrath of God, we must have faith in Him and live godly lives.

Genesis 31:36
Romans 1:18 CEV
Psalm 18:58–59
John 3:36

XERXES.

A Persian king. Xerxes was married to Queen Esther. He had a prime minister named Haman who was an evil man. Haman told Esther's cousin Mordecai to bow down to him. But Mordecai wouldn't do it. This made Haman very angry. He asked the king to have all the Jews killed. He also made plans to have Mordecai hanged. When Esther heard this, she went to her husband, the king. She convinced him that it was wrong to kill Mordecai and the Jews. King Xerxes listened to her advice. He agreed that Haman was evil. The king ordered that Haman be hanged instead of Mordecai. In some Bibles, Xerxes is known as Ahasuerus.

Esther 3:2
Esther 3:5–6
Esther 7:10

YAHWEH.

An ancient name for God. It is a very holy name. In Hebrew, you write it using these four letters יהוה. If you were reading the Hebrew word, you would read the letters from right to left. In English, it looks like these four consonants: YHWH. Many Bibles today translate the word *Yahweh* as Lord or Jehovah.

YOKE.

An animal collar. A yoke was a big, heavy collar made from wood. It was put around the necks of large animals like horses and cattle. These animals helped to plow fields. The plow was attached to the yoke. When the animal walked, it dragged the plow behind it.

Deuteronomy 21:3
Hosea 10:11

YOKEFELLOW.

A companion or friend. A yokefellow has nothing to do with eggs! And it isn't always a fellow. A yokefellow is someone with whom you have something in common. Are your classmates yokefellows?

Philippians 4:3 KJV

ZACCHAEUS.

A short, tree-climbing tax collector. One day, Jesus traveled through Jericho surrounded by a crowd. Zacchaeus was a short man. So he climbed a tree to get a better look at Jesus. When Jesus saw him in the tree, He told him to come down. He wanted to rest at Zacchaeus's house. Zacchaeus hurried down and went to Jesus. He told Him that he would give half of his money to the poor. He promised to pay back anyone he had cheated. Jesus was pleased with Zacchaeus's decision. Read all about it in Luke 19:1–10.

ZACHARIAS.

John the Baptist's dad. Zacharias was a priest. He was a good and godly man. Zacharias was very old when the angel Gabriel told him that he would have a son. Zacharias did not believe Gabriel. So Gabriel made him speechless! Zacharias could not speak until the day that John was named— eight days after he was born. (See Luke 1:18–24; 57–64.)

ZAMZUMMIMS.

Giants. The Zamzummims were a group of giants. Some versions of the Bible call them Zamzummites. They lived in a land that God had promised to the Ammonites. God got rid of them so the Ammonites could move in.

Deuteronomy 2:19–21 KJV

ZEAL.

Pursuing something with passion. Zeal is when you want very much to do something. If you are determined to play your best at soccer or to get better grades, that's zeal. Romans 12:11 says: "Never be lacking in zeal, but

b
c
d
e
f
g
h
i
j
k
l
m
n
o
p
q
r
s
t
u
v
w
x
y
z

keep your spiritual fervor, serving the Lord" (NIV). That means, never give up following and serving God.

ZECHARIAH. ———————

A prophet. In the Bible, there are lots of men named Zechariah. But this Zechariah is the one who wrote the Old Testament book that has his name. He is best known for encouraging the people to rebuild the temple in Jerusalem. Zechariah had visions. In his mind, he saw that Jesus would come. Israel would grow into a great nation. And God would rule forever.

Ezra 5:1–2
Zechariah 9:9–10
Zechariah 10
Zechariah 14:3–21

ZEPHANIAH. ———————

An important Bible name. There are four men named Zephaniah in the Bible. One of them was a priest and a friend of Jeremiah. He served as a messenger between Jeremiah and King Zedekiah. Another Zephaniah was one of God's prophets. He wrote the Old Testament book that has his name. He wrote about God's judgment against the nation of Judah. He told the people to behave before it was too late.

Jeremiah 37:3
Zephaniah 2:1–3

ZERUBABBEL. ———————

A Jewish leader. Zerubbabel was among a group of Jews held captive in Babylonia. He, and some of the others, returned to their homeland, Jerusalem. Zerubbabel supervised the rebuilding of the temple, which the Babylonian army had destroyed. He encouraged the people to worship God. Zerubbabel was also known as Zorobabel and Sheshbazzar.

Ezra 2
Ezra 3:8
Zechariah 4:9

ZION. ———————

One of the hills on which Jerusalem was built. Long ago, an ancient fortress stood there. It belonged to the Jebusites. David took Zion from the Jebusites and made it his city. When David's son King Solomon ruled, his temple was in Zion. If you visited the Holy Land today, you could see Zion. It is called by several names: Mount Zion (Mount Sion), the Southwestern Hill, and the Upper City. Sometimes the name Zion is used for the whole city of Jerusalem.

2 Samuel 5:7
1 Kings 3:1

ZIPPORAH. ———————

Wife of Moses. Zipporah's dad was Jethro, the priest of Midian. She and Moses had two sons. Their names were Gershom and Eliezer.

Exodus 18:1–5

ZOPHAR. ———————

A friend of Job. When God tested Job, Zophar came to help Job and to give him advice. At first, Zophar told Job to get right with God and not to question His justice. In the end, Zophar and two other friends offered a sacrifice for Job. Zophar wasn't perfect, but he was a friend to Job. You can be a good friend to others. How? By sharing this Bible dictionary with them!

Job 2:11
Job 11; 20

KiDS' Bible Handbook

TRACY M. SUMNER

Interior design and layout by ThinkPen Design.

WHAT'S IN THIS BOOK

BEFORE YOU GET STARTED

Chances are, you've got at least one copy somewhere in your home. Maybe more than one copy. And maybe more than one version.

What are we talking about?

The bestselling book of all time.

The Bible!

It only makes sense that the Bible, also called "God's Word" or "the Word of God," is the world's all-time bestseller. After all, it's been around for almost 2,000 years (actually, the books of the Old Testament have been around for a lot longer than that) and has been translated into hundreds of languages.

The Bible is easy to find in most parts of the world. In America, we have dozens of translations and styles available in just about any bookstore. There are study Bibles, children's Bibles, pocket-size Bibles, hardcover and softcover Bibles, and Bibles that include easy-to-follow reading plans for people who want to read through the entire Bible in a year.

Did you know that the word *Bible* actually means "book"? In reality, the Bible isn't just one book. It's a collection of 66 books (39 in the Old Testament and 27 in the New Testament), written by about 40 different writers over a period of several centuries. The oldest books of the Bible (including Job and the first five books of the Old Testament) were written 3,000 to 3,100 years ago; and the youngest book (Revelation, written by the apostle John) was written around 2,000 years ago.

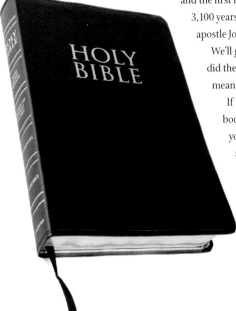

We'll get into more detail about the Bible's writers and when they did their writing later on, but first let's focus on what the Bible means to us.

If someone were to ask you what the Bible is (other than a book that's been around for a really long time), how would you answer? Would you say that the Bible is a collection of stories about God's people going back thousands of years? Would you say it's God's book of promises for people who put their faith in Him? Would you say it's a book of God's commands for people who want to please Him in the way they live, talk, and think?

Well, none of those answers would be wrong. In fact, they're all 100 percent correct. But there's a lot more to the Bible than that. You see, the Bible is more than a collection of stories about a bunch of people who died a long time ago, and it's more than a book of God's promises and commands. The Bible is the account of how God has communicated with the most prized part of His creation—His people!—from the beginning of time until the beginning of the Christian church. And it's also about how God communicates with you and me today.

With so many Bibles in the world, it's easy sometimes to start taking God's Word for granted. That's partly why I've written *this* book. I want to help you come to a greater appreciation for the Bible, and I want to give you some of the basics that will help you understand where it came from, how it became the book it is today, and how you can better read the Bible and understand what it is all about.

This book will give you a brief look at all 66 books of the Bible, including information about the people who wrote the books, the men and women they were written to, what the books mean, and how the message of the Bible applies to your life today.

Each of the 11 chapters in this book includes a story about how the Bible came to be, as well as some fun and interesting features about the Bible and what you'll find in it.

Here are some of the fun features you'll find in this book:

Power Words: Important verses you can memorize from different books of the Bible.

Who, What, Where? Important people, things, and places mentioned in the Bible, as well as the people and events God used to give us the Bible.

Fun Bible Trivia: Some not-so-well-known facts about people and events you can find in the Bible.

What's in It for Me? How you can apply what you read in the Bible to your own life.

Did You Know. . . ? Fun facts about the Bible itself and how it came to be the book it is today.

This book won't teach you everything there is to know about the Bible. To do that, it would have to be many times longer than it is. What it will do, though, is give you a good place to start as you read, study, and learn what the Bible has to say and what it means to you.

When you're finished reading this book, you'll have a pretty good idea of how wonderful and amazing the Bible really is. And you'll probably think to yourself, *Wow! The Bible is a really cool book!*

CHAPTER 1

How Did We Get This Book Anyway?

The Work God Did—and the People He Used—to Give Us the Bible

Take a look at your own copy of the Bible. If you don't have it nearby, take a minute to go get it. Then just look at it for a moment. You've probably read at least some of the Bible, and you might even have a pretty good idea about what it says. But have you ever stopped to think about what it took to give you an opportunity to have your very own copy?

A lot of Christians, even some who know the Bible very well, don't really understand how we got the 66 books that make up the Bible. That's what this chapter is all about. It gives you a quick look at how God used different people from all sorts of backgrounds to record His words, to gather them all together to make up one book, and to help make the Bible available in the language that you speak, write, and read.

So read on! You're about to discover the amazing story of how God's Word became the book we know as the Bible.

Writing Down God's Words

The first thing you should know about the Bible—if you don't already—is that God didn't just give someone a completed manuscript and send him off to a printing press. Actually, the story of how we got the Bible is a lot more interesting than that.

You probably know—even if you haven't given it a lot of thought—that someone had to write down the words that are in your Bible. Actually, the books of the Bible were written by about 40 men (and possibly a few women). These writers came from a lot of different backgrounds and professions. For example, Moses was a shepherd, Amos was a fig farmer, Matthew was a tax collector, and Peter and John were fishermen.

DID YOU KNOW. . . ?

The apostle Paul writes, "All Scripture is inspired by God" (2 Timothy 3:16). The idea behind the word *inspiration* is that God "breathed out" or "spoke" the words that are in the Bible. In other words, the words you read in the Bible are the words of God Himself!

Yet all these people, from different backgrounds, writing over a span of about 1,500 years, together produced a unified book that never disagrees with itself, never moves from its main message, and always presents God's perfect plan for the salvation of humanity.

How did such a group of writers—most of whom never met one another—pull that off? The answer to that question is in the word *inspiration*. One of the Bible's main writers, the apostle Paul, writes, "All Scripture is *given* by *inspiration of* God" (2 Timothy 3:16, italics added). What Paul means is that God, through His Holy Spirit, spoke through the Bible's writers and gave them His very own words to record. In other words, the people who wrote the books of the Bible were tools that God miraculously used to give us His written Word.

This means that, even though the Bible was written by dozens of people from different backgrounds and points of view, it has one ultimate author: God Himself. That's why you can count on the Bible as your final source for everything you need to know about how to live a life that pleases God.

...WER WORDS

No prophecy in Scripture ever came from the prophet's own understanding, or from human initiative. No, those prophets were moved by the Holy Spirit, and they spoke from God.

2 Peter 1:20-21

Why *These* Books?

All 39 of the books in the Old Testament had been written by about 400 BC (*before* the birth of Christ), and all 27 of the New Testament books were finished by the end of the first century AD (*after* the birth of Christ).

But these weren't the only books written that contained teachings and history that are very much like what we have in the Bible today. For example, during the first few centuries after Jesus' life here on earth, dozens of letters and other "gospels" were circulated in the Christian church.

So how do we know that all the books in the Bible are the ones God wanted? The answer lies in the great care He put into making sure all the words He inspired the biblical writers to record were kept in the book He has prepared and given us.

By the time of Jesus' birth, the collection of books included in the Hebrew Bible (the Old Testament) was pretty much decided. The Jewish people recognized that Moses,

DID YOU KNOW. . .?
Moses and Jesus both spent part of their lives in Egypt!

the prophets, and other writers were God's messengers, so they accepted their work as the inspired Word of God. This collection is sometimes called the "canon of Scripture," and the act of declaring individual books as part of the Bible is called "canonization."

By the mid-third century AD, almost all Christian leaders agreed that the books we now have in the Old Testament belong in the canon of Scripture. But there was some disagreement about certain books that are not in the Bible but are part of what is called the Apocrypha (see the Did You Know. . .? sidebar on this page).

The process of accepting the New Testament books as part of the Bible began in the first century AD and continued on into the fourth century. By the beginning of the fourth century, Christians had already accepted most of the books now in the New Testament as God's Word. But a few books still needed final approval before they would be accepted as part of the canon.

Around AD 363, about 30 Christian leaders from what was then called Asia Minor (now part of the nation of Turkey) held a meeting called the Council of Laodicea. One of the things they talked about was the final acceptance of the canon of Scripture. This council decided that only the Old Testament, including the Apocrypha, and the 27 books in the New Testament could be read in the churches. Two other meetings—the Council of Hippo in AD 393 and the Council of Carthage in AD 397—also agreed that those same 27 books would be part of the New Testament.

Same Message, Different Languages

Okay, now you have a basic idea of how we got the books we have in the Bible today. But there is more to the story. Not only did God use some very brave people to record His words; He also used some very dedicated men to keep the original words in the Bible from being changed. That's why we can count on the fact that the message of the Bible is the same today as it was when it was first recorded thousands of years ago.

One thing that *has* changed is the languages people use. Very few people in the world today speak Hebrew or Greek, the languages used when the Bible was written. That means God's Word has had to be translated into languages that people could understand. God again used gifted and devoted

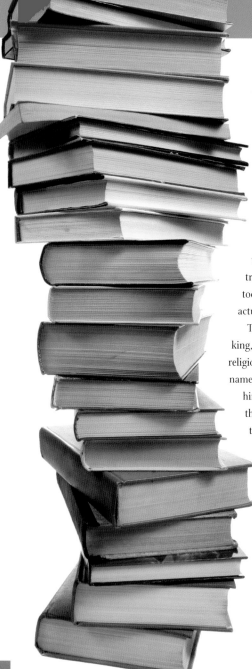

men to do His work, making it possible for people to read and understand the Bible in their own languages.

The translation of the Bible into other languages actually began even before Jesus was born. Starting around 285 BC, a group of 72 men began translating the Old Testament books from their original language of Hebrew into Greek—the common language that most people spoke back then. This translation was called the Septuagint.

The word *Septuagint* is Greek for 70, which approximates the number of translators who worked on the project. According to one story about this translation of the Hebrew Old Testament into Greek, it took the 72 translators 72 days to finish the project. But it actually took a lot longer than that!

The project was started because Ptolemy, the Egyptian king, wanted to include the literature of all the world's ancient religions in his library at Alexandria. Ptolemy contacted a man named Eleazar, the Jewish chief priest at the time, and asked him to assign Hebrew scholars from Jerusalem to work on the translation. Six men were chosen from each of the 12 tribes of Israel, which accounts for the 72 translators. At first, they translated only the five books of the Old Testament, the Law of Moses; but after a while, they translated the other books and added them to the collection.

By the time Jesus was born, the Septuagint was read by most Greek-speaking Jews. It was also read in church gatherings during the first century AD—because the New Testament had not yet been completed, the first Christians didn't have it to read like we do now.

The Bible in the "Common Language"

Most of the New Testament was originally written in Greek. But as the years passed, Latin replaced Greek as the language that most people spoke in the Roman Empire—which meant that someone would have to translate the New Testament into Latin.

That someone was Jerome, a church leader who lived from about AD 347 to 420.

Around AD 382, Pope Damasus I asked Jerome to translate both the Old Testament and the New Testament into Latin. Jerome used the Greek copies of scripture as his starting point. He began by translating the Gospels—Matthew, Mark, Luke, and John—and the Old Testament. Jerome finished his work around AD 400, and it came to be known as the Vulgate.

The Vulgate was used in the Christian—mostly Catholic—church from the 4th century to the 15th century. Even though the primary language of the people continued to change, there were no new official translations done during this time. That's mostly because the Catholic Church, which was very powerful at the time, wouldn't allow anyone to translate the Bible into the people's spoken and written languages. So only the pope and the priests, who learned to read and write in Latin, could read and understand the Bible.

That began to change when brave men such as John Wycliffe and William Tyndale risked everything—including their lives—to make sure that people could read the Bible for themselves.

clanging ... the gift of prophecy, and ca... fathom all mysteries and all knowledge, and if I have a faith that can move moun- tains, but have not love, I am nothing. 3If I give all I pos- sess to the poor and surren- der my body to the flames,8 but have not love, I gain nothing.
4Love is patient, love is kind. It does not envy, it does not boast, it is not proud. 5It is not rude, it is not self-seeking, it is not easily angered, it keeps no record of wrongs. 6Love does not delight in evil but rejoices in

cymbal
προφητείαν prophecy
καὶ and
πᾶσαν all
τὴν –
πίστιν faith
δὲ 1but
μὴ I have no
πάντα all
τὰ the
τὸ the
σῶμά body
δὲ 1but
μὴ I ha

καὶ and
εἰδῶ know
τὰ 2the
μυστήρια 3mysterie
τὴν –
γνῶσιν, knowledge,
κἂν and if I
ὥστε o as
ὄρη mountains
μεθιστάν to remo
ἔχα

DID YOU KNOW. . . ?

Even though there wasn't much Bible translation going on between the 4th and 15th centuries, some translations of the New Testament into the language of the Anglo-Saxons—an early form of English—began showing up late in the tenth century (the AD 900s).

A Big Step toward an English-Language Bible

John Wycliffe was a Catholic priest who lived in England in the 1300s. Even though he was a Catholic, he believed—and said—some things that got him in trouble with the church. One of the things he believed was that every Christian should have the right to read the Bible without the interference of the church.

Wycliffe knew that the Roman Catholic Church wouldn't allow anyone to translate the Bible into the languages that the "common" spoke and read. But he was willing to risk trouble with the authorities, so he moved ahead with his plans to translate the Bible into English.

Wycliffe—and probably several of his closest friends—began their work by translating Jerome's Latin Vulgate into English. It is believed that Wycliffe translated the four Gospels himself and that he may have translated the entire New Testament. The work of translating the whole Bible into English wasn't finished until several years after Wycliffe died of a stroke in 1384.

Wycliffe's work was just the beginning when it came to translating the Bible into English. Another Englishman, William Tyndale, picked up where Wycliffe left off.

This is Merton College at Oxford University, where William Tydale attended college.

William Tyndale Gives His All

William Tyndale was an amazing man who attended college at Oxford University, one of England's best schools. By the time he graduated, he had mastered seven languages, including Greek and Hebrew. Because he knew those languages so well, he was able to read the Bible for himself—in its original languages.

Tyndale knew what he wanted to do more than anything else, and that was to translate the Bible into English so that even the most uneducated Englishman could read it for himself. But he also knew that the Catholic Church was against the idea and that working on translating the Bible into English could cost him everything—including his life.

At first, he asked the church authorities for permission to translate the Bible into English. But because the leaders of the church believed that only the pope and priests were educated enough to truly understand the Bible, the answer was a big no!

Still, Tyndale wouldn't stop talking about how he disagreed with the church about many subjects, including translating the Bible into English. He began his translation work while he was still in England; but when the authorities found out what he was doing, he had to leave England. He traveled to Germany, where he could continue his work.

DID YOU KNOW. . . ?

It took a lot of courage for William Tyndale to work on translating the Bible into English. As an example of how brave he really was, consider this story: One day, Tyndale shouted at an English bishop who told him that the common people didn't need to read the Bible but only needed to listen to the words of the pope. "I defy the pope and all his laws!" Tyndale said. "And, if God spares me, I will one day make the boy that drives the plow in England to know more of the scriptures than the pope does!"

WHO, WHAT, WHERE?

Even though he never worked on translating the Bible, a German inventor named Johannes Gutenberg played a huge part in making the Bible available to all people. Gutenberg developed the movable type printing press, which made it possible to mass-produce printed materials—including the Bible. In fact, the world's first printed book was the *Gutenberg Bible*, a 1,286-page printed version of the Latin Vulgate that came off the presses in the 1450s.

DID YOU KNOW...?

By the time William Tyndale arrived in Germany, a man named Martin Luther had already begun translating the Bible into the German language. In 1523, Luther published the first five books of the Bible in German. By the 1530s, he had published the entire Bible in German.

Translating the Bible into English was no easy job, and it took Tyndale more than a year just to complete the New Testament. After he finished, he and some of his friends arranged for the English Bibles to be smuggled into England. The people loved the "new" Bibles, but the authorities weren't impressed. They made plans to stop Tyndale for good.

Tyndale knew he could not return home to England. He loved his native land and missed his friends and family there, but he knew that going home would mean almost certain death. Instead, he left Germany and traveled to Antwerp, Belgium, where, in 1530, his translation of the first five books of the Old Testament was printed. He also planned to translate the remainder of the Old Testament.

Tyndale didn't live long enough to realize his dream of an English translation of the entire Bible. In May 1535, he was arrested in Antwerp and thrown in a prison cell. Later that year, he was executed.

Finishing What William Tyndale Started

After William Tyndale's death, one of his friends, a man named Miles Coverdale, completed the translation of the Old Testament. In 1535, Coverdale printed the first complete Bible in the English language. It was called the Coverdale Bible. Two years after that, John Rogers, another friend of Tyndale's, printed the second complete English Bible. He translated his Bible directly from Hebrew and Greek manuscripts. It was called Matthew's Bible.

In 1539, Coverdale published what is now known as the Great Bible (it is called that because it was really big—about 14 inches thick). Even though the "common" people still weren't allowed to own copies of the Bible or to read the Bible on their own, the Great Bible brought English Christians a step closer.

The King James Bible—the World's Number 1 Bestseller

In 1604, King James I of England appointed 54 of the world's best Bible scholars and language experts of the time to translate the Bible into English. Each of these men knew the Hebrew, Greek, and Aramaic languages well. It wasn't easy work, and it took several years to finish it. Their final product came to be known as the King James Bible (also known as the Authorized Version), and it was completed and printed in 1611.

At first, the people of England—and other English-speaking places—didn't like the King James Bible as much as other translations. They preferred the Geneva Bible, an English translation that had been around for several decades. But in time, the King James Bible became more and more popular. Eventually, it became the world's all-time bestselling book. By the end of the 18th century, the King James Bible had become the only Bible used in English-speaking Protestant (non-Catholic) churches.

Look How Far We've Come!

You're fortunate enough to live in a time when you can walk into any bookstore and buy your own copy of the Bible. Not only that, but you can buy one of literally dozens of translations. All you have to do is find one that is easy for you to read and understand, plunk down your money, and take home your very own Bible.

Translation of the Bible didn't stop with the King James Bible. Since the King James Bible was first printed and distributed in 1611, Bible translators have worked tirelessly through the years to adapt the language of the Bible—while keeping the content the same.

POWER WORDS

"People are like grass; their beauty is like a flower in the field. The grass withers and the flower fades. But the word of the Lord remains forever."

1 Peter 1:24–25

Here are some of the versions translators have produced since the King James Bible first came on the scene:

- 1885—The English Revised Version, the first major revision of the King James Bible
- 1900–01—The American publishing company Thomas Nelson & Sons publishes the American Standard Version
- 1952—The Revised Standard Version
- 1965—The Amplified Bible
- 1971—The New American Standard Bible and *The Living Bible* (a paraphrase)
- 1976—*The Good News Bible*
- 1978—The New International Version
- 1982—The complete New King James Version
- 1989—The New Revised Standard Version
- 1995—The Contemporary English Version
- 1996—The New Living Translation
- 2001—The English Standard Version
- 2002—*The Message* (a paraphrase)
- 2004—The Holman Christian Standard Bible

With all these versions of the Bible—and many others—around, it's hard to believe there was a time when ordinary people weren't even allowed to *read* the Bible themselves, let alone own one. But it's true.

We can be grateful that God used so many people to put His thoughts and deeds down on paper, and then to make the Bible available to anyone who wants one.

As you're starting to see, the Bible really is an amazing book. . .and the God who gave it to you really is an awesome God!

CHAPTER 2

In the Beginning...
and Beyond

How It All Started (Genesis through Deuteronomy)

The Bible begins with five books that, as a group, are called the Pentateuch. The word *Pentateuch* is a Greek word that means "five rolls" or "five cases." Jewish people call the first five books of the Bible the *Torah*.

The first five books of the Old Testament are a set of books about beginnings—the beginnings of the universe and the world around us, the beginning of the human race, the beginning of God's plan for the salvation of humankind, the beginning of the Hebrew people and the nation of Israel, and the beginning of God's rules, laws, and guidelines for living.

By the time you finish reading those five books—Genesis through Deuteronomy—you will have read everything the Bible says about human history, starting with Adam and Eve and ending with the death of Moses.

Does that sound like fun reading?
Let's get started!

Genesis

What It's About: The word *genesis* means "beginnings," and that's what the book of Genesis is all about. This book is about the *beginning* of the universe and the world around us, the *beginning* of life, the *beginning* of the human race, the *beginning* of sin, and the *beginning* of a special race of people through whom God chose and prepared to bring salvation to the world.

Important Characters/People: Adam and Eve, Noah, Abraham, Sarah, Lot, Isaac, Rebekah, Jacob, Esau, Joseph, Potiphar, Pharaoh

Adam and Eve

Noah

Abraham and Sarah

Jacob and Esau

Joseph

The Writer: None of the first five books of the Bible names its writer, but many centuries of tradition say that Moses wrote all of them. Moses lived around the 1400s BC.

What You'll Find in the Book of Genesis

Knowing what the word *genesis* means, doesn't it make sense that the book of Genesis begins with the words "In the beginning"? This was the moment when God began the miraculous six-day process of creating everything you see around you—the universe, our solar system, our planet, and every living thing that inhabits the earth.

The first two chapters of Genesis give us a bare-bones outline of what God created and when He created it. You won't find a lot of detail about the process of creation in Genesis—or anywhere else in the Bible, for that matter. How God did it remains a mystery. But as someone once wisely said, "I don't know *how* God did it; I just believe Him when He says, 'In the beginning, God created. . .'"

Genesis 1 divides the process into six days of creation. On the first day, God laid the groundwork for all life on earth when He created light. Without light—light from the sun, that is—nothing could live, grow, or reproduce here on earth.

Here is a basic list of what God created on each creation day:

Day 1: The earth itself and light (1:2–5)
Day 2: The sky and the oceans (1:6–8)
Day 3: Dry land and plants (1:9–13)
Day 4: The sun, moon, and stars (1:14–19)
Day 5: Birds and fish (1:20–23)
Day 6: Other animals. . .and people! (1:24–31)

When God finished the job of creation, He looked at everything He had done and "saw that it was very good" (Genesis 1:31). God had just made *paradise*, and He told Adam and Eve, the world's first two humans, to reproduce and to care for His creation.

Everything was perfect, *until. . .*!

It Was All Downhill from Here

The third chapter of Genesis tells us that the serpent—actually the devil in the guise of a snake—deceived Adam and Eve and got them to do the one thing God had told them not to do: eat from the tree of the knowledge of good and evil. And when they did that, they brought on another beginning from the book of Genesis: the beginning of sin.

From that moment on, it was all downhill for the human race. Adam and Eve were kicked out of the Garden of Eden. Genesis 4 reports how jealousy, anger, and even murder became a part of human life. And as the years went on, things only got worse. In fact, things got so bad that God decided to scrap the whole thing and start over.

DID YOU KNOW. . . ?

The Old Testament is filled with what are called "messianic prophecies"—predictions of the coming Messiah, Jesus Christ. The first prophecy is found in Genesis 3:15, where God says to the serpent (Satan), "I will cause hostility between you and the woman, and between your offspring and her offspring. He will strike your head, and you will strike his heel." This meant that the Messiah would be born from a woman and that He would one day destroy the devil.

Water, Water Everywhere—the Flood

You've probably read or heard the story of Noah (Genesis 6–9). Several hundred years after God kicked Adam and Eve out of Eden, humans had become so sinful and violent that God decided to send a huge flood to destroy the whole human race—except for Noah and his family.

God told Noah to build a huge boat called an ark. The plan was for Noah, his family, and some of each kind of animal to get in the ark before the rains came and stay there until dry land appeared again. Five months after the flood started, the ark came to rest on a mountain called Ararat. A few months later, more land started to appear. Several more months later, Noah and his family—along with all those animals—left the ark and began repopulating the earth all over again.

Abraham and Some Other Biblical "Fathers"

The book of Genesis shifts gears in chapter 12. While the first 11 chapters tell us the story of the beginnings of the universe and of human history, chapter 12 is the start of what is called *patriarchal history*.

The word *patriarch* is kind of a fancy name for "father." The four patriarchs of the book of Genesis are Abraham (Genesis 12–25:8), Isaac (21:1–35), Jacob (Genesis 25:21–50:14), and Joseph (Genesis 30:22–50:26). When you call these men patriarchs, what you're really saying is that they are fathers of the nation of Israel.

There are a lot of important characters in the book of Genesis, but probably the most important is Abraham, the man God chose to be the father of the Hebrew nation. You can read all about Abraham (or Abram, as he was called earlier in his life before God gave him a new name) in Genesis 12–24.

Even though Abraham wasn't a perfect man—he made more than his share of mistakes—he was still a man who believed that God kept His promises. That made a difference in nearly everything Abraham did!

When you first start reading about the patriarch Abraham, you may wonder if someone misspelled his name in the first few chapters that tell his amazing life story. But the name *Abram* is not a typo. Abram and Abraham are the same guy. After God called Abram and told him to move to Canaan, He promised Abram he'd be the father of a great nation and a blessing to the entire world.

Abraham (we'll use this name from now on to avoid further confusion) is first mentioned in Genesis 11; but it's in chapter 12 where his life gets really interesting. Abraham was 75 years old when God told him to leave Ur and travel to Canaan. But he never questioned God—he just did what he was told.

It probably helped that God made him an amazing promise: "I will make you a great nation; I will bless you and make your name great; and you shall be a blessing. I will bless those who bless you, and I will curse him who curses you; and in you all the families of the earth shall be blessed" (Genesis 12:2–3 NKJV).

WHO, WHAT, WHERE?

Ur was a place—probably a large city—located in what is now Iraq, about 600 miles east of Canaan, which is the land in and around Israel today. Ur was the birthplace of Abraham and Haran, his brother. Abraham and his family lived in Ur before God commanded him to travel to Canaan.

The Promise of a Son...and Millions of Family Members

POWER WORDS

And Abram believed the LORD, and the LORD counted him as righteous because of his faith.

Genesis 15:6

WHAT'S IN IT FOR ME?

The story of Isaac's birth is a good reminder of two things: God always keeps His promises, even when it doesn't seem humanly possible; and we need to wait patiently—sometimes for years—for God to keep His promises. You can never go wrong when you simply trust God to do what He says He will do.

Later, as you can read in Genesis 17, God repeated His promise to Abraham, only this time He was a little more specific. God promised Abraham that He would begin a new race of people through him and his wife, Sarah—even though Abraham was 99 years old and Sarah was way too old to have children. God promised He would make Abraham the father of many nations and that he would have millions of descendants. This is when God renamed him Abraham and renamed his wife Sarah as well (she was called Sarai before that).

In time—after Abraham and Sarah hatched a plan to produce a son through Sarah's servant, Hagar (you can read this story in Genesis 16)—God kept His promise. Genesis 17 says that Sarah became pregnant and gave birth to the son God had promised them. They named him Isaac, as God had told them to, and he later became the founder of the nation God had promised Abraham and his family.

This Is Only a Test...

Abraham knew beyond all doubt that his son Isaac was the result of God's keeping His promises. But one day, Abraham had to wonder what God could possibly be thinking when He told Abraham to do the unthinkable: sacrifice Isaac on an altar.

Genesis 22 tells the story of Abraham hearing that command and then obediently taking Isaac to a place called Moriah, where he built an altar and prepared to take his son's life. Abraham had placed Isaac on top of the altar, and was about to sacrifice him, when an angel of the Lord stopped him and told him not to harm the young man.

In the end, Abraham sacrificed a ram—caught by its horns in a thicket—instead of his son Isaac.

It was all a test. God wanted Abraham to discover just how deeply he trusted God and just how committed he was to obeying God's every command. Because Abraham proved how faithful he was, God again promised to bless Abraham with countless millions of descendants—all of whom would also be descendants of his son Isaac.

More Branches on the Family Tree

After the death of Sarah, Abraham arranged a marriage for Isaac. He sent a servant to his brother Nahor's home to find a wife for Isaac. The servant returned with Nahor's daughter Rebekah. Isaac married Rebekah, and after much prayer—because Rebekah at first couldn't get pregnant—she had twin sons: Esau and Jacob.

Esau was Isaac's favorite son, but when Isaac was very old, Jacob tricked his blind father into giving him the blessing meant for the firstborn child in that culture. (You can read this story in Genesis 27.) That meant that Jacob, not Esau, would become the forefather of the Hebrew people.

Later, Jacob himself was tricked into marrying a woman named Leah—when he really wanted to marry her sister, Rachel. In those days, men were allowed to have more than one wife, so he also married Rachel. Jacob, whom God renamed Israel, became the father of 12 sons, and his family came to be known as the 12 tribes of Israel.

One of those sons was named Joseph, and his story takes up the last 20 chapters of the book of Genesis.

> **FUN BIBLE TRIVIA**
>
> The book of Genesis doesn't say what Abraham was thinking as he prepared to sacrifice his son Isaac, but in the New Testament, the book of Hebrews suggests that Abraham believed that if he had actually slain his son, God would have raised Isaac from the dead. (You can look it up in Hebrews 11:17–19.)

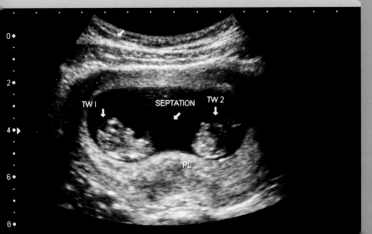

Modern technology allows us to see twins in their mother's womb—but Jacob and Esau were born 4,000 years before ultrasounds!

TW 1   SEPTATION   TW 2

PL

> **DID YOU KNOW. . . ?**
>
> The name Jacob means "supplanter," which is another word for someone who replaces someone, often by trickery or force. This makes sense, because Jacob—with the help of his mother—tricked his father into giving him a birthright meant for his older brother, Esau. Though God doesn't approve of trickery and deception, Jacob's story is an example of how God uses imperfect people to carry out His perfect plans.

185

That's Some Jacket You're Wearing, Joseph!

Joseph was the second-youngest of 12 sons born to Jacob. You can only imagine the kind of problems he faced being one of 12 boys, but to make matters worse, he was Jacob's favorite, which made the other brothers mad. Not only that, Joseph was a bit of a tattletale, who brought his father bad reports of some of the things the other boys were doing. To top it off, Jacob set Joseph apart by giving him a beautiful robe (called a "coat of many colors" in some Bible versions).

When Joseph's 10 older brothers saw the robe their father had given Joseph, they became very jealous. They disliked him so much that they wouldn't even say anything nice to him. Things only got worse for Joseph when he told his brothers about a couple of strange dreams he had—both of which showed him that his brothers would bow down to him.

A few days later, Jacob asked Joseph to check up on his brothers, who were working in the fields. When the brothers saw him coming, they made plans to kill him. But Reuben, the eldest brother, had another idea: he said they should just throw Joseph into a well and leave him there to die. (Reuben's real plan was to come back later by himself and rescue Joseph.)

After the brothers stripped off Joseph's coat and tossed him into the empty well, a group of men came by on their way to Egypt. That gave Judah, another one of the brothers, an idea. Why not sell Joseph to the men as a slave? That way, the brothers would be innocent of killing him—and they would make a nice profit besides!

So Joseph was off to Egypt, where he was sold to an important man named Potiphar. Meanwhile, Joseph's brothers dipped Joseph's robe in animal blood and took it to Jacob, who believed a wild animal had killed his favorite son.

Joseph started out his life in Egypt as a slave, but because he was faithful to God—and because God blessed him—Joseph became an important person in Egypt. He even got to talk to Pharaoh himself and told him the meaning of some of his dreams.

WHAT'S IN IT FOR ME?

When you read about how Joseph's brothers treated him—how they sold him to a bunch of strangers—you might be tempted to say, "That's not fair!" But keep in mind that God used what happened to Joseph to help keep the Hebrew race from starving to death. Joseph is an example of how God can use everything that happens in your life—even the tough times you have to go through—for your own good.

One of those dreams meant that there would be a terrible time in the surrounding world when people wouldn't have any food to eat. So Joseph advised Pharaoh to save up lots of food during the good times, so people wouldn't starve to death later.

When the hard times came, people came from all over to buy grain from Joseph. That included Joseph's brothers, who bowed to him—just as he had told them they would—because he was such an important person.

Joseph had the authority to have his brothers punished—even put to death—for what they had done to him. But he wasn't about to do that. Instead, he told them not to be afraid of him or angry at themselves for selling him, because God had used what they had done to keep a lot of people from dying.

So Jacob, Joseph's brothers, and their families left Canaan and moved to Egypt to live with Joseph. They had all the food they needed, and their families got bigger and bigger. Because they were Joseph's family, they had the best of everything.

Joseph died in Egypt at the age of 110. But before he died, he promised his brothers that God would one day rescue them and take them back to Canaan. The book of Genesis ends with Joseph's body being placed in a coffin in Egypt.

Now it's time to look ahead about four centuries to see what became of Joseph's descendants in Egypt—and how God made good on Joseph's promise. ❌

Exodus

What It's About: The word *exodus* literally means "departure," and that's what the story in the book of Exodus is all about. The book of Genesis ends with Abraham's descendants living in Egypt as guests of Joseph. After spending more than four hundred years in Egypt, the Hebrews—by now, hundreds of thousands of families—were living in a foreign land as slaves. That all changed when God assigned His own chosen man, Moses, to bring the people of Israel out of Egyptian slavery and set them on their way to the Promised Land of Canaan.

Important Characters/People: Moses, Aaron, Miriam, Pharaoh, Jethro, Joshua

The Writer: Moses (see page 20)

187

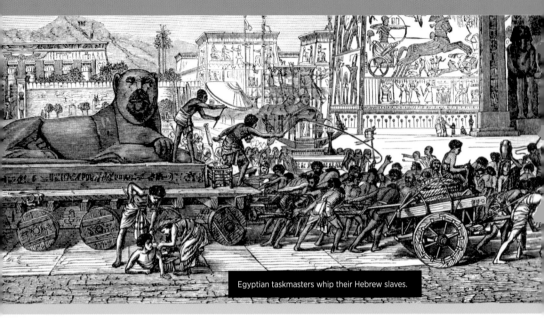

Egyptian taskmasters whip their Hebrew slaves.

What You'll Find in the Book of Exodus

The Israelites had it pretty good in Egypt while Joseph was alive. But after Joseph died, the new pharaoh saw the tribes of Israel not as welcome guests but as a threat to his nation. So Pharaoh made the Israelites slaves in Egypt. God saw what was happening to His chosen people, and He heard their cries for a deliverer. So He called a shepherd named Moses to lead them out of slavery in Egypt.

At first, Moses wasn't sure he was the man for the job. Even though God appeared to him in a miraculous way— out of a bush that looked like it was on fire, even though it wasn't burned up—Moses made excuses about why he couldn't lead the Hebrews out of Egypt. (You can read this story in Exodus 3–4.)

But God wasn't going to have it any other way. Eventually, He convinced Moses that he was the right person to lead the Hebrews, and Moses went to Pharaoh with this demand: "Let my people go!" (Exodus 5:1).

Pharaoh knew he had a good thing going with all the free labor provided by the Hebrew slaves, and he wasn't about to let them just walk away—at least not without some heavy persuasion from above! Chapters 7–12 of Exodus tell the story of a series of 10 plagues that God sent on Egypt because Pharaoh wouldn't let the Hebrew nation go free. First it was the water in the Nile River turning to blood, then plagues of frogs, gnats, and flies. Then came the death of the livestock in Egypt, boils breaking out on the people, hail, locusts, and three days of darkness.

Still, Pharaoh wouldn't budge—not until God sent the final plague: the death of all firstborn male children in Egypt. When Pharaoh saw what had happened, he *begged* Moses and his people to leave Egypt for good. The Egyptian people wanted the Hebrews to leave so much that they let them take anything they wanted with them—as long as they left right away!

POWER WORDS

God replied to Moses, "I Am Who I Am. Say this to the people of Israel: I Am has sent me to you."

Exodus 3:14

WHO, WHAT, WHERE?

Where would Moses have been without his big brother, Aaron? When Moses complained that he wasn't a very good speaker, God appointed Aaron as Moses' spokesman, a position he held for almost 40 years. Aaron was also the first priest of Israel and the father of a line of priests that continued for more than 1,000 years.

189

Time to Hit the Road. . .for the Promised Land!

What a sight it must have been! Hundreds of thousands of people gathering for their exodus from Egypt!

Even though the people of Israel were beginning a journey to the Promised Land, they didn't take the shortest way there—which would have been a straight line through the desert. Instead, they headed toward a place called the Wilderness of Sinai, which is located near the southern tip of the Sinai Peninsula. It was here that God called Moses to the top of Mount Sinai to give him rules to govern the Hebrew people, including the Ten Commandments.

FRESH FRESH
THOU SHALT NOT STEAL

A Mountaintop Experience, the Laws of God. . .and a Calf Made of Gold

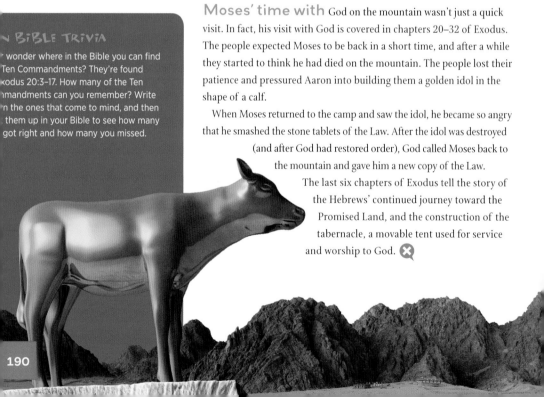

Moses' time with God on the mountain wasn't just a quick visit. In fact, his visit with God is covered in chapters 20–32 of Exodus. The people expected Moses to be back in a short time, and after a while they started to think he had died on the mountain. The people lost their patience and pressured Aaron into building them a golden idol in the shape of a calf.

When Moses returned to the camp and saw the idol, he became so angry that he smashed the stone tablets of the Law. After the idol was destroyed (and after God had restored order), God called Moses back to the mountain and gave him a new copy of the Law.

The last six chapters of Exodus tell the story of the Hebrews' continued journey toward the Promised Land, and the construction of the tabernacle, a movable tent used for service and worship to God.

BIBLE TRIVIA

wonder where in the Bible you can find Ten Commandments? They're found xodus 20:3–17. How many of the Ten mandments can you remember? Write n the ones that come to mind, and then them up in your Bible to see how many got right and how many you missed.

Leviticus

What It's About: Once God had delivered the people of Israel out of slavery in Egypt, He instructed them how to live and how to worship Him. That included a system of sacrifices that would one day be replaced by the onetime sacrifice of Jesus Christ on the cross.

Important Characters/People: Moses, Aaron, Nadab, Abihu, Ithamar, Eleazar

The Writer: Moses (see page 20)

What You'll Find in the Book of Leviticus

The people of Israel lived as slaves in Egypt for more than 400 years. As a result of living among a people that worshipped many false gods, the way the Hebrews viewed God was warped. The words recorded in the book of Leviticus are the words of a God who wanted to bring His people back into fellowship with Him.

The people of Israel were imperfect—just like everyone else—but they were *God's* people, and He provided the words recorded in Leviticus to give them instructions on how to have a relationship with a holy God. That's why you'll see the word *holy* throughout the book of Leviticus. God is holy, and He wants His people to be holy, too. And in those days, the only way for that to happen was through sacrifices to pay for the people's sins.

God *hated* it when His people worshipped silly idols!

The first seven chapters of Leviticus cover the various offerings and sacrifices that God required from the people. The first three chapters are about what are called *voluntary offerings*, which were meant as worship to God.

POWER WORDS

"For I am the Lᴏʀᴅ your God. You must consecrate yourselves and be holy, because I am holy."

Leviticus 11:44

Chapters 4 and 5 address offerings made to cover people's sins. Chapters 6 and 7 record laws and regulations about the different kinds of offerings.

Chapters 8–10 cover the rules and regulations for the priesthood of that time. Chapters 11–16 explain to the Hebrew people what to do in order to deal with different kinds of "uncleanness." The last 10 chapters are instructions and guidelines for holy living.

Numbers

What It's About: Even though God brought the nation of Israel out of slavery in Egypt—and performed some amazing miracles for everyone to see—the people were ungrateful and unbelieving. As a result, they were forced to wander in the wilderness of Sinai for 40 years.

Important Characters/People: Moses, Aaron, Joshua, Balaam, Eleazar, the 70 elders, Caleb, Korah, Dathan, Abiram, the 12 spies, Gad, Reuben

The Writer: Moses (see page 20)

What You'll Find in the Book of Numbers

At the beginning of the book of Numbers, God instructs Moses to count all the young men of Israel—which is how the book got its name. God told Moses and his brother, Aaron, along with leaders of the 12 tribes, to do the counting.

Most of the events in the book of Numbers take place in the wilderness between Egypt and Canaan. The book begins 14 months after the people had left Egypt, and long after they should have entered the Promised Land. But even though they should have completed the journey in less than two weeks, they were still decades away from claiming the land that God had promised to give them. That's because God was punishing them for their constant complaining and rebellion.

The book of Numbers includes probably the best—or the worst—example of the people's rebellion and lack of faith. It happened while the people were camped out at a place called Kadesh, which was located in the Desert of Zin. They were just days away from entering the Promised Land when Moses sent representatives from each of Israel's 12 tribes ahead to check out the land. When they returned, they told the people that everything they had been told about the land was true and that it would be a great place to live and raise their families.

So what was the problem?

Two of the spies—Joshua and Caleb—told the people to get ready to take the land and that there was no way they could fail, because God would be with them. But 10 of the spies told the people about giants living in the land—giants so big that they made the men of Israel look like grasshoppers in comparison.

Sadly, the people of Israel chose to listen to the 10—and they rebelled against Moses and against God and refused to move out to take the land. Because they rebelled, and because they failed to believe God, many of them died at Kadesh. (You can read the whole story in Numbers 13–14.)

Sadly, a whole generation of people who were just days away from enjoying life in a land flowing with milk and honey instead died in the wilderness. Moses had prayed to God for the rebellious people, and God forgave them. But He wasn't going to reward them for their lack of faith

Moses sent 12 men to "spy out" the Promised Land.

WHO, WHAT, WHERE?

Caleb, who was a member of the tribe of Judah, was one of the 12 spies Moses sent to spy out the land of Canaan. He is an example of what can happen in the life of someone who trusts God instead of allowing fear to rule. The Bible says that Caleb trusted God and acted on that trust, so he became an example of the kind of faith God honors and rewards (see Joshua 14:6–15). Do you have that kind of faith in God?

WHAT'S iN iT FOR ME?

It's not pleasant reading about thousands of people dying in a desert because they refused to believe God but instead focused on a bunch of giants. But the story of what happened at Kadesh is a great reminder to focus on the size of our God and not on the size of the giants in your life. When you do that, you'll be more than willing to do exactly what God asks you to do—and you'll enjoy the good things God has for you as a result!

Ten of the 12 spies said they didn't want to face the giants in the Promised Land!

and obedience. They would have to wander in the wilderness until everyone over the age of 20 had died.

Even Moses wasn't allowed to enter the Promised Land. But Joshua and Caleb, the two spies who had tried their best to rally the people and get them to claim what God had already given them, were allowed to enter the land of Canaan. ✖

Deuteronomy

What It's About: Moses, who had led Israel out of captivity and slavery in Egypt, speaks to the Hebrew people four times to remind them where they had come from, where they had been, whom they belonged to (God), and how belonging to God should affect their lives.

Important Characters/People: Moses, Joshua, the Canaanites, the Hittites, the Girgashites, the Amorites, the Perizzites, the Hivites, the Jebusites

The Writer: Moses (See page 20)

What You'll Find in the Book of Deuteronomy

Chapters 1–4 of Deuteronomy record Moses' words to his people reminding them of their 40 years in the wilderness. Moses didn't talk to the people about that time just to give them a history lesson. He wanted them to remember *why* they had wandered in the wilderness—because of their disobedience and lack of faith.

In chapters 5–11, you can read about how Moses repeated the Ten Commandments (5:6–21), reminded the people of the importance of doing what God had told them to do, and promised the people they would soon enter the Promised Land.

Moses begins this part of his address by telling the people, "Listen carefully, Israel. Hear the decrees and regulations I am giving you today, so you may learn them and obey them!" (5:1).

WHAT'S IN IT FOR ME?

God promises that when you come to Him to confess your sin, He will completely forgive you and cleanse you. It's true now, and it was true in the days of Moses. So why would Moses remind the people of what they had done wrong after they left Egypt? So they would remember their mistakes and not make the same ones again! When you think about the things you've done that displease God, don't beat yourself up. Instead, thank God for His forgiveness. . .and for the lessons He has taught you when you made bad decisions.

The book of Deuteronomy is a written record of Moses' spoken sermons to God's people.

POWER WORDS

"And you must love the LORD your God with all your heart, all your soul, and all your strength."

Deuteronomy 6:5

In chapters 12–26, Moses reminds the Hebrews of the laws and rules that God wants them to obey once they enter the Promised Land. In chapters 27–30, he tells them what kinds of blessings they would receive for obeying those laws.

Chapters 31–33 are Moses' final words to the people before his death—his final good-byes. Chapter 34 is the account of Moses' final days, which he spent on Mount Nebo on the plains of Moab. From there, God showed him the Promised Land, which the people of Israel would soon enter.

After Moses' death, Joshua—the same Joshua who years before had so bravely tried to encourage the people of Israel to possess the land—took over as leader of the Hebrew people.

That's what you'll read about in the next chapter!

Moses sees the Promised Land from far away, in a 19th-century painting by James Joseph Jacques Tissot.

CHAPTER 3

His Story...
and Their Story

The History of God's People (Joshua through Esther)

Someone once said that the Bible isn't just history, but that it's "His story," meaning the story of how God relates to the human race.

The first five books of the Bible—the collection called the Pentateuch—are books about beginnings and the Law of Moses. The next 12 are books of history, and they're the ones that tell the story of the rise and fall, and then the rise again, of the nation of Israel.

These books of history cover more than 1,000 years, starting with the appointment of Joshua to lead the Israelites into the Promised Land (around 1452 BC) and ending after the return of the Jews to Israel following what is called the Babylonian Captivity (which you'll read about later in this chapter).

The people of Israel enjoyed some good times during this period, but they also went through some bad times. As you'll see in this chapter—and in the books of the Bible it covers—those bad times happened because of some bad decisions on the part of Israel's leaders and on the part of the people.

As you read through this part of the Bible, you'll learn how the people of Israel moved into the Promised Land, how they became a kingdom with a human king, how Israel was divided into two kingdoms called Judah and Israel, and the good and bad (mostly bad) things the kings who ruled over Judah and Israel did during their reigns.

Joshua

What It's About: After wandering in the wilderness for 40 years, the people of Israel—now led by Joshua—capture and settle the Promised Land, also known as the land of Canaan.

Important Characters/People: Joshua, Caleb, Rahab, Eleazar, Achan

The Writer: The book of Joshua doesn't name its writer, but most experts agree that Joshua himself wrote most of it. (The last five verses describe Joshua's death and legacy, so someone else would have written those verses.)

POWER WORDS

"This is my command—be strong and courageous! Do not be afraid or discouraged. For the LORD your God is with you wherever you go."

Joshua 1:9

What You'll Find in the Book of Joshua

This book picks up where the book of Deuteronomy leaves off. Moses has died, and now it's up to Joshua the "son of Nun" (1:1) to finish what Moses started and lead the people of Israel into the Promised Land.

Before his death, Moses appointed Joshua as the new leader of the Hebrews (see Deuteronomy 34:9). As the book of Joshua begins, God gives Joshua the encouragement and command to "be strong and courageous" (Joshua 1:6, 7, 9). Almost all of the rebellious people who had earlier lost out on their chance to enter the Promised Land have died, leaving a group of people who are ready to follow Joshua's lead and take what God had already said was theirs.

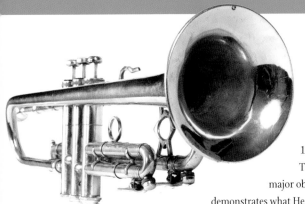

The book of Joshua is split into two 12-chapter sections. The first 12 chapters tell the story of the Israelites' conquest of the people and armies that stood in their way; the last 12 chapters tell the story of how the Israelites divided the land of Canaan among the 12 tribes of Israel.

The city of Jericho is the Israelites' first major obstacle under Joshua's leadership. But God demonstrates what He can do when His people obey His commands. God commanded Joshua's army to march outside Jericho. . .blowing trumpets and shouting! When they did that, God knocked the city walls flat, and the Israelites defeated the city. After that, Joshua's armies drove idol-worshipping people such as the Hittites, Amorites, Canaanites, Perizzites, Hivites, and Jebusites from Canaan. ✖

FUN BIBLE TRIVIA

Joshua is a Hebrew name that means either "Jehovah is his help," "Jehovah the Savior," or "Jehovah is salvation." The name *Jesus* essentially means the very same thing!

WHO, WHAT, WHERE?

Rahab was a woman in Jericho who played a big part in the Israelites' defeat of the city. When Joshua sent two spies to check out the city before Israel attacked it, Rahab hid them from the king of Jericho. In return for her kindness, the men promised she and her family would be spared if she hung a scarlet cord from her window when Israel attacked. Rahab is mentioned in the New Testament as a woman of great faith (Hebrews 11:31; James 2:25). You can read the story of Rahab in Joshua 2:1–24.

Judges

What It's About: Judges is a book of ups and downs—followed by still more ups and downs. It tells the 350-year story of how the people of Israel strayed away from God, the punishment the people suffered as a result, and their turning back to God. Each time Israel abandoned God, He appointed leaders, called judges, to lead them back to Him.

Important Characters/People: Othniel, Ehud, Shamgar, Deborah, Gideon, Abimelech, Tola, Jair, Jephthah, Ibzan, Elon, Abdon, Samson, Barak, Jael, Micah, the Midianites, the Amalekites, the Philistines, the Ammonites

The Writer: Experts aren't certain who wrote the book of Judges, but most believe it was the prophet Samuel.

FUN BIBLE TRIVIA

Some of the Judges listed in the book of Judges had very unusual families. For example, Jair had 30 sons (10:4) and Abdon had 40 sons (12:14). Ibzan had 30 sons and 30 daughters (12:9). Jephthah, on the other hand, had only one child, a daughter he foolishly vowed to sacrifice to God in exchange for a military victory (11:30-40).

What You'll Find in the Book of Judges

This book picks up not long after the book of Joshua leaves off. It tells the stories of 13 people—12 men and one woman—who lead the nation of Israel against the enemies who took over because of the Israelites' disobedience.

The stories in the book of Judges aren't pleasant ones. You can read about how the nation of Israel spent almost four centuries falling away from God, suffering the consequences, and then being rescued by one of the 13 judges.

These are the 13 judges listed in this book and where you can read about them:

Othniel (Judges 3:7–11)—Caleb's brother, who delivered Israel from the king of Mesopotamia and judged Israel for 40 years.

Jair had 30 sons who rode 30 donkeys.

Ehud (Judges 3:12–30)—He defeated the oppressing Moabites. Ehud killed Eglon, the king of Moab, with a dagger while pretending to be on a peace mission.

Shamgar (Judges 3:31)—He fought bravely against the Philistines, killing 600 soldiers with an ox goad—a pointed rod used to prod along oxen as they pulled a cart.

Deborah (Judges 4–5)—She was Israel's only female judge and prophetess. Deborah called Barak to lead warriors into battle against a Canaanite army commander, but Barak would fight only if Deborah went with him.

Gideon (Judges 6–8)—God raised him up to lead Israel against the Midianites.

Abimelech (Judges 9)—He was Gideon's son. He killed all but one of his brothers and was made king of Shechem. He was killed when a woman dropped part of a millstone on his head.

Tola (Judges 10:1–2)—He judged Israel for 23 years.

Jair (10:3–5)—He led Israel for 22 years. He was known for having 30 sons who rode 30 donkeys.

Jephthah (Judges 10:6–12:7)—He was Gilead's son, and he judged Israel for six years.

Ibzan (Judges 12:8–10)—He led the nation for seven years. Ibzan sent his daughters abroad and brought in 30 foreign women as wives for his sons.

Elon (Judges 12:11–12)—He judged Israel for 10 years.

Abdon (Judges 12:13–15)—He led the nation of Israel for eight years. He was known for having 40 sons and 30 nephews who each rode a donkey.

Samson (Judges 13–16)—He was a Nazirite, which meant he had taken a vow not to eat or drink anything from a grapevine, drink alcohol, cut his hair, or eat anything unclean. Samson performed amazing feats of strength, but he had some weaknesses that led to his downfall. ❌

Samson peformed amazing feats of strength.

WHO, WHAT, WHERE?

Gideon was the fifth judge of Israel, and probably the best known of all the judges. God appointed Gideon to lead his nation against the Midianites. The angel of the Lord appeared to Gideon when he was hiding from the enemy, told him God was with him, and called him a "mighty man of valor." Gideon had many doubts, but they did not keep him from obeying God. You can read his story in Judges 6-8.

Ruth

What It's About: Ruth was a loyal daughter-in-law of a Hebrew woman named Naomi. After Ruth's husband died, she went on to become an example of faithfulness to God and an object of God's love and care. Ruth and her new husband, Boaz, are the great-grandparents of King David.

Important Characters/People: Ruth, Naomi, Boaz

The Writer: The writer of the book of Ruth isn't named, but some people believe the prophet Samuel wrote the story.

What You'll Find in the Book of Ruth

The story's main character, Ruth, probably lived around 1100 BC, during the time of the judges.

What makes the book of Ruth different from most other Old Testament books is that Ruth wasn't a Hebrew; she was a native of a place called Moab. She married a Jewish man named Mahlon. Mahlon's mother was a Jewish woman named Naomi. Ruth lived with her husband and his family in Moab.

POWER WORDS

Ruth replied, "Don't ask me to leave you and turn back. Wherever you go, I will go; wherever you live, I will live. Your people will be my people, and your God will be my God."

Ruth 1:16

FUN BiBLE TRiViA

Ruth and Boaz are mentioned in the New Testament as ancestors of Jesus. Matthew 1:5 lists them as the parents of Obed, the grandfather of King David.

When Naomi's husband, Elimelech, and her two sons (including Ruth's husband) died, Naomi decided to move back to Bethlehem. Naomi told Ruth and her other daughter-in-law, Orpah, to stay in Moab, but Ruth refused to leave Naomi. The two women traveled to Bethlehem, where Ruth gathered leftover barley during the harvest—a practice called gleaning—so that she and Naomi would have enough food to survive.

As Ruth gathered grain one day, Boaz, the wealthy owner of the field where she was working, noticed her and ordered his workers to protect her and to leave some grain behind for her to collect. When Ruth went home that night, she told Naomi about Boaz, and her mother-in-law recognized him as a relative of Ruth's late husband. Naomi encouraged Ruth to pursue Boaz and make herself available to him.

Boaz was flattered by Ruth's attention, and he eventually married her. Together, they had a son named Obed, who would one day become the grandfather of King David. ❌

1 Samuel

What It's About: The 12 tribes of Israel unite under a king. Even though God never wanted His people to live under the rule of a human king, He allows them to set up an earthly kingdom and even chooses the men who would rule over them.

Important Characters/People: Hannah, Eli, Samuel, Saul, David, Jonathan, the Philistines, Abigail

The Writer: The writer of the book of 1 Samuel isn't named, but some experts believe Samuel himself wrote most of it. Some of the history in this book takes place after Samuel's death, and it is not known who wrote the remainder of the book.

What You'll Find in the Book of 1 Samuel

This book tells two stories. First, there's the life of the prophet Samuel, who was Israel's last judge (chapters 1–12). Then there is the life of Saul, Israel's first king (chapters 13–31). It starts out with a miracle birth, as a woman named Hannah prays for a son and promises to dedicate him to God's service. God answers by giving her Samuel.

Samuel was one of Israel's greatest prophets. He spoke out against dishonesty in the priesthood and led the people of Israel to turn away from idolatry and back to their God. Samuel spent his entire life as a judge and prophet in Israel.

This Is Not What God Wanted!

The book of 1 Samuel includes a big change in the nation of Israel. The people ask Samuel for a human king so that they could be just like the other nations around them. Samuel doesn't want Israel to have a king, but he reluctantly prays and tells God what the people want. Even though God warns that having a human king will be disastrous for Israel in the long run, He tells Samuel to appoint a man named Saul as the first king of Israel.

WHO, WHAT, WHERE?

Eli was a priest during the period of the judges at a place called Shiloh, which was about 10 miles north of Jerusalem. After Hannah's miracle son, Samuel, was weaned, she kept a promise to God and brought him to Eli for service and training. One night, Eli realized God had spoken to Samuel and encouraged the boy to listen and respond. In his first prophecy, Samuel spoke out against the dishonesty of Eli's sons, Hophni and Phinehas, who were both priests.

Saul's reign as king starts out well, but later he makes several bad decisions. Because he disobeys God several times, God removes his blessing from Saul and appoints a young shepherd named David as Israel's second king.

Chapter 16 is the story of Samuel's journey to Bethlehem to anoint David as Israel's next king. Chapter 17 covers David's famous battle with a giant Philistine named Goliath. David's victory over Goliath makes him a hero to everyone in Israel except King Saul, who tries several times to kill David. With God's help, David escapes from Saul several times. (You can read the whole story in chapters 19–26.)

In the final chapter of 1 Samuel, Saul's three sons, including Jonathan (a close friend of David's), die in battle with the Philistines, and Saul commits suicide, clearing the way for David to take the throne of Israel. ⊗

David, a statue by the Italian artist Michelangelo, was created between the years 1501 and 1504.

2 Samuel

What It's About: This book picks up where 1 Samuel leaves off. David becomes king of Israel. Even though David was far from a perfect man, he becomes Israel's greatest king.

Important Characters/People: David, Joab, Abner, Ishbosheth, Absalom, Michal, Bathsheba, Uriah, Nathan, Hushai

The Writer: Unknown, but it wasn't Samuel, because the events recorded in this book take place after his death. Some suggest that Abiathar the priest was the author (15:35).

What You'll Find in the Book of 2 Samuel

Second Samuel covers about 40 years of Israel's history—the entire reign of David as king of Israel. After King Saul died, David took the throne of the tribe of Judah. Seven years later, after the death of Ishbosheth, the son of Saul and king of the northern tribes, David became king over all Israel.

After capturing Jerusalem from the Jebusites, David made Jerusalem the capital city of Israel. That was the first of many military victories for Israel under King David. After that, Israel became a powerful and rich nation.

One spring, though, David stayed home from battle and committed a terrible sin with Bathsheba, the wife of Uriah, one of his most devoted soldiers. To cover up what he had done, David arranged to have Uriah killed in battle. Even though David repented for his sins and was forgiven, the consequences of what he did affected the rest of his reign—as well as his own family.

David's son Absalom tried to take the throne of Israel from his father. David had to run for his life away from Jerusalem. Eventually, Absalom died in battle, and David returned to Jerusalem to take back the throne. The final three chapters of 2 Samuel tell the story of David's final days. ⊗

1 and 2 Kings

What They're About: First Kings starts with the reign of Solomon, David's son, as king of Israel, and 2 Kings ends with both parts of a divided kingdom—the northern kingdom (Israel) and the southern kingdom (Judah)—being defeated and their people taken into captivity. The northern kingdom was defeated by the Assyrians, and the southern kingdom was defeated by the Babylonians.

Important Characters/People: David, Adonijah, Solomon, Rehoboam, Jeroboam, Abijam, Asa, Jehoshaphat, Ahab, Jezebel, Nathan, Ahijah, Elijah, and Micaiah in 1 Kings; Elijah, Elisha, Jehoram, Ben-Hadad, Hazael, Ahaziah, Jehu, Jezebel, Ahab, Joash, Ahaz, Isaiah, Hezekiah, Josiah, and Nebuchadnezzar in 2 Kings

The Writer: First Kings and 2 Kings were originally one book in the Hebrew Bible. No writer is mentioned, but tradition teaches that the prophet Jeremiah—the same one who wrote the book of Jeremiah—recorded this time in biblical history.

POWER WORDS

"Give me an understanding heart so that I can govern your people well and know the difference between right and wrong. For who by himself is able to govern this great people of yours?"

1 Kings 3:9

What You'll Find in the Books of 1 and 2 Kings

First Kings covers events from around 970 BC to 850 BC. It begins with the last days of King David, moves through the reign of King Solomon, and ends with the story of Elijah, a powerful prophet of God.

The first 11 chapters of 1 Kings tell the story of the reign of King Solomon, who started his reign as king of Israel very well. He asked for and received wisdom from God, built the Temple in Jerusalem, and ruled over Israel as it reached its high point in power and standing in that part of the world.

Solomon had it all—power, riches, and respect from his neighbors. Sadly, though, he didn't finish his time as king of Israel the way he started it. In fact, he led God's chosen people down a terrible path that would end with a divided nation at war with itself.

It's All Downhill from Here—Again

Like his father, David, Solomon had a weakness for women that would eventually bring him and his nation down. After spending seven years constructing the Temple for God, Solomon spent the next 13 years building a palace for himself. He also married 700 women, many of whom were foreigners who persuaded him to worship their false gods.

After Solomon's death, his son Rehoboam made some big mistakes that led to the division of the nation of Israel. When all was said and done, the 10 northern tribes formed their own nation under Jeroboam, a former official under Solomon. That nation is called Israel. The two southern tribes made up a nation called Judah.

WHO, WHAT, WHERE?

Both Israel and Judah were led by a series of kings who didn't do what God wanted them to do. There were a few exceptions, though. Three kings of Judah—Asa (1 Kings 15:9–24), Jehoshaphat (1 Kings 22:41–50), and Hezekiah (2 Kings 18–20)—stood out as men who did what pleased God and who encouraged their people to follow Him, too.

Starting in 1 Kings 12, you can read about the kings (and one queen) of Israel and Judah. Each nation was ruled over by about 20 kings during that time. For the most part, it's not a very positive story. None of the kings of Israel followed God, and only a few of Judah's kings were godly men. They took part in idol worship and encouraged their people to do the same.

Even though God's prophets warned these kings and the people to turn back to God, both countries strayed further and further from Him as time went on. Eventually, God sent judgment in the form of outside invaders, who brought death, destruction, and slavery.

Second Kings ends with the nation of Israel falling to the Assyrians (chapters 16 and 17) in around 722 BC, and Judah falling to the Babylonians (chapters 24 and 25) in about 585 BC.

Second Kings chapter 25 tells how the armies of Babylonian king Nebuchadnezzar surrounded Jerusalem and then destroyed the city and the Temple and took everything of value from the Temple and the king's palace. The Babylonians also captured thousands of captives and took them away to Babylon, where they stayed for several decades in what is called the Babylonian Captivity. ⊗

This "ball and chain" was put on a prisoner's ankle to keep him from trying to run away. The Babylonians probably didn't use balls and chains—but they sure took a lot of prisoners from Jerusalem.

1 and 2 Chronicles

What They're About: These books cover much of the same history you read about in 1 and 2 Samuel and 1 and 2 Kings, but with more emphasis on the spiritual side of the stories you read in those other books. The books of Chronicles were written after the Babylonian Captivity to give the people returning to Israel an understanding of how to worship God.

Important Characters/People: Saul, David, Nathan, Gad, Solomon, Joab, Jashobeam, and Eleazar in 1 Chronicles; Solomon, Rehoboam, Jeroboam, Abijah, Asa, Jehoshaphat, Ahab, Jehoram, Ahaziah, Joash, Amaziah, Uzziah, Jotham, Ahaz, Hezekiah, Manasseh, Josiah, and Jehoahaz in 2 Chronicles

The Writer: Like most of the books of the Old Testament, 1 and 2 Chronicles don't name their writers, but centuries of tradition hold that Ezra the priest wrote them.

What You'll Find in the Books of 1 and 2 Chronicles

First Chronicles is a detailed picture of King David's reign over the nation of Israel. It starts with a nine-chapter family history of King David, starting as far back as Adam and his family. Starting with chapter 10, it picks up with David taking the throne of Israel. It ends with Solomon, David's son, taking the throne after his father's death.

We often think of "worship" as a music style. But for the people of Israel, it was a whole way of life.

DID YOU KNOW. . .?

The books titled 1 Chronicles and 2 Chronicles in our Bibles today were originally written as one really long book with a title that meant "the words of the days." The book was divided in two in the third century BC, when the Hebrew Bible (also known as the Old Testament) was translated into Greek.

Second Chronicles covers more than 400 years of history. It begins with the construction of Solomon's Temple and ends with Cyrus's announcement that the Jews would be allowed to rebuild the Temple following the Babylonian Captivity. This book focuses mostly on the southern kingdom of Judah and barely mentions the northern kingdom of Israel. It mentions the invasion of Judah by the Babylonians, but focuses more on the good things that happened there.

Ezra

What It's About: After about 70 years of captivity in Babylon, the Jews return to Israel, where for a time they live lives of obedience and devotion to God.

Important Characters/People: Darius, Cyrus, Artaxerxes, Ezra, Zerubbabel, Zechariah, Haggai

The Writer: The book of Ezra doesn't name its writer, but thousands of years of tradition hold that Ezra himself wrote it. Ezra's name first appears in the book in chapter 7—the same time that the writer changes from writing in the third person to the first person (from "he" to "I").

What You'll Find in the Book of Ezra

This book covers about one hundred years of history, starting in about 530 BC. The book of Ezra begins where the book of 2 Chronicles ends. King Cyrus of Persia declares that the captive Jews will be allowed to return to their homeland, where they will rebuild the Temple, which had been destroyed when the Babylonians raided Jerusalem seven decades earlier.

The first six chapters of the book of Ezra tell the story of how a first group of Jews, led by a man named Zerubbabel, left Persia and traveled home to Jerusalem to build the second Temple. In between chapters 6 and 7 is a gap of about 58 years, and chapters 7–10 cover the ministry of Ezra, a priest who was accompanied by Israel's religious leaders.

Zerubbabel led a group of people who would build the new Temple. Ezra led a group who reestablished what the Temple stood for in Jerusalem: a growing relationship with God.

WHO, WHAT, WHERE?

Cyrus was the king of Persia who commanded that the Jewish people be released from captivity so they could return to their home country. He also ordered his people to give donations to help the Jews and returned the Temple vessels that Nebuchadnezzar of Babylon had taken when he took the people of Judah into captivity.

WHAT'S IN IT FOR ME?

The story told in the book of Ezra shows just how willing God is to offer His people second chances. God had punished the people of Judah for their disobedience, but now He is giving them a fresh start in their homeland. Here's the really cool thing you need to remember: the same God who gave those wayward people a second chance is more than willing to do the same thing for you after you've made a bad decision.

211

Nehemiah

What It's About: The Jewish people, who have just returned to Israel from Babylon, rebuild the walls of the city of Jerusalem.

Important Characters/People: Nehemiah, Artaxerxes, Sanballat, Tobiah, Geshem

The Writer: This book starts out, "The words of Nehemiah" (1:1 NKJV), but according to Jewish tradition, Ezra wrote the book of Nehemiah.

POWER WORDS

"Go and enjoy choice food and sweet drinks, and send some to those who have nothing prepared. This day is sacred to our Lord. Do not grieve, for the joy of the Lord is your strength."

Nehemiah 8:10 NIV

WHO, WHAT, WHERE?

Nehemiah and the rest of the Jews received plenty of opposition as they worked to rebuild Jerusalem's walls. Three guys, named Sanballat, Tobiah, and Geshem, plotted to attack Jerusalem, which forced the Jews to guard the uncompleted walls. Tobiah and Sanballat hired a man to warn Nehemiah that he would be killed, and Tobiah sent threatening letters to scare Nehemiah.

What You'll Find in the Book of Nehemiah

Nehemiah lived around the same time as Ezra and led the third and final group of Jews from Persia back to their homeland of Judah. He served as Persian King Artexerxes's cupbearer—the man whose job it was to taste the king's food and wine to make sure someone hadn't put poison in them. The king liked Nehemiah, and when Nehemiah heard that the walls around the city of Jerusalem hadn't been rebuilt, Artaxerxes gave him permission to return to Jerusalem.

The Temple had been rebuilt, but there were no walls around the city to protect it from its many enemies. Nehemiah wanted to go to Jerusalem and encourage the people to get busy rebuilding the city walls.

The book of Nehemiah tells us how he led a team of builders from Persia to Jerusalem to rebuild the city's walls. With Nehemiah cheering them on—and giving them a little push from behind—the people gave money, supplies, and manpower toward rebuilding the walls. Even though Israel's enemies didn't want the walls rebuilt, the work was completed in just 52 days—a feat that even Israel's enemies saw was the result of God's power.

Not long after the walls were finished, Ezra the priest read the Law of Moses to the people out loud "from early morning until noon" (8:3). That was just the beginning of a spiritual renewal among the people of Israel. Nehemiah also helped reestablish true worship through prayer and encouraged the people to read and obey the Word of God.

Esther

What It's About: Esther, a beautiful Jewish girl who becomes queen of Persia through her marriage to King Ahasuerus (also known as Xerxes), helps save her people from slaughter.

Important Characters/People: Xerxes, Mordecai, Haman, Esther, Hathach

The Writer: The book of Esther doesn't name its author, but one of the most popular traditions is that Mordecai, Esther's cousin, wrote it. Some believe that Ezra or Nehemiah wrote this book.

What You'll Find in the Book of Esther

The story of Esther takes place during the 58-year gap in the book of Ezra (the one between chapters 6 and 7). Many of the Jews who had been held captive all their lives in Persia wanted to stay there. It was, after all, the only place they'd ever known as home.

The book of Esther tells the story of how Esther becomes queen of Persia then finds herself and her people threatened by a plot to kill all the Jews in Persia. Esther knew that speaking up to her husband, the king, was dangerous, but she was willing to risk her own life to save the lives of the Jews still living in Persia.

Esther's courage to save God's chosen people is celebrated in the annual Jewish festival of Purim, which is still celebrated today.

CHAPTER 4

Words to Live By

God's Written Wisdom (Job through Song of Solomon)

So far, we've covered books with a lot of history—how things began and what happened after they got their start. Now we're moving on to five books that are often called the Bible's *wisdom literature*.

You can learn a lot about how God wants you to live by reading just about any part of the Bible, but these books are devoted to teaching wisdom for life. In these books are simple instructions for how to maintain your relationship to God, how to get along with other people, and how to be the kind of person God wants you to be.

Out of all the wisdom books, only one—Job—tells someone's story. The rest are mostly collections of thoughts on certain subjects. . .and about God Himself.

Job

What It's About: Job was a good man who loved God but who went through a terrible time of suffering after God allowed Satan to take everything Job had, including his family, his wealth, and his health.

Important Characters/People: Job, God, Satan, Eliphaz, Bildad, Zophar, Elihu

The Writer: Many experts believe that Job is the oldest book in the Bible—even older than Genesis. Jewish tradition says that Moses wrote the book of Job, but the writer isn't known for certain.

What You'll Find in the Book of Job

The story of Job takes place during the time of the patriarchs (Abraham, Isaac, Jacob, and Joseph). Job lived with his family—his wife and seven sons and three daughters—in a place called Uz, and he had everything going for him. He owned 7,000 sheep, 3,000 camels, 500 teams of oxen, and 500 female donkeys. In those days, a person's wealth was measured by how many animals he owned, so it's no wonder the Bible calls Job the wealthiest man living in Uz.

But Job's riches aren't the first thing the Bible tells us about him. The very first verse in the book of Job says, "He was honest inside and out, a man of his word, who was totally devoted to God and hated evil with a passion" (Job 1:1 MSG).

Job was such a great example of godliness and character that God bragged on him a little bit when He said to Satan, "He is the finest man in all the earth. He is blameless—a man of complete integrity. He fears God and stays away from evil" (Job 1:8).

Job sounds like just the kind of guy God would protect from suffering and loss, doesn't he? But if you know anything at all about the book of Job, you know that Job went through a time of terrible suffering and loss.

The devil wasn't impressed with what God had to say about Job, and he challenged God to allow him to take away from Job everything he had—his family, his livestock, and his health. When that happened, the devil said, Job would curse God to His face.

God told Satan he could do what he wanted with Job, but with one limit: the devil wasn't allowed to take Job's life. What followed for Job was suffering on a level that most of us would find hard to imagine. Not only did Job lose his children and his wealth, but he was also covered from head to toe in painful sores called boils. To make matters worse, Job's wife provided no comfort, and when his three best friends came to Uz to "comfort" him, they spent most of their time accusing him of committing some terrible sin against God that led to his suffering.

Most of the book of Job (chapters 3–37) is an account of conversations between Job and his friends—Eliphaz, Bildad, and Zophar—as they try to make sense out of something that made no earthly sense: a good man's horrible suffering, even when he hadn't done anything wrong.

Job cannot understand why all this has happened to him, and finally he calls on God to help him understand. Chapters 38–41 are an account of another conversation—between Job and God. God confronts Job with question after question about His own character and power. Job has no answer for any of them. In the end, Job realizes that even when he can't make sense of his suffering, he must still remain loyal to the God who had blessed him with so much and then allowed it to be taken away.

WHAT'S IN IT FOR ME?

Have you ever gone through a tough time when you wondered if you had done something to deserve it? One of the lessons from the book of Job is that bad things *do* happen to good people, even when they haven't done anything wrong. But don't worry— the Bible promises that God will use everything that happens to you for your own good and for His benefit (see Romans 8:28).

Psalms

What It's About: The book of Psalms is actually a collection of songs, poems, and other writings that showcase the different writers' praise, prayers—and complaints—to God as well as their thoughts *about* God.

Important Characters/People: David, Asaph, Solomon, the sons of Korah, Moses, Heman, Ethan

The Writers: At least seven different writers contributed to the book of Psalms. Of those, King David is credited with the most—at least 73. Other notable psalmists (people who wrote psalms) include Solomon, Moses (yes, the same Moses who led the people of Israel out of Egypt), Asaph, Ethan, and the sons of Korah. Forty-eight of the 150 psalms are not attributed to a specific writer.

What You'll Find in the Book of Psalms

The book of Psalms includes writings by people who were going through some of the same things you will experience at different times in your life—happiness, sadness, anger, pain, fear, and other strong feelings. Sometimes it's good to read the psalms so you can understand that you're not alone, that other people have felt the same feelings you might be feeling right now.

FUN BiBLE TRIViA

If you were to take your Bible in your hand and try to open it so that you were in the very middle, you'd probably see one of the psalms. The middle chapter of the Bible is Psalm 117 and the middle verse is Psalm 118:8.

The Bible includes 150 psalms. The book of Psalms is by far the longest book in the Bible. It also includes the shortest chapter in the Bible (Psalm 117) and the longest chapter (Psalm 119).

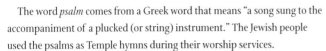

The word *psalm* comes from a Greek word that means "a song sung to the accompaniment of a plucked (or string) instrument." The Jewish people used the psalms as Temple hymns during their worship services.

The book of Psalms, which is also called the Psalter, was written over a long time period: from about 1100 BC to around 430 BC. Psalm 90, which was written by Moses, is clearly the oldest of the psalms.

Because the psalms were written as poetry, they use a lot of word pictures to describe what God is like. Here are just a few of the many, many ways God is presented in the psalms:

Creator (8:3–4)
Deliverer (18:2)
Father (68:5–6)
King (93:1–2)
Refuge (46:1)
Shepherd (23:1)
Shield (3:3)
Teacher (25:8–9)
Warrior (35:1–3)

While the psalms describe the many parts of God's character, they also put into words people's feelings about Him. In the psalms, you'll find words of praise for God, confessions of sin to God, expressions of confidence in God. You'll even find words of disappointment and frustration with God from people who were going through difficult times and wondered if God was really there for them. (Hint: The psalmists usually came around to the

WHO, WHAT, WHERE?

The Asaph who wrote Psalms 50 and 73–83 was a descendant of Abraham through Jacob's son Levi. He was one of the key musicians serving in the Jerusalem Temple during the time of King David. David appointed Asaph's descendants "to proclaim God's messages to the accompaniment of lyres, harps, and cymbals" (1 Chronicles 25:1).

POWER WORDS

The LORD is my shepherd; I have all that I need. He lets me rest in green meadows; he leads me beside peaceful streams. He renews my strength. He guides me along right paths, bringing honor to his name.

Psalm 23:1–3

DID YOU KNOW. . . ?

The book of Psalms is divided into five smaller collections, based on the time periods in which historians believe they were written or compiled. The five books are as follows:

Book One (Psalms 1–41): Psalms compiled, and mostly written, by David.

Book Two (Psalms 42–72): Psalms written by the sons of Korah and by David; likely compiled while Hezekiah was king of Judah.

Book Three (Psalms 73–89): Psalms written during the reigns of kings Hezekiah and Manasseh, but compiled while King Josiah ruled.

Book Four (Psalms 90–106): Includes the rest of the psalms written prior to the Babylonian Captivity, including one by Moses and a couple by David; the rest are by unknown writers.

Book Five (Psalms 107–150): Psalms written during the Jews' return from the Babylonian Captivity. Books four and five may have been compiled during the time of the prophet Nehemiah.

219

conclusion that God really was there, even when it seemed He was millions of miles away!) Many of the psalms ask God some really tough questions!

Proverbs

What It's About: This book is mostly a collection of short sayings and thoughts to encourage people of different ages and life situations to follow God and seek out wisdom. The book of Proverbs is different from most other books of the Bible in that it doesn't have a story line, but is instead a collection of practical tips for wise and godly living.

Important Characters/People: Solomon, Agur, Lemuel

The Writers: Most experts agree that the first 29 chapters of the book of Proverbs were written by a man known for his wisdom: King Solomon, the third king of Israel and son of King David. Solomon wrote his proverbs during his reign as king of Israel, which began around 1015 to 1020 BC. Chapter 30 of the book of Proverbs is credited to someone named Agur, who may have been a friend of Solomon's or who may have been Solomon himself, writing under another name. Chapter 31 is credited to King Lemuel. It is suggested by some that Lemuel is the name Bathsheba, Solomon's mother, gave to Solomon, so this may be a proverb from Bathsheba.

What You'll Find in the Book of Proverbs

Solomon's purpose for writing the proverbs—as well as the rewards for living by them—is found early in the book, in Proverbs 1:2–6. Solomon writes that he intends for these proverbs to give wisdom, instruction, and understanding to the reader, to teach his readers to live carefully.

God told Solomon that He had given the young king wisdom and understanding (1 Kings 3:12). Later in his life, Solomon didn't apply the wisdom God had given him, and it cost him and his kingdom dearly. But he recorded a lot of wisdom in this book and in the next book of the Bible, Ecclesiastes.

Solomon writes that he intends for these proverbs to give wisdom, instruction, and understanding to the reader, to teach his readers to live carefully.

WHAT'S IN IT FOR ME?

Many times in the book of Proverbs, Solomon calls his readers "my son." In the Hebrew culture of that time, all male descendants of a king were considered that king's sons, so Solomon wrote to give future kings of Israel wisdom and understanding. The book of Proverbs is still a great source of teaching for all young people. Read the book through once and see what kind of wisdom God might be trying to teach you.

During most of Solomon's reign, the nation of Israel was at an all-time high in a lot of areas. The people worshipped God and lived in a time of prosperity. The surrounding nations treated Israel and its king with amazing respect. Leaders from all over the known world traveled to Israel to hear Solomon speak (see 1 Kings 4:34).

Chapter 31 begins by discouraging the use of strong drink, and continues by describing the perfect wife.

Sometimes, the proverbs included together in the same chapter seem completely unrelated to one another, but they all speak to important life issues, such as work, money, relationships, temptation, drinking, laziness, discipline, seeking God, and raising children.

Ecclesiastes

What It's About: "These are the words of the Teacher, King David's son, who ruled in Jerusalem" (1:1). The book of Ecclesiastes points out that life is futile and meaningless when we don't seek and follow God as our top priority.

Important Characters/People: The Teacher, God, wise men, fools

The Writer: The book of Ecclesiastes doesn't name its author, but several verses imply that it was King Solomon. Some experts believe Solomon wrote this book late in his life to help teach others the lessons he had learned from his own wrong choices.

What You'll Find in the Book of Ecclesiastes

Early in his reign as king of Israel, Solomon followed his father's instructions to the letter. He followed God and kept all His commandments. God rewarded Solomon's faithfulness by giving him power, prosperity, popularity, and other earthly blessings. Sadly, later in his life, Solomon abandoned his God and chased after worldly pleasures he had been warned about. The results were disastrous—for Solomon himself and for the kingdom of Israel.

Solomon reigned as king from around 970 BC to about 930 BC. Bible experts believe he wrote the book of Ecclesiastes near the end of his reign—around 935 BC. If Solomon is the author of this book, then it is the reflections of a man who had learned some very hard lessons. He had every earthly blessing a man could want—money, power, respect, just to

POWER WORDS

Don't let the excitement of youth cause you to forget your Creator. Honor him in your youth before you grow old and say, "Life is not pleasant anymore."

Ecclesiastes 12:1

WHAT'S IN IT FOR ME?

Solomon wrote, "Whatever you do, do well" (Ecclesiastes 9:10). That's great advice. Ask yourself, do you do everything you do to the best of your ability? Are you the best son or daughter you can be? The best brother or sister you can be? Are you the best student you can be?

WHAT'S iN iT FOR ME?

In the end, after writing about a life of futility and hopelessness apart from God, the Teacher in the book of Ecclesiastes concludes with these wise words: "Fear God and keep His commandments, for this is man's all. For God will bring every work into judgment, including every secret thing, whether good or evil" (12:13–14 NKJV). That's great advice for anyone to follow!

name a few—but he understood that none of those things was enough to give him a life of joy and happiness. True fulfillment came only when he made God the center of everything he did.

Throughout Ecclesiastes, the word *vanity* (other translations use the word *meaningless*) and the phrase "under the sun" occur repeatedly. The lesson of this book is that everything we can enjoy in this world (under the sun) will one day be left behind; and it all means nothing if we don't make God the center of everything we do, say, and think.

The first seven chapters of this book are the words of a very unhappy man. He has tried to find fulfillment in knowledge, worldly wisdom, riches, work, and other things. But he realizes these things, though they may bring some pleasure for a while, won't give him the purpose, fulfillment, and happiness that can be found only in eternal things.

The final four chapters of Ecclesiastes are the Teacher's advice on how we should live if we want to find purpose, fulfillment, and happiness. He has left God and tried everything else "under the sun" and has learned (the hard way) that the very best this world has to offer is nothing compared with living a life centered on loving God and keeping His commandments. (Read the Teacher's words in chapter 12.) ✖

Song of Solomon (also known as Song of Songs)

What It's About: Solomon writes about the beauty of married love. Though the name of God is never mentioned in this book, some experts believe the Song of Solomon was written to compare the love of a devoted spouse to the love of God, who is deeply devoted to His people.

Important Characters/People: The husband and his wife

The Writer: King Solomon wrote more than 1,000 songs, but he calls this his "Song of Songs." Some experts believe it's possible that Solomon didn't write this book but that it was written *about* him.

What You'll Find in the Song of Solomon

The two main characters in this book are Solomon and his wife, the beautiful young Shulamite woman. The words in the poem are those of Solomon, the young woman, and the daughters of Jerusalem.

POWER WORDS

He escorts me to the banquet hall; it's obvious how much he loves me.

Song of Solomon 2:4

In one of the Bible's weirdest visions, the prophet Ezekiel sees dry, long-dead skeletons being covered with muscles and skin, and coming back to life. This painting, from 1630, is an artist's idea of how Ezekiel 37 might have looked.

CHAPTER 5

God's Messengers

Major and Minor Prophets (Isaiah through Malachi)

The Old Testament includes 17 "prophetic" books—books that warn people of God's judgment and encourage them with promises of forgiveness and restoration if they will turn back to Him.

The Old Testament includes the writings of five "major" prophets and 12 "minor" prophets. The difference isn't that the minor prophets are less important than the others, but that their books are much shorter than those of Isaiah, Jeremiah (who also wrote Lamentations), Ezekiel, and Daniel.

The books of Old Testament prophecy include some of the best-known stories in the Bible. For example, you can read about Daniel in the lions' den and his friends Shadrach, Meshach, and Abednego in the book of Daniel, and you can read about the prophet Jonah finding himself stuck in a giant fish's belly in the book of Jonah.

Isaiah

What It's About: Even though the people of Israel had fallen away from God and would suffer the consequences of their sin, God promises a Messiah to provide forgiveness and save them from their sins.

Important Characters/People: Isaiah, King Hezekiah, the Messiah, kings of Judah and Israel

The Writer: The prophet Isaiah was the son of a man named Amoz, and his ministry to the people of Judah began during the reign of King Uzziah and ended during the reign of King Hezekiah. Isaiah preached during the reigns of four kings. The book of Isaiah was written between 701 and 681 BC.

What You'll Find in the Book of Isaiah

Like the other Old Testament prophets, Isaiah warned the people that they faced God's punishment for their sin. But He also wrote about the coming Messiah, a Savior who would take the punishment for the people's sins and give them peace with God. In fact, chapters 40–66 of Isaiah's long prophecy describe God's restoration of Israel, His promised salvation, and His eternal kingdom.

The prophet Isaiah preached mostly to the kingdom of Judah. At that time, Judah's relationship with God was up and down. There were times when the people stuck close to God, but there were also times when they rebelled against Him.

One interesting fact about the book of Isaiah: it is the Old Testament prophetic book most often quoted in the New Testament (the Psalms are the most quoted book overall). The New Testament directly quotes Isaiah 66 times. Also, Isaiah contains more prophecies about Jesus than any other Old Testament book of prophecy.

The book of Isaiah contains literally dozens of prophecies about the life and work of Jesus. These include His virgin birth (7:14), that His ministry would include healing people of sickness and disease (35:5–6), and that He would suffer and die willingly to give people forgiveness and peace with God (53).

POWER WORDS

He was pierced for our rebellion, crushed for our sins. He was beaten so we could be whole. He was whipped so we could be healed. All of us, like sheep, have strayed away. We have left God's paths to follow our own. Yet the Lord laid on him the sins of us all.

Isaiah 53:5-6

WHAT'S IN IT FOR ME?

Look up Isaiah 9:1-2 and you'll find a wonderful promise that the Jewish Messiah—Jesus—would come not only for the Jews but for all people. That means that no matter what race or people group you come from, Jesus came to earth and lived, died, and was raised from the dead for you!

Isaiah contains more prophecies about Jesus than any other Old Testament book of prophecy.

Jeremiah

What It's About: The prophet Jeremiah warns the people of Judah of coming punishment and suffering because they have abandoned God.

Important Characters/People: Jeremiah, King Jehoiakim, Hananiah, Baruch

The Writer: Jeremiah was a young boy when God called him to be a prophet (1:6). He was the son of a priest named Hilkiah. His ministry started during the reign of King Josiah (about 617 BC) and ended several years after the Babylonians destroyed Jerusalem, an event he foretold in his writings.

What You'll Find in the Book of Jeremiah

Jeremiah's message to the people of Judah was pretty much all bad news. God had given the people warning after warning through earlier prophets to turn back to Him, but they had refused. Jeremiah warned that God would send the Babylonians to destroy Jerusalem and take the people of Judah into captivity.

The people of Judah—especially the leaders—didn't like what Jeremiah had to say. They made fun of Jeremiah, beat him, and imprisoned him. But Jeremiah's words came true. Chapter 52 of his prophetic book describes the Babylonian invasion of Judah. ✖

POWER WORDS

"O Israel, can I not do to you as this potter has done to his clay? As the clay is in the potter's hand, so are you in my hand."

Jeremiah 18:6

WHO, WHAT, WHERE?

Baruch was an assistant to Jeremiah who wrote down all the words the prophet received from God and then went to the Temple and read those prophecies to the people. When Baruch read the prophecies to the princes of the land, the princes warned him and Jeremiah to hide. After Jehoiakim, the king of Judah, destroyed the first copy of the prophecies, Baruch rewrote it from Jeremiah's dictation.

Lamentations

What It's About: The prophet Jeremiah grieves over the destruction that has come on the city of Jerusalem and the people of Judah—the same destruction he had warned about in the book of Jeremiah.

Important Characters/People: Jeremiah, Zedekiah, the Babylonians

The Writer: Jeremiah the prophet

What You'll Find in the Book of Lamentations

Jeremiah has often been called "the weeping prophet," and the book of Lamentations shows why. It isn't very pleasant to read the words of a godly man who saw the death and destruction in his homeland and mourns over what has happened. ✖

Ezekiel

What It's About: Even though things look hopeless for the people of Judah, who are living in captivity in Babylon, God promises that their nation will one day be restored.

Important Characters/People: Ezekiel, Pelatiah, Jaazaniah, Nebuchadnezzar, Pharaoh

The Writer: Ezekiel was a priest and the son of Buzi. He was about 25 years old when he was among the people of Judah who were taken to Babylon after King Nebuchadnezzar attacked Judah and took many of the people of Jerusalem away. About five years later, while Ezekiel was in Babylon, God came to him in a vision and called him to minister to the rebellious Israelites. The book of Ezekiel was probably written between 593 and 565 BC.

What You'll Find in the Book of Ezekiel

Like Jeremiah, Ezekiel wrote a lot about God's judgment. But he also wrote about God's love and mercy for His people. Yes, God had judged and punished the people of Judah, but He would also forgive them and one day would allow them to return to their homeland.

The book of Ezekiel can be split into four sections. Chapters 1–24 are about the ruin of Jerusalem when the Babylonians attacked, and chapters 25–32 are about God's judgment on the nations around Jerusalem. In chapter 33, Ezekiel records God's call for His people to turn back to him. Chapters 34–48 are chapters of hope for the nation of Israel, because they promise that Israel will be restored and rebuilt in the future.

Daniel

What It's About: Daniel—as well as some of his friends—remain true to God while in captivity in Babylon. God blesses their faithfulness, even though they are in a really tough situation.

Important Characters/People: Daniel, Nebuchadnezzar, Darius, Belshazzar, Shadrach, Meshach, Abednego

The Writer: Daniel was a young man when the Babylonians destroyed Jerusalem and took many of the people of Judah captive. During the 70-year Babylonian Captivity, Daniel remained true to God in every way and was rewarded with knowledge, wisdom, and power. The book of Daniel was probably written between 540 and 530 BC.

What You'll Find in the Book of Daniel

During the Babylonian Captivity, the prophet Daniel served in King Nebuchadnezzar's royal court. He also served several rulers who succeeded Nebuchadnezzar. In the book of Daniel, you can read about the prophet's actions and the visions and prophecies he received during this time.

Daniel describes and interprets several dreams in this book, including one dream Nebuchadnezzar had about an image of several metals and clay. (You can read the whole story in Daniel 2.) Daniel revealed the meaning of a second dream to Nebuchadnezzar, predicting his downfall until he worshipped God. (That story is found in chapter 4.)

During the reign of King Belshazzar, Nebuchadnezzar's son, Daniel interpreted the meaning of some mysterious handwriting that appeared on the wall during a banquet. As a result, Belshazzar made Daniel the third highest ruler in the kingdom; but later that night, Belshazzar died.

When Darius took over the kingdom of Babylon, he planned to make Daniel head of the whole kingdom, but other leaders plotted against Daniel. They knew he would never worship anyone but God, and they tricked the king into punishing any person who worshipped anyone but the king. For disobeying this law, Daniel was thrown into the lions' den. But when Daniel came out safely, Darius honored the God who had kept Daniel safe. (You can read the whole story in Daniel 6.)

Daniel's prophecies predicted the coming of several important world figures, including Alexander the Great, Cleopatra, and (most important) Jesus Christ.

Rembrandt's painting *Belshazzar's Feast*

Hosea

What It's About: God calls a prophet to marry an immoral woman named Gomer. When she runs away from Hosea with another man, God tells Hosea to go after her and try to win her back.

Important Characters/People: Hosea, Gomer

The Writer: Hosea served the people of Israel around the time of the reigns of kings Uzziah of Judah (around 792-750 BC), Jotham of Judah (750-735 BC), Ahaz of Judah (735-715 BC), Hezekiah of Judah (715-697 BC), and Jeroboam of Israel (793-753 BC).

What You'll Find in the Book of Hosea

God called Hosea to live a very difficult family life. He commanded Hosea to marry Gomer, a woman Hosea no doubt knew wouldn't be faithful to him. Gomer wasn't faithful to Hosea, but he went after her to try to win her back to himself. God used Hosea's family life to show the people how He loved them despite their unfaithfulness to Him and how He was working to bring them back to Him. ❌

Joel

What It's About: Swarms of grasshoppers descend on the nation of Israel, devouring every living plant in their path. The grasshoppers are an example of God's judgment on a sinful people. In the middle of this plague, God promises salvation to those who turn to Him.

Important Characters/People: Joel, leaders in Jerusalem and Judah

The Writer: Joel, the son of Pethuel (Joel 1:1), was an educated man who knew the words of the earlier prophets. It isn't known for certain when Joel prophesied, but some experts believe it was around the time of the reign of King Joash (835-796 BC). The book of Joel was probably written around that time.

What You'll Find in the Book of Joel

It isn't certain whether swarms of grasshoppers actually devoured all of Israel's crops or if they were part of a story God used to make a point. Either way, however, Joel used the example to warn the people of what would happen if they didn't turn back to God. If they didn't turn back, armies from surrounding nations would invade and "devour" the land, just as the grasshoppers had devoured all the plants there. But if the people did turn back to God, He would forgive them and bless them. ⊗

Amos

What It's About: God wanted His people to understand that He wanted them to treat people fairly and justly, not just to observe a bunch of religious rules.

Important Characters/People: Amos, Jeroboam II, Uzziah, Amaziah

The Writer: The prophet Amos was a shepherd and fruit picker from a small village in Judah. He was an uneducated man who ministered during the reigns of King Uzziah of Judah and King Jeroboam II of Israel. This book was probably written around 756 BC.

What You'll Find in the Book of Amos

Amos's message was mostly directed to the nation of Israel. Things were going pretty well in Israel at that time, but the people committed many sins, including idolatry, greed, and mistreatment of poor people. Mostly, the people of Israel ignored Amos's warning of God's judgment for their sins.

The first part of this book includes warnings of judgment on the nations around Israel, and then on the nation of Judah. The second part warns of even worse judgment on Israel. Amos's message is clear: God's judgment is coming soon. The book ends like many other Old Testament books of prophecy—with the promise of better things in the future for some of the people of Israel. ⊗

Obadiah

What It's About: God announces that the city of Edom will be judged for taking part in Jerusalem's destruction.

Important Characters/People: Obadiah, Edom's leaders

The Writer: The prophet Obadiah. The Bible says nothing about Obadiah's family or personal life. The book of Obadiah was probably written around 845 BC.

What You'll Find in the Book of Obadiah

Obadiah is the shortest book in the Old Testament—only 21 verses. The prophet Obadiah delivers the message that the nation of Edom will be destroyed because the Edomites celebrated the bad things that had happened to Israel and because they fought against Israel after the Israelites asked for Edom's help against their enemies. ❌

FUN BIBLE TRIVIA

The name Obadiah means "serving God." The prophet Obadiah is one of 13 men by that name in the Old Testament.

Jonah

What It's About: A prophet runs the other way when God tells him to go to a city called Nineveh to preach. Because of his disobedience, Jonah is swallowed by a giant sea creature and stays in its stomach for three days.

Important Characters/People: Jonah, the king of Nineveh, the sailors

The Writer: This is Jonah's story, but it is written in the third person ("he" instead of "I"), so another writer probably recorded the words. This book was written around 760 BC.

Nineveh was a large city located on the eastern bank of the Tigris River. The city was built by a descendant of Noah named Asshur (Genesis 10:11), who also built the cities of Rehoboth and Calah (see Genesis 10:11). During the time of Jonah, Nineveh was the capital of the Assyrian Empire.

WHAT'S IN IT FOR ME?

The obvious lesson from the book of Jonah is that it's always the best choice to obey when God tells us to do something. But there's another lesson here, and it's one Jesus taught when He told His followers, "Love your enemies! Pray for those who persecute you!" (Matthew 5:44).

What You'll Find in the Book of Jonah

Jonah lived and preached around the time of King Jeroboam II of Israel. When God called him to travel to Nineveh to preach to the people there, Jonah refused. Being a prophet, Jonah knew that the people of Nineveh would become Israel's mortal enemies. He wasn't about to do anything to help them!

Rather than go to Nineveh, Jonah hightailed it to a port city called Joppa, where he boarded a ship bound for Tarshish—exactly the opposite direction God had told him to go. When a violent storm struck, threatening to sink the ship and kill everyone aboard, Jonah confessed to the sailors that he was running from God, and they threw Jonah overboard.

Jonah was swallowed by a big sea creature, and while inside the animal, he had time to think about his actions—and the fact that he was running from God. When Jonah praised God, the creature vomited him onto dry land.

Jonah went to Nineveh, just as God had told him to do, and preached there. Amazingly, the people of Nineveh, led by their king, turned to God, who spared the city.

Micah

What It's About: God announces that Judah (the southern kingdom) and Israel (the northern kingdom) will be judged for worshipping idols instead of God and for their mistreatment and abuse of the poor and needy around them.

Important Characters/People: Micah, Jotham, Ahaz, Hezekiah

The Writer: The prophet Micah was a native of Moresheth in southern Judah who ministered during the reigns of Kings Jotham, Ahaz, and Hezekiah of Judah (750–686 BC). This book was written around 700 BC.

What You'll Find in the Book of Micah

Micah preached against idolatry and cheating the poor and warned that both Judah and Israel would be destroyed by outside invaders.

Like many other prophets, Micah preached a message of God's judgment but also of God's mercy. God would forgive the sins of His people and would not remain angry with them forever—simply because He loves showing mercy. ❌

POWER WORDS

O people, the Lord has told you what is good, and this is what he requires of you: to do what is right, to love mercy, and to walk humbly with your God.

Micah 6:8

Nahum

What It's About: The powerful city of Nineveh, which had repented a century earlier when Jonah preached there, will be destroyed for its evilness.

Important Characters/People: Nahum, the king of Nineveh

The Writer: The prophet Nahum. Nahum lived in a place called Elkosh. He preached to Judah after Assyria had captured Israel. This book was written between 663 and 612 BC.

What You'll Find in the Book of Nahum

This book of prophecy is kind of a sequel (continues a story begun in another book) to the book of Jonah. Even though God had shown mercy on the city after the people repented when they heard Jonah preach, they returned to their old ways. The city was destroyed not long after Nahum preached to the people there. ❌

Habakkuk

What It's About: A prophet questions God—and receives an answer—when he learns that God will allow the evil Chaldeans to destroy the nation of Judah.

Important Characters/People: Habakkuk, the leaders of Judah, Jehoahaz

The Writer: The prophet Habakkuk. Nothing is known of his personal life or his family. He served during the reign of King Josiah of Judah. This book was written around 600 BC.

WHAT'S iN iT FOR ME?

Ever been in a situation where you just wanted to tell God, "It's not fair!" If you haven't, you most likely will at some point. Then you can follow Habakkuk's example: Talk to God about your situation. Tell Him what you think is unfair about it. Then wait. Even if you don't have an answer, even if things seem more unfair than ever, trust God and allow Him to use your situation for your best.

What You'll Find in the Book of Habakkuk

Being a prophet of God, Habakkuk knew what was ahead for his nation. It was only a matter of time before Judah's mortal enemies, the Chaldeans, attacked and destroyed Judah.

Habakkuk understood that God had to punish his people's sinful, idolatrous behavior. What he couldn't understand was why God would use such an evil, godless people to do it.

In time, Habakkuk had his answer. And even though it wasn't the answer he wanted, he still accepted that God knew what He was doing and why He was doing it the way He was. ❌

Zephaniah

What It's About: God warns of a coming "day of the Lord," when His people will face judgment, but He also promises restoration for the nation of Israel.

Important Characters/People: Zephaniah, Josiah, Nebuchadnezzar

The Writer: Zephaniah was the son of Cushi and great-grandson of King Hezekiah, the godly king of Judah. He preached in the days of King Josiah of Judah (around 640–610 BC). This book was written during that time.

What You'll Find in the Book of Zephaniah

Like Jeremiah, Zephaniah preached of a terrible time of judgment and suffering by the people of Judah because they had moved so far away from their God. Also like Jeremiah, Zephaniah pleaded with the people to seek God before it was too late (Zephaniah 2:1–3).

Zephaniah's book closes with a promising message. Though the prophet agreed that hard times were ahead for his people, he also delivered a message of salvation and restoration (3:8–20).

> **POWER WORDS**
>
> "For the LORD your God is living among you. He is a mighty savior. He will take delight in you with gladness. With his love, he will calm all your fears. He will rejoice over you with joyful songs."
>
> Zephaniah 3:17

Haggai

What It's About: The Jews return to Jerusalem after being held captive in Babylon and are commanded to rebuild God's Temple.

Important Characters/People: Haggai, Joshua, Darius, Cyrus, Zerubbabel, Shealtiel

The Writer: The prophet Haggai preached after the Jews had returned from captivity in Babylon to their homeland. The Bible says nothing about his personal life or his family. This book was written in 520 BC, in the second year of Darius the king (1:1).

What You'll Find in the Book of Haggai

What the people saw when they returned to Jerusalem from the Babylonian Captivity broke their hearts. The beautiful Temple that King Solomon had built centuries before was nothing but a pile of rubble—thanks to the efforts of King Nebuchadnezzar's men, who had attacked and destroyed the city 70 years earlier.

God had promised that this second Temple would be greater than the original Temple that Solomon had built. The people had begun the work of rebuilding the Temple, but when opposition from surrounding kingdoms arose, the work stopped and the people pursued their own interests.

The unfinished Temple sat in place for 16 years before Haggai came on the scene with this simple message: Finish what you've started! When you do, God will give you prosperity.

POWER WORDS

Be strong, all you people still left in the land. And now get to work, for I am with you, says the LORD of Heaven's Armies.

Haggai 2:4

Zechariah

What It's About: The Jewish people are commanded to get busy rebuilding the Temple—and watch for the arrival of their Messiah.

Important Characters/People: Zechariah, Zerubbabel, Joshua, Darius, Heldai, Tobijah, Jedaiah

The Writer: Zechariah, who is identified in the Bible as the son of Berekiah (1:1), wrote most or all of the book of Zechariah, but some experts believe a second, unnamed writer contributed chapters 9–14. This book was probably written between 520 and 475 BC.

What You'll Find in Zechariah

Like Haggai, Zechariah preached to the people of Judah after their return from Babylon. Also like Haggai, Zechariah's words were written and spoken to encourage the people to dedicate themselves to finishing the new Temple.

Zechariah preached a message of encouragement, for the Temple would one day be home to the Messiah Himself. The first eight chapters of this prophecy focus on the need to finish the project, while the last six focus on the blessings in store for the Jewish people once the task is completed.

FUN BIBLE TRIVIA

Zechariah's prophecy of the Messiah riding a donkey into Jerusalem (9:9) was fulfilled perfectly in Jesus' "triumphal entry" (Matthew 21:1-11). Also, the prophecy "They will look on me whom they have pierced" (12:10) refers to the Roman soldier's spearing of Christ after the Crucifixion (John 19:34).

Malachi

What It's About: God warns the Jewish people to be more careful with their attitude toward Him and what He had told them to do.

Important Characters/People: Malachi, Persian rulers, Jewish religious leaders

The Writer: Other than what is in his book, not a lot is known about the prophet Malachi. He lived during the time of Nehemiah and Ezra, but he is not mentioned in the books of Nehemiah or Ezra. The book of Malachi was written between 440 and 400 BC.

What You'll Find in the Book of Malachi

The words in the book of Malachi are directed toward the Jews in Jerusalem about 100 years after the end of the Babylonian Captivity. The people were doing what they thought God wanted them to do, but in their hearts they had strayed from God.

Sadly, they were doing the same things and committing the same sins that had led to their captivity in the first place! The men were divorcing their wives to marry foreign women, the people weren't giving of their income the way God had instructed them, and the priests weren't giving God the best when they offered the required sacrifices.

God wanted His people to know how much He loved them, but He wanted them to see that they weren't returning that love. So, speaking through Malachi, God called the people to return to true worship and true love of God.

CHAPTER 6

The Bible's Main Man

The Story of Jesus (Matthew through John)

The time between the writing of the final book of the Old Testament—Malachi—and the birth of Jesus is sometimes called "the silent years," simply because God did not speak through prophets during those 400 years.

But God finally broke the silence with the arrival of the long-awaited Messiah, Jesus Christ. The story of His life is told in what are called the Gospels, the four books you'll read about in this chapter.

As you read through the Gospels, the first four books of the New Testament, you'll notice that they cover many of the same events in the life of Jesus. Even so, from one book to the next, the events may look very different—at least at first. Some of the Gospels include information you won't find in the others. Likewise, some Gospels leave out events that are included in one or more of the other Gospels.

That's because the Gospels were written by men with different life experiences and different ways of looking at things. What was really important to one writer may not have been as important to the others. When they wrote their Gospels, they focused on the things about Jesus' life they thought were most important—or most important to their readers.

Now, let's take a look at what you'll find in the four Gospels, starting where the New Testament starts: with the Gospel of Matthew.

DID YOU KNOW. . . ?

The four Gospels included in the Bible (Matthew, Mark, Luke, and John) were not the only stories of the life and ministry of Jesus written during the first and second centuries. Far from it! Dozens and dozens of "gospels" were written during that time, and Christian leaders discussed—and often disagreed about—which ones were accurate accounts and which were not. The four Gospels in the Bible today were approved for inclusion at meetings—called councils—of Christian leaders in the fourth century.

The Gospel of Matthew

What It's About: The apostle Matthew writes about the things Jesus did and the words He spoke—and how they fulfilled Old Testament prophecies.

Important Characters/People: Jesus, Mary and Joseph, the wise men from the East, John the Baptist, Herod, the centurion, the 12 apostles

The Writer: Most Bible experts agree that the writer of the Gospel of Matthew was Matthew (also known as Levi), one of Jesus' 12 original disciples. Luke 5:27-28 tells us that Matthew left everything to follow Jesus when Jesus called him. Some experts believe that Matthew wrote his Gospel between AD 60 and 65, but others believe he wrote it as many as 20 years later.

POWER WORDS

"Love your enemies! Pray for those who persecute you! In that way, you will be acting as true children of your Father in heaven. For he gives his sunlight to both the evil and the good, and he sends rain on the just and the unjust alike."

Matthew 5:44-45

WHO, WHAT, WHERE?

If you were going to pick someone to write the story of Jesus' life and ministry here on earth, it probably wouldn't be a guy like Matthew. Before Jesus called him to be a disciple, Matthew was a tax collector for the hated Roman government—a job that most Jews despised because the tax collectors worked for the Romans and engaged in dishonest business practices.

What You'll Find in the Gospel of Matthew

The Gospel of Matthew contains a lot of great messages for any Christian, but it was written specifically for the Jewish people of Matthew's time, especially to the first Jewish Christians.

For centuries, the Jews had suffered under foreign rule, and many of them were more than ready for their Messiah to come. Though Jesus wasn't exactly what most of the people expected, He was everything the Old Testament prophets said He would be.

Many times over, Matthew points out to his readers the things that Jesus did or said that fulfilled Old Testament prophecies about the coming Messiah. His Gospel quotes about 60 references to Old Testament prophecies and directly quotes the Old Testament about 40 times.

As you read the Gospel of Matthew, you'll notice that he uses the word *fulfilled* many times. Here are a few examples:

- "Joseph obeyed. He got up, took the child and his mother under cover of darkness. They were out of town and well on their way by daylight. They lived in Egypt until Herod's death. This Egyptian exile *fulfilled* what Hosea had preached: 'I called my son out of Egypt'" (2:14 MSG).

- "That evening a lot of demon-afflicted people were brought to him. He relieved the inwardly tormented. He cured the bodily ill. He *fulfilled* Isaiah's well-known sermon: He took our illnesses, He carried our diseases" (8:16 MSG).

- "All Jesus did that day was tell stories—a long storytelling afternoon. His storytelling *fulfilled* the prophecy: I will open my mouth and tell stories; I will bring out into the open things hidden since the world's first day" (13:34 the MSG).

- "All this was done that it might be *fulfilled* which was spoken by the prophet, saying: 'Tell the daughter of Zion, "Behold, your King is coming to you, lowly, and sitting on a donkey, a colt, the foal of a donkey"'" (21:4–5 NKJV).

- "Then they crucified Him, and divided His garments, casting lots, that it might be *fulfilled* which was spoken by the prophet: 'They divided My garments among them, and for My clothing they cast lots'" (27:35 NKJV).

> **POWER WORDS**
>
> *"Keep on asking, and you will receive what you ask for. Keep on seeking, and you will find. Keep on knocking, and the door will be opened to you. For everyone who asks, receives. Everyone who seeks, finds. And to everyone who knocks, the door will be opened."*
>
> Matthew 7:7-8

In a nutshell, Matthew's message for his audience was this: "Brothers and sisters, Jesus—the man I spent more than three years of my life with—is the Messiah we have been waiting for. But don't just take my word for it. Look at scripture and you'll see that His words and actions, as well as the things that happened to Him, prove who He is!"

The Gospel of Matthew starts out by referring to Jesus as "the son of David" NIV (the first fulfillment of prophecy that Matthew points out) and then traces Jesus' family tree from Abraham all the way through the centuries (and 14 generations) to Jesus' earthly father, Joseph. It then records the story of Jesus' birth and childhood (1:18–2:23), the ministry of John the Baptist (3:1–12), Jesus' baptism (3:13–17), His temptation by the devil (4:1–11), the calling of some of His disciples (4:12–22), and the beginning of His earthly ministry.

The Best Sermon Ever Preached!

Matthew is the only Gospel to include a fairly long and very detailed set of Jesus' teachings called the Sermon on the Mount (even though Luke 6:17–49 is a shortened version of the same teaching). In chapters 5–7, you can read about some tough—but very practical— teachings by Jesus on a wide variety of subjects.

If you want to know what Jesus had to say about what God wants you to be, how He wants you to approach Him, and how you are to treat other people, take some time to read Matthew 5–7. And don't miss out on what Jesus had to say about prayer in Matthew 7:7–12.

WHAT'S IN IT FOR ME?

The Sermon on the Mount starts out with eight statements called Beatitudes, which means "statements of blessing":

"Blessed are the poor in spirit, for theirs is the kingdom of heaven" (Matthew 5:3 NKJV).

"Blessed are those who mourn, for they shall be comforted" (Matthew 5:4 NKJV).

"Blessed are the meek, for they shall inherit the earth" (Matthew 5:5 NKJV).

"Blessed are those who hunger and thirst for righteousness, for they shall be filled" (Matthew 5:6 NKJV).

"Blessed are the merciful, for they shall obtain mercy" (Matthew 5:7 NKJV).

"Blessed are the pure in heart, for they shall see God" (Matthew 5:8 NKJV).

"Blessed are the peacemakers, for they shall be called sons of God" (Matthew 5:9 NKJV).

"Blessed are those who are persecuted for righteousness' sake, for theirs is the kingdom of heaven" (Matthew 5:10 NKJV).

The Gospel of Mark

What It's About: This Gospel tells how Jesus proved that He is the Savior of all people, not just the Jews, by serving others, by suffering, by dying, and by being raised from the dead.

Important Characters/People: Jesus, John the Baptist, Herod, Pontius Pilate, the 12 apostles, the women who followed Jesus, the Pharisees

The Writer: The Gospel of Mark does not name its writer, but it is generally agreed that the writer was John Mark, who wasn't one of the original 12 disciples but who was a close associate of the apostle Peter. It is believed that John Mark received from Peter an eyewitness account of everything that appears in this Gospel. The Gospel of Mark was probably written around AD 57, making it one of the oldest books—if not *the* oldest book—of the New Testament.

What You'll Find in the Gospel of Mark

The Gospel of Mark is the shortest of the four Gospels. That's because Mark left out a lot of details you'll find in the other Gospels—especially Matthew and Luke. For example, Mark doesn't mention anything at all about Jesus' family tree, and he doesn't mention anything about the virgin birth. Also missing is any part of the famous Sermon on the Mount, which is covered in three chapters in Matthew and one in Luke.

Even though this book tells basically the same story as Matthew, one of the things you might notice is that it doesn't focus on how Jesus fulfilled Old Testament prophecies. In fact, Mark quotes the Old Testament only twice. This is because Mark wasn't writing to a Jewish audience the way Matthew was. Instead, he was writing to Gentile (non-Jewish) Christians, who wouldn't have been as concerned about Old Testament prophecies as their Jewish brothers and sisters.

POWER WORDS

Jesus called out to them, "Come, follow me, and I will show you how to fish for people!"

Mark 1:17

Mark understood what Jesus taught during His time on earth—and what the Old Testament prophecies about Jesus said: that Jesus was the Messiah or Savior, not just for the Jews+ but for people of all races.

As you read this book, you'll see that Jesus didn't just talk about serving others and sacrificing Himself for them—He put actions behind those words. After introducing his readers to Jesus with an account of His baptism by John the Baptist in the Jordan River, Mark writes about Jesus' life, death, and resurrection. Mark includes some of Jesus' teaching—including some of the parables—but he focuses more on the things Jesus did.

Starting in chapter 11, Mark's Gospel tells the story of Jesus' arrival in Jerusalem, where He would spend most of the last week of His life on earth. Chapters 11–13 cover Jesus' teaching and actions in the city of Jerusalem before His arrest and crucifixion. During that time, He also dealt with people who didn't like what He was doing and teaching and who wanted to kill Him because of His words and actions. He also taught His disciples about the things that would happen in the future (chapter 13).

Chapters 14 and 15 tell the story of Jesus' suffering and death, and chapter 16 covers His resurrection and some of the things He did and said before He returned to heaven to be with His Father. ❌

The Gospel of Luke

What It's About: Luke writes about how God's offer of salvation through Jesus is available to all people, not just the Jews. The Gospel of Luke focuses on Jesus as a perfect man—as the One who was fully God but also fully human. . . and perfect as both. In Luke, we can see Jesus as a man of amazing love and compassion for people around Him.

Important Characters/People: Jesus, Mary and Joseph, Zacharias and Elizabeth, the shepherds, Anna, Simeon, the 12 disciples, the Pharisees, Pilate, Herod

The Writer: Luke was a physician, historian, writer, and missionary, who accompanied the apostle Paul on his third of three missionary journeys. Luke was not one of Jesus' original disciples or even an eyewitness to His life here on earth. It isn't known for certain when he became a Christian. Luke is the only Gentile (non-Jew) to write a book of the Bible—in fact, he wrote two: the Gospel of Luke and the book of Acts. Luke probably wrote his Gospel between AD 58 and 65.

What You'll Find in the Gospel of Luke

Luke's Gospel is the only one of the four that is written *chronologically*, meaning in the order that everything happened. It is written to someone named Theophilus (his name means "lover of God"). Luke begins his Gospel by explaining to Theophilus that he had investigated all the accounts written in the book.

Luke was apparently quite the historian, because his Gospel includes a lot of information not included in the other Gospels. For example, Luke gives his readers a detailed story of Jesus' birth—as well as the birth of John the Baptist. Many of the stories you hear told around Christmastime come from Luke's Gospel—including the angel's announcement to the shepherds that their Messiah had been born. (You can read that story in Luke 2:8–20.)

Luke also is the only Gospel writer to include anything about Jesus' childhood. In Luke, you can read about Jesus' circumcision, His presentation at the Temple, His visit with a godly man named Simeon and a prophetess named Anna, and the way He amazed Jewish religious scholars with His understanding when he was only 12 years old. (You can read these stories in Luke 2:21–52.)

WHO, WHAT, WHERE?

The angel named Gabriel, who appeared to Mary to tell her she would be the mother of the Messiah (see Luke 1:26–38), is also mentioned in Daniel 9. Gabriel and Michael are the only angels mentioned by name in the Bible. Gabriel's name means "champion of God."

POWER WORDS

"Seek the Kingdom of God above all else, and he will give you everything you need."

Luke 12:31

WHO, WHAT, WHERE?

Golgotha, also known in Latin as "Calvary," is mentioned in Luke 23:33 as the place where the Romans executed criminals. Jesus was crucified there. Golgotha, which means "skull," is not far outside the city of Jerusalem.

Luke's Gospel includes 25 parables—stories Jesus told to illustrate important truths about the kingdom of God—including 17 that appear only in his Gospel. Two of Jesus' most famous parables—the good Samaritan (10:25–37) and the prodigal son (15:11–32)—appear only in Luke. He also records seven miracles of Jesus that aren't found in the other three Gospels.

Luke presents Jesus as a man who showed compassion to all people, including some the Jewish people of that time wanted nothing to do with. That includes the poor (6:20), Roman soldiers (7:1–10), widows (7:11–17), the "sinful" (7:36–50), the sick (8:43–48), Samaritans (10:33), lepers (17:11–19), and many others—including a dying thief on a cross beside Him (23:40–43).

Jesus is also seen in Luke as a man who valued women in His ministry. For example, in chapter 1, Mary and Elizabeth play important roles in the story, and in chapter 10, He visits the home of Mary and Martha of Bethany.

Like the other three Gospel writers, Luke wrote about Jesus' death and resurrection. He also added detailed accounts of Jesus' appearances to two believers on the Emmaus road and the 11 remaining disciples. At the end of Luke's Gospel, Jesus ascends to heaven to be with His Father.

The Gospel of John

What It's About: Jesus is God in the flesh—the Son of God—and the Savior of all people.

Important Characters/People: Jesus, John the Baptist, the Samaritan woman at the well, Mary Magdalene, Lazarus, Mary and Martha of Bethany, Pilate

Who Wrote It: The writer of the fourth Gospel is the apostle John, the brother of the apostle James. (Don't get him mixed up with John the Baptist.) John and James were the sons of a fisherman named Zebedee, and they were two of Jesus' original 12 disciples. In his Gospel, John refers to himself as "the disciple whom Jesus loved." John's Gospel was the last one of the four written. It was completed between AD 80 and 100. Experts believe John wrote his Gospel when he was very old, while he lived in a Greek city called Ephesus, where he served as a leader of the Ephesian church.

What You'll Find in the Gospel of John

The apostle John wastes no time in telling his readers what his Gospel is all about: "In the beginning was the Word, and the Word was with God, and the Word was God" (John 1:1 NKJV). The "Word" whom John wrote about is Jesus, and John wanted his readers to know that Jesus was no ordinary man and that He wasn't just a great teacher—He was God in the flesh!

The Gospel of John is different from the other three (Matthew, Mark, and Luke, which are called "synoptic Gospels" because they focus on many of the same events) in several important ways. John left out all of Jesus' parables and recorded only seven of His miracles.

John's Gospel focuses more on the spiritual part of Jesus' life and works. John records Jesus' explanation for coming to earth and His discussion of His relationship with God. As you read the Gospel of John, you'll notice that Jesus is often quoted as telling people that God had sent Him and that God was His Father.

John didn't include any of Jesus' parables in his Gospel, but he included some of Jesus' best-known miracles. In chapter 2, you can read the account of Jesus turning water into wine at a wedding in a place called Cana. Chapter 9 includes the story of Jesus healing a man who had been born blind and His teaching about that healing, and chapter 11 tells the story of Jesus raising His good friend Lazarus from the dead.

More than half of John's Gospel is devoted to the events of Jesus' life and teaching during His final week on earth. John records how, just hours before Jesus' arrest, He spoke to the disciples and gave them some final words of encouragement. Jesus told them:

- They should not be troubled by what was happening but to trust in Him (14:1–4).
- They were to trust in Him as the One whom God had sent (14:5–14).
- They were to continue obeying Him—with the help of the Holy Spirit (14:15–31).

FUN BIBLE TRIVIA

John and his brother James, along with Peter, were part of what is called Jesus' "inner circle" of disciples. These three men were the closest to Jesus and often accompanied Him to places and events the others weren't allowed to see. For example, they were the only three allowed to be with Jesus at an event called the Transfiguration. (You can read that story in Matthew 17:1–9; Mark 9:2–10; and Luke 9:28–36.)

POWER WORDS

"For God loved the world so much that he gave his one and only Son, so that everyone who believes in him will not perish but have eternal life."
John 3:16

- They were to "abide" (remain) in Him (15:1–8).
- They were to love one another just as He had loved them (15:9–17).
- He would ask the Father to send the Holy Spirit to them (15:26–16:16).
- Their sadness would be turned to joy (16:17–28).

WHO, WHAT, WHERE?

Jesus spoke the words of John 3:16—probably the best-known verse in the whole Bible—to a Jewish religious leader named Nicodemus, who visited Him late one night to find out more about Him. While most of the religious leaders of that time opposed Jesus, Nicodemus stood up for Him when they hatched the plan to arrest Him. Nicodemus also provided the expensive spices used on Jesus' body when He was buried.

Like the other three Gospels, John's includes the story of the apostle Peter's denial that he was one of Jesus' followers after Jesus was arrested. But John is the only Gospel writer to include the scene where Jesus spoke to Peter, forgave him, and invited him to continue following Him. (You can read that story in John 21:15–23.)

Now that we've covered the four written accounts of Jesus' life, let's take a look at the men who took His message to the world after Jesus returned to heaven. You'll find their stories in the next book in the Bible: the Acts of the Apostles, or simply Acts. ✖

DID YOU KNOW. . .?

Even though the Gospel of John is now many Christians' favorite Gospel, there was a time when church leaders questioned whether it should have been included in the Bible. Some even thought that John's Gospel included false teaching! But it was eventually accepted as part of the canon of scripture, even though many didn't believe it belonged there.

CHAPTER 7

How the Church Got Its Start

(Acts of the Apostles)

The first four books of the New Testament—Matthew through John—tell the wonderful story of how Jesus came to earth from heaven, was born to a virgin girl named Mary in a town called Bethlehem, lived and ministered among the Jewish people of that time, died on a cross, and was raised from the dead.

That sounds like a great ending to the story, doesn't it? But there's more. Lots more! When we continue on from the end of John's Gospel and begin in the next New Testament book, the Acts of the Apostles (Acts for short), we read about how God started what is called "the Church" with a group of 120 believers gathered in Jerusalem, and then used some brave, dedicated men and women to spread the Good News of Jesus throughout the known world of that time.

Let's take a look at the book of Acts and the amazing story it has to tell.

Acts

What It's About: Jesus' promise of the Holy Spirit comes true, and believers receive the power He told the apostles they would receive. The Church gets its start in Jerusalem and then spreads all over the known world.

Important Characters/People: Peter, John, Gamaliel, Stephen, Philip, Aquila and Priscilla, Paul, Barnabas, Herod, Agrippa, Festus, Apollos, Silas, Lydia, Luke, Timothy

The Writer: The book of Acts was written by Luke, the same writer who wrote the Gospel of Luke. Just as he did with his Gospel, Luke wrote Acts to a man named Theophilus (but the Bible gives us no other information about Theophilus).

What You'll Find in the Book of Acts

Acts picks up almost exactly where the Gospel of Luke leaves off. The risen Jesus appeared to the apostles several times during the 40 days He remained on earth after God raised Him from the dead.

Not long after those 40 days had passed, Jesus appeared to the apostles one more time at a place called the Mount of Olives, which was located just outside the city of Jerusalem. He reminded them of His promise that God would send the Holy Spirit to give them power so that they could boldly tell the world around them about salvation through Jesus. After that, Jesus was "taken up into a cloud while they were watching, and they could no longer see him" (Acts 1:9).

What Now?

After Jesus returned to heaven, that group of 120 believers, including the apostles, continued to meet together, waiting for God to do something amazing. God never disappoints someone who waits for Him, and that first group of believers was no exception!

One day, about seven weeks after Jesus was raised from the dead, while that small group of believers was gathered in a house in Jerusalem, the Holy Spirit came. It was an amazing scene! What looked like tongues of fire appeared and rested on each person in the room. Everyone there was filled with God's Spirit, and they began talking in languages they didn't even know!

Not long after that, Peter—the same Peter who just weeks before was too scared to admit that he even knew Jesus—delivered an amazing sermon. When he was finished, that small group of 120 Christians was now a much bigger group—more than 3,000 people!

This gathering of believers called the Church continued to grow in numbers, mostly through the preaching of Peter and John. There were lots of miracles taking place, a few problems to solve, and some of the apostles got themselves in trouble with the local authorities. But through it all, the Church continued to grow, with new members being added every day.

But now it was time for the message of Jesus to spread from the cozy confines of Jerusalem.

POWER WORDS

"There is salvation in no one else! God has given no other name under heaven by which we must be saved."

Acts 4:12

You Can't Keep a Good Message Down (Acts 7–8)

As the Church continued to grow, both the Jewish religious leaders and the Roman government wondered what this new group was all about. Jesus had told the apostles that Christians would have to suffer terrible treatment because of Him. Up until now, however, the worst that had happened was that some of the apostles had been arrested for preaching about Jesus.

That all changed in a big way one day when a brave Christian named Stephen spoke to a group of Jewish religious leaders and told them things they didn't like to hear. He told them how Jesus was the Messiah they had been waiting for but that they had rejected Him.

The things Stephen said made these religious leaders so angry that they took him outside the city and killed him by throwing rocks at him. As he died, he prayed, "Lord, don't charge them with this sin!" (7:60).

Stephen's death was just the beginning of a time of terrible treatment of Christians in the city of Jerusalem. While some Christians stayed there, a lot more left the city and moved to places they thought would be safer.

You might think that when the Christians began to suffer it would bring about the end of Christianity in that part of the world; but it turned out to be only the beginning. You see, when the Christians left Jerusalem, they took with them their faith, and many of them preached to people in places like Judea and Samaria.

Paul: Jesus' Most Unlikely Servant

The Christians in Jerusalem suffered through terrible treatment. Some had their property taken away, some were beaten, and some even lost their lives.

One of the men responsible for this persecution was a Jewish religious leader named Saul (later called Paul). In chapter 9 of Acts, we read how Saul was on his way from Jerusalem to a city called Damascus to attack the Christians there. But something happened to Saul on the road to Damascus—something that would lead to the spread of Christianity all over the world.

As Saul neared Damascus, a bright light came from heaven, so intense that it blinded him and caused him to fall to the ground, and a voice said to him, "Saul! Saul! Why are you persecuting me?" (9:4).

It was Jesus talking to Saul!

Jesus told Paul to go to Damascus and wait for further instructions. Three days after Saul arrived in Damascus, he miraculously received his sight back. But more important than that, he received the Holy Spirit. He would never be the same again!

باب العامود

Damascus

הר הצופים

If you think some of the Christians who heard that Saul was God's choice to preach the gospel to the non-Jewish world were a little skeptical, you'd be right! Ananias, who took care of Saul during his first three days in Damascus, could hardly believe his ears when God told him that Saul would preach to Gentiles, kings, and the people of Israel. But Ananias took care of Saul, just as God had told him to do, making him an important part of the story. (You can read the whole story in Acts 9:10–19.)

The Christians in Jerusalem were also a little wary of Saul. In fact, when he first showed up to meet with them in Jerusalem, they were afraid of him! They thought he was only pretending to be a Christian and that he had something up his sleeve. But after they found out how he had met Jesus on the road to Damascus and how he had so courageously preached there afterward, they accepted him as one of their own.

A New Name...and a Road Trip

When you get to Acts 13:9, the first thing you will probably notice is that something else had changed about Saul: his name! This is the first time the Bible calls the man formerly known as Saul by the name Paul.

Chapter 13 of Acts records the beginning of the first of three journeys Paul took during his lifetime to preach the message of Jesus. By this time, Antioch, a city in Syria, had replaced Jerusalem as the Church's headquarters.

Paul began this trip with a man named Barnabas and with a young assistant named John Mark, who was a relative of Barnabas's. This long road trip took about three years and is covered in Acts 13:1–15:35.

WHO, WHAT, WHERE?

When we first meet Paul in the Bible, he is watching the stoning of Stephen and giving his approval. Later in the book of Acts, we find more details about Paul's life before he started attacking Christians. For example, he was born in a Roman city called Tarsus (22:3), he was a Pharisee and the son of a Pharisee (23:6), he studied Jewish law under a teacher named Gamaliel (22:3), he was a citizen of Rome (22:25–28), and he had a sister who lived in Jerusalem (23:16).

POWER WORDS

"We are here to proclaim that through this man Jesus there is forgiveness for your sins. Everyone who believes in him is declared right with God—something the law of Moses could never do."
Acts 13:38-39

After a time of fasting and prayer, the three men set sail for the island of Cyprus, Barnabas's home, where they traveled from town to town preaching the gospel (13:1–4). From there, they moved on to Perga. It was here that John Mark left them and returned to Jerusalem. After that, Paul and Barnabas traveled to a town called Pisidian Antioch, where they established the world's first Gentile church.

During the rest of the trip, Paul and Barnabas saw a lot of people coming to faith in Jesus, but they also had to run for their lives a few times. In one city, Lystra (14:8–19), Paul and Barnabas were treated as gods after they performed a miracle healing; but then they were nearly stoned to death after people came from other cities and stirred up the crowds against them.

Their last stop was a city called Derbe (14:20–21), where many people came to faith in Jesus. On their return trip to Antioch, they revisited some of the places they'd been before, and this time they appointed leaders in the newly formed churches (14:21–26).

Road Trip, Part 2 (Acts 15:36–18:22)

After hanging out in Antioch for a while, Paul set out on his second missionary journey. This time, he traveled with a new partner, a man named Silas. The plan was to have Paul, Barnabas, and Silas travel together, but when Paul and Barnabas disagreed over whether or not to take John Mark with them again (Paul was against the idea), they separated, leaving only Silas as Paul's traveling companion.

Along the way, Paul and Silas added two new members to their group: Timothy, who joined them while they were in Derbe and Lystra; and Luke, who joined them while they were in Troas, a Roman colony (see the Fun Bible Trivia sidebar on this page).

On one of their stops—a city called Philippi—Paul and Silas were beaten and thrown in jail. (You can read the whole story in Acts 16:13–40.) Then a miraculous earthquake shook the prison, giving the two men a chance to make their escape. Instead, they stayed put. Because they didn't escape, the jailer, who would have been in trouble if they had escaped, became a Christian.

FUN BIBLE TRIVIA

During Paul's second missionary journey, Luke the physician—the same Luke who wrote the Gospel of Luke and the book of Acts—joined the team. We know this because, starting with Acts 16:10, Luke refers to the team as "we," meaning he was with them everywhere they went.

Paul and Silas were beaten and thrown in jail.

DID YOU KNOW. . . ?

On Paul's second missionary journey, he visited four cities that became homes to churches he later wrote letters to—letters that later became part of the New Testament. Those cities (and the books of the Bible they are named after) are Philippi (Philippians), Thessalonica (1 and 2 Thessalonians), Corinth (1 and 2 Corinthians), and Ephesus (Ephesians).

POWER WORDS

"Believe in the Lord Jesus and you will be saved, along with everyone in your household."
Acts 16:31

WHO, WHAT, WHERE?

Acts 17:11-12 describes the people of Berea as "more open-minded" than the people of Thessalonica and as people who eagerly heard his message and searched the scriptures to see if what he said was true. Many Jews in Berea believed in Jesus as a result of their searching.

After leaving Philippi, Paul and Silas traveled to Thessalonica (17:1–4), Berea (17:10–12), Athens (17:16–33), Corinth (18:1–18), Ephesus (18:19–20), and Jerusalem (18:22). After making those stops, Paul and Silas returned to Antioch, Syria.

In Athens, which is now the capital city of Greece, Paul was sad to see all the idols erected to the Greek "gods." But when he saw one with an inscription that read, "To an Unknown God," he took the opportunity to tell the people about a God they could know through Jesus Christ.

Paul and Silas stayed in Corinth for about 18 months. While there, they met Aquila and Priscilla, a married couple who later traveled with Paul. Paul also wrote his two letters to the Thessalonians while he was in Corinth.

The Parthenon of Athens was dedicated to Athena, the Greek goddess of war, civilization, and justice.

Modern-day Athens, Greece

The First Two Trips Were So Good, We're Taking a Third (Acts 18:23–21:14)

Paul's third and final missionary journey was the longest of the three, beginning in about AD 53 and ending around AD 58.

After spending some time in Antioch, Paul set out to the cities in Galatia and Phrygia, including Tarsus and Iconium. He then traveled to Ephesus, where he stayed for almost three years (Acts 19:1–41).

God did a lot of great work through Paul in Ephesus. Paul preached and taught and did many great miracles—including healing the sick and casting out evil spirits (Acts 19:11–12). His work was so amazing that even magicians stopped their evil practices and burned very expensive books they used for their magic (Acts 19:17–20).

Later, Paul was nearly killed when he exposed the dishonesty of men who were in the business of making and selling idols (19:24–27). Even though Paul was a very busy man, he also found time to write his first letter to the Corinthian church and his letter to the Galatians, both of which are now in the Bible.

Paul then traveled to Macedonia and Greece (20:1–3), where he wrote his second letter to the Corinthians. From there he traveled to Troas (20:6–12) and then to Assos (20:13–14) and then back to Ephesus (20:17–35). The final three stops on his third missionary journey were in Tyre (21:3–6), Ptolemais (21:7), and Caesarea (21:8).

On to Jerusalem and Rome (Acts 21:15–23:15)

WHO, WHAT, WHERE?

Malta, where the apostle Paul and others stayed after their ship wrecked on the way to Rome, is a southern European archipelago (a large group of islands) located in the Mediterranean Sea, about 60 miles south of the southeastern tip of Sicily, Italy.

The last eight chapters of the book of Acts take place after Paul's third and final missionary journey. But that doesn't mean Paul was finished preaching and teaching the Good News about Jesus. And it also doesn't mean an end to the threats on his life.

Even though Paul had been warned there would be trouble if he traveled to Jerusalem, he still went there. This time, the Christians in Jerusalem welcomed him, but his reception among the Jews in the city wasn't as friendly. He was arrested in the Temple after a riot broke out because of the things he preached (21:26–36).

After Paul learned of a plot to kill him, he was sent to Caesarea, where he stayed two years before he was sent to Rome. On the way to Rome, the ship he was sailing on shipwrecked during a terrible storm, and he ended up on the island of Malta, where he continued preaching. (You can read this story in Acts 27:14–28:10.)

When Paul finally arrived in Rome, he was placed under house arrest. He was allowed to live by himself—with a Roman soldier to guard him. During his two years in Rome, he wrote several more letters that were later included in the Bible: Ephesians, Philippians, two letters to Timothy, and Philemon.

While Paul was in Rome, he continued to preach—"boldly proclaiming the Kingdom of God and teaching about the Lord Jesus Christ. And no one tried to stop him" (28:31).

The Bible doesn't say exactly when Paul died or how. But historians teach that he was killed by the Roman emperor Nero around AD 67.

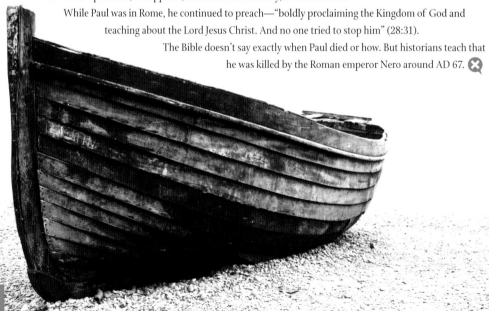

CHAPTER 8

Letters That Became Books of the Bible

Epistles from Paul, Peter, and the Rest (Romans through Jude)

If you've ever read through your Bible from Genesis to Revelation, right after you finished reading about the life, words, and deeds of Jesus Christ (Matthew through John), you moved on to the adventures of the men He appointed to continue His work in the then-known world (Acts).

If you're like a lot of people who have just finished reading the Gospels and the book of Acts, you might be wondering, *Okay, now that I know a little something about what Jesus and the men who followed Him have done, what does it mean to me?*

The next 21 books of the Bible—books that are called the Epistles—give you an amazing number of answers to that question. In these books, you'll find some very practical instructions on what you are to believe, how you are to live, and how you are to treat other people.

The Bible's epistles are actually personal letters written by men called apostles. At least five (and probably six) men wrote letters that ended up in the New Testament. The apostle Paul wrote most of the epistles included in the New Testament. He is known for certain to have written 13 of the letters (Romans, 1 and 2 Corinthians, Galatians, Ephesians, Philippians, Colossians, 1 and 2 Thessalonians, 1 and 2 Timothy, Titus, and Philemon) and is thought by some to have written Hebrews (more on that later).

DID YOU KNOW. . . ?

Though Paul is credited with writing the first 13 epistles in the New Testament, he didn't work alone. Romans 16:22 credits an assistant of Paul's named Tertius with helping the apostle write down his letter to the Roman Christians; and 1 Corinthians 1:1 credits a man named Sosthenes with assisting Paul in his first letter to the Christians in Corinth. Nothing else is known about either man.

Romans

What It's About: The apostle Paul explains to the Roman Christians that everyone born since the days of Adam and Eve comes into this world as a sinner—someone who is not at peace with God. But there is a way of salvation—and only one way—and that's through faith in Jesus Christ.

Important Characters/People: Paul, Phoebe, Priscilla, Aquila, and many others mentioned in Romans 16

The Writer: Paul, with help from Tertius (16:22), wrote this letter in about AD 56, while he was in the city of Corinth.

What You'll Find in the Book of Romans

POWER WORDS

And we know that God causes everything to work together for the good of those who love God and are called according to his purpose for them.

Romans 8:28

Romans is different from Paul's letters to the other churches, because he wrote it to a church he'd never personally visited. In fact, he had never even seen the city of Rome at the time he wrote this letter. Paul hoped to see the Roman Christians face-to-face when he traveled to Spain (15:23–24). It's not known if Paul ever made it to Spain, but he did end up in Rome at the end of his life.

Some people have called Romans the "Gospel according to Paul," because it gives its readers such a detailed but simple plan for salvation.

The book of Romans starts out by describing in detail the sad condition of all people. In the first two chapters and most of the third, Paul writes about God's anger over human sin. He points out that even the best people in the world don't live the way God wants them to live. Not only that, but he writes that simply following God's written laws isn't enough to make us right with Him.

Modern-day Rome, Italy

It seems like a pretty hopeless situation, but in chapter 3, Paul begins to explain why there is still hope. It's almost as if Paul were saying, "Here's the bad news, but stay with me while I tell you the Good News!" Sure, everyone sins and falls shorts of God's standard (3:23), but God Himself has lovingly provided the way for people to overcome that sin and have peace with Him: "Yet God, with undeserved kindness, declares that we are righteous. He did this through Christ Jesus when he freed us from the penalty for our sins" (3:24).

Paul wanted the Christians in Rome to understand that it wasn't about being a better person or about making an effort to follow God's rules. It's not that it wasn't a good idea to do those things, but they would never be enough to get a person into heaven. Salvation comes through one simple thing: trusting in Jesus Christ, who died as a sacrifice for our sins.

In chapters 6–8, Paul encourages his readers with the promise that they can live the way God wants them to live because God has given them power through the Holy Spirit. In chapters 9–11, he expands on how God worked His perfect plan to make people at peace with Him. Chapters 12–15 are some practical instructions for the Christian life. ⊗

WHAT'S IN IT FOR ME?

Paul writes in Romans 8:15 that Christians can call God "Abba, Father." *Abba* is an Aramaic word for the word *father* that implies a really close relationship—kind of like when you call your father "Daddy." Paul uses this very same word to describe our relationship with God in Galatians 4:6.

1 Corinthians

What It's About: The people in the church in the city of Corinth weren't living the way Christians should live and weren't treating one another the way they should, so Paul wrote this letter to correct them and encourage them.

Important Characters/People: Paul, Apollos, Priscilla, Aquila, Timothy, Crispus, Sosthenes, Stephanas

The Writer: The apostle Paul, with help from Sosthenes (1:1)

What You'll Find in the Book of 1 Corinthians

POWER WORDS

Three things will last forever—faith, hope, and love—and the greatest of these is love.

1 Corinthians 13:13

WHAT'S IN IT FOR ME?

Chapter 13 of 1 Corinthians is well known as the "love chapter" of the Bible. Take some time to read this chapter and ask yourself how you can better show your love for your family, friends, people at church, and others around you.

Paul helped establish the Corinthian church during his second missionary journey (Acts 18). But after Paul moved on to Ephesus, he found out that the Corinthians were having some serious problems. There were arguments in the church, ungodly living, and even lawsuits among the Christians there. Chapters 1–6 cover Paul's warnings and encouragements for the Christians at Corinth about unity in the church and right living for Christians.

In 1 Corinthians, Paul teaches on marriage (chapter 7), problems with food and idols (chapter 8), Christian freedom (chapter 9), the Lord's Supper (11:17–34), spiritual gifts (chapters 12–14), the resurrection of the dead (chapter 15), and giving (chapter 16).

2 Corinthians

What It's About: The apostle Paul writes another letter to the Corinthians, this time to defend his ministry.

Important Characters/People: Paul, the Corinthian church leaders, Titus

The Writer: The apostle Paul, with help from Timothy (1:1)

What You'll Find in the Book of 2 Corinthians

The Corinthian Christians had dealt with some of the problems Paul wrote to them about in his first letter to them, but some troublemakers in Corinth questioned Paul's authority and attempted to divide the church. In the first seven chapters of 2 Corinthians, Paul describes his work as an apostle.

Chapters 8 and 9 of this book are Paul's instructions for giving and sharing in the church, including his words "God loves a person who gives cheerfully" (9:7). In the next three chapters, Paul defends his position as an apostle and tells the Corinthians why he writes with the authority he does. ✖

FUN BIBLE TRIVIA

In 2 Corinthians 12:7, Paul mentions a "thorn in my flesh" that God used to keep him humble. Paul doesn't say exactly what that "thorn" is, but some believe it might have been a physical problem like bad eyesight, migraine headaches, or epilepsy. Others believe it might have been attacks in the spiritual or human realm.

Galatians

What It's About: Paul writes to the Galatian Christians to remind them to trust in only Jesus for their salvation and not in Jewish laws and customs. Paul wanted the Galatians to understand that the Christian life isn't about observing a lot of rules and regulations but about living under the power of the Holy Spirit.

Important Characters/People: Paul, Abraham, Sarah, Hagar, Ishmael, Isaac

The Writer: The apostle Paul. He wrote his letter to the Galatians around AD 50. This letter was actually written to several churches in a larger area called Galatia, which was located in Asia Minor (now Turkey).

What You'll Find in the Book of Galatians

The Galatian Christians had started their lives of faith in Jesus well, but then a big problem came along. Men called "Judaizers" were trying to convince the Galatians, including the Gentiles, that they needed to observe Jewish rituals and customs in order to be true Christians.

Paul starts out his letter by telling the Galatians that he is shocked that they would turn way from God and His love and mercy (1:6) and follow a different path. He even writes of the Judaizers, "Let God's curse fall on anyone, including us or even an angel from heaven, who preaches a different kind of Good News than the one we preached to you " (1:8). Paul called the Galatian Christians "foolish Galatians" (3:1), because many of them had tried to take the salvation God had given them freely through Jesus Christ and add Jewish customs and rituals to it.

The main theme of the book of Galatians is *freedom*, and Paul wanted all Christians, including us today, to understand that because we have Jesus, we are free to love God and others without adding rituals, customs, or any human effort to our Christian lives. ✖

Ephesians

What It's About: Paul writes to the church in the city of Ephesus (in Asia Minor) to explain their true identity as Christians and what it should mean to them in their daily lives.

Important Characters/People: Paul, Timothy, Tychicus

The Writer: The apostle Paul

What You'll Find in the Book of Ephesians

If you want to have a good understanding of what God has done for you through Jesus and who He says you are as a Christian, the book of Ephesians is a great place to start.

Paul started the church in Ephesus during his second missionary journey. (You can read the story in Acts 19.) Even though Paul had spent two years in the city, he later wrote to the Ephesians from his prison cell in Rome to explain the meaning of their relationship to Jesus Christ and how it should change their way of living and thinking.

The first three chapters of Ephesians teach what God has done in bringing people to Himself through Jesus. Paul told the Ephesians that through Jesus, God had brought both Jews and Gentiles together to Himself (2:11–18). The final three chapters explain what this new life in Jesus should look like—both in the church and in the home and other places. ✖

Philippians

What It's About: Paul writes a heartfelt letter of love, friendship, and encouragement to the believers at the church in the city of Philipi.

Important Characters/People: Paul, Epaphroditus, Timothy, Euodia, Syntyche

The Writer: Paul, along with Timothy (1:1)

What You'll Find in the Book of Philippians

When you're going through a hard time and are feeling a little sad, discouraged, or worried, then maybe you should crack your Bible open to the book of Philippians, one of the most positive, upbeat, encouraging books in the whole Bible.

The apostle Paul was probably sitting in a stinky, cold Roman prison cell when he wrote this letter. He had helped establish the Philippian church during his second missionary journey, and this letter shows that he had some very positive, warm feelings for the Christians there.

One of the things you'll notice as you read Philippians is that Paul uses the words *joy* and *rejoicing* over and over. That includes a verse you may have sung as a song at Sunday school: "Rejoice in the Lord always. Again I will say, rejoice!" (4:4 NKJV). Paul knew for himself that no matter what kinds of circumstances he was in, he could always find joy in Jesus. He wanted the Christians in Philippi—and you—to understand that.

One thing Paul never says in this letter is that life is always going to be easy or fun. He was in a bad place himself (he knew his life could be nearing an end), and he warned the Philippians that they could expect to have to suffer for Jesus (1:29–30). Still, he wrote a book filled with words of joy for the life God had allowed him to live and the things God had allowed him to do.

Colossians

What It's About: To fight against false teaching that had arisen in the church in Colossae, Paul writes to the Colossian Christians to remind them that Jesus is higher and greater than everything and everyone.

Important Characters/People: Paul, Barnabas, Aristarchus, Justus

The Writer: The apostle Paul, along with Timothy (1:1)

DID YOU KNOW. . . ?

In Colossians 4:16, Paul mentions a letter he wrote to the church in Laodicea. This was one of probably dozens of letters Paul wrote that didn't make it into the Bible as part of the New Testament. Paul also asked that the letter to the Colossians be read to the Christians in Laodicea.

What You'll Find in the Book of Colossians

The Colossian church—like so many others of that time—had been the target of false teaching (or, as Paul calls it in Colossians 2:4, "well-crafted arguments") that had caused some of the Christians in Colossae to add unhelpful things to their Christian faith. When Paul found out about the situation, he wrote this letter to remind the people that Jesus was all they needed—not additional rules and regulations, false thinking, angels, or anything else.

To demonstrate who Jesus is and what He meant to them, Paul reminded the Colossians that Jesus is the image of the invisible God (1:15), is the firstborn over all creation (1:15), is the creator of all things (1:16), is before all things (1:17), holds all things together (1:17), and is the head of the church (1:18). ❌

POWER WORDS

Think about the things of heaven, not the things of earth.

Colossians 3:2

1 Thessalonians

What It's About: Paul writes to the church in the Macedonian city of Thessalonica to instruct the Christians on living the way God wants them to live and also to assure them that Jesus will one day return to earth.

Important Characters/People: Paul, Silas, Timothy

The Writer: The apostle Paul, along with Silvanus (Silas) and Timothy (1:1). Paul, along with Silas, his traveling companion, had started the church in Thessalonica during his second missionary journey (Acts 17:1-9). He wrote his first letter to the Thessalonians around AD 50.

What You'll Find in the Book of 1 Thessalonians

The first three chapters of this book are Paul's greetings and words of encouragement to a church he knew was growing strong in the faith. In chapter 4, he gives them instructions on living a godly life and encourages them with the promise that Jesus will return and Christians who have already died will go to heaven when He comes back. ❌

WHAT'S IN IT FOR ME?

The book of 1 Thessalonians contains many promises for you as a Christian—including the promise that because you are a Christian, you will one day be together in heaven with all your Christian family members and friends (4:13-18).

2 Thessalonians

What It's About: Paul writes a follow-up letter to the Thessalonian church to encourage them not just to wait around until Jesus returns, but to continue the work God has for them to do.

Important Characters/People: Paul, the "man of lawlessness"

The Writer: The apostle Paul, along with Silvanus (Silas) and Timothy (1:1)

What You'll Find in the Book of 2 Thessalonians

Paul wrote this letter to help calm the shaken and troubled (2:2) Thessalonians, who had been told that Jesus had already returned to earth. Some of the Thessalonian Christians had quit their money-earning jobs and stopped doing the work God had for them to do here on earth.

In this letter, Paul assures them that Jesus' second coming is still in the future and that they should continue the work they had been doing before. In chapter 2, Paul tells the Thessalonians not to pay any attention to those who tell them Jesus has already returned and gives them an outline of what will take place in the "Day of the Lord." He explains that this day won't come until the "man of lawlessness" is revealed (2:8).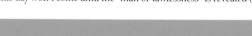

1 Timothy

What It's About: Paul's letter of instruction and encouragement for the church in Ephesus and to a young pastor named Timothy. In this letter, Paul gives Timothy the requirements for church leadership.

Important Characters/People: Paul, Timothy, church leaders, Hymenaeus, Alexander

The Writer: The apostle Paul

What You'll Find in the Book of 1 Timothy

The apostle Paul wasn't just the greatest missionary in the history of Christianity, and he wasn't just the writer of many of the books in the New Testament. Paul was also a teacher and a mentor, and one of his students was Timothy, a young man who had been with Paul on his missionary journeys.

Paul begins his first letter to young Timothy by warning him against some of the false teaching that had made its way around the churches in that part of the world. He encourages Timothy to "fight well in the Lord's battles" and "cling to your faith in Christ, and keep your conscience clear" (1:18–19). In chapter 2, Paul lists some guidelines for the conduct of the church. Then, in chapter 3, he lists the qualifications for pastors and deacons, who were the church leaders of that time.

Chapters 4–6 cover a variety of topics, including more advice for church leaders, including Timothy himself (4:4–16), caring for widows (5:1–21), and avoiding the love of money (6:10–17).

WHO, WHAT, WHERE?

Timothy was a young man who worked side by side with the apostle Paul, who assigned him the tough job of pastoring the church in Ephesus. In his letters to Timothy, Paul addresses him as a loving father would a son.

2 Timothy

What It's About: Paul's final words of encouragement to his much-loved partner and spiritual son, Timothy

Important Characters/People: Paul, Timothy, Demas, Crescens, Carpus, Titus, Luke, John Mark, Alexander

The Writer: The apostle Paul, who wrote this letter in approximately AD 67, shortly before he was put to death in Rome

DID YOU KNOW. . . ?

The first nine epistles in the New Testament were written to churches. The next four were written to individuals. Both letters to Timothy and the one to Titus were written to church leaders who had traveled with Paul. That is why they are sometimes called "pastoral epistles."

What You'll Find in the Book of 2 Timothy

Sitting in a Roman prison cell, Paul wrote this letter to Timothy, his young friend and "true son in the faith" (1 Timothy 1:2). Paul knew his life was probably going to end soon, and he might have known that this letter would be his "last words." But even though Paul was in a terrible place, he didn't dwell on his own circumstances but took the time to express his concern for other Christians, especially Timothy.

In this letter, Paul encourages young Timothy to continue loving Jesus passionately and to preserve the truth he had learned from Paul. He pushes him to live the way God wants him to live as an example to Christians around him. Paul also warns Timothy to expect trouble as a result of living for Jesus (3:12) but also encourages him with the promise that God will always be faithful.

Titus

What It's About: Paul instructs Christian leaders on how to live and how to lead their churches.

Important Characters/People: Paul, Titus

The Writer: The apostle Paul

What You'll Find in the Book of Titus

The apostle Paul had left a young traveling companion named Titus on the Mediterranean island of Crete so that Titus could appoint church leaders and correct some of the problems in the new church there.

The people of Crete were known back then for their bad behavior, and they needed a strong leader who would hold them accountable for their actions. Titus was just that kind of leader.

Paul's letter to Titus encourages him to choose godly leaders and to set an example for the Christians on Crete by living the kind of life God wanted him to live. But this book applies to more than just church leaders—it gives good advice for any Christian to follow.

Who, What, Where?

Titus was a Gentile (non-Jewish) friend and helper of the apostle Paul who accompanied Paul and Barnabas on a journey to Jerusalem (see Galatians 2:1) and who was with Paul during his imprisonment in Rome (2 Timothy 4:10). The Bible says he was completely selfless and trustworthy (2 Corinthians 12:18).

Philemon

What It's About: Paul encourages a slave owner named Philemon to treat his runaway slave like he would any other fellow Christian: with love, compassion, and forgiveness.

Important Characters/People: Paul, Timothy, Philemon, Onesimus

The Writer: The apostle Paul. He wrote his letter to Philemon in about AD 60 while in prison in Rome.

WHAT'S iN iT FOR ME?

The story of Philemon and his runaway slave is an example of how a Christian should treat someone who has done something wrong. Paul knows Philemon has every right under the law to have Onesimus harshly punished, but Paul begs his friend to treat Onesimus with forgiveness and compassion.

What You'll Find in the Book of Philemon

A slave named Onesimus had robbed Philemon and run away to Rome, where he met Paul and became a Christian. Paul wanted to keep Onesimus in Rome as a helper, but because Philemon didn't approve, Paul sent Onesimus back to Colossae. Paul then writes a very personal letter in which he asks Philemon to forgive his runaway slave, who faced severe punishment under Roman law for running away from his master. ✖

Hebrews

What It's About: The writer of this letter shows his readers that Jesus is better than any Old Testament sacrifice or ritual. In fact, while those sacrifices and rituals were an imperfect way to approach God, Jesus provided the one and only perfect way to God.

Important Characters/People: Moses, Joshua, Melchizedek, the Hebrew patriarchs, Jesus

The Writer: One of the biggest mysteries in the entire New Testament is this: who wrote the book of Hebrews? It is believed the letter was written around AD 65, but there is no real agreement on who wrote it. Some experts believe the apostle Paul wrote this letter. Others believe the writer was Barnabas, who traveled with Paul on his first missionary journey. Others believe it was a man named Apollos, a Jewish preacher from Alexandria who had been taught by a married couple named Aquila and Priscilla (Acts 18:26).

What You'll Find in the Book of Hebrews

The writer of Hebrews was probably addressing new Jewish Christians (that's why it's called "Hebrews") who might have been tempted to avoid persecution from other Jews and return to the system of sacrifices and other Old Testament–style ceremonies. The writer of Hebrews wanted his readers to understand that Jesus' sacrificial death eliminated the need for those kinds of observances.

In chapter 10, the writer to the Hebrews tells his readers that Jesus was far better than the Old Testament system of sacrifices. For one thing, the sacrificial system required people to make sacrifices once every year through a human priest to cover their sins. The perfect sacrifice of Jesus on the cross was a once-and-for-all sacrifice that allows each individual Christian to approach God without the help of a priest.

The writer of Hebrews encourages Jewish Christians to hold to their faith in Jesus, and also warns them not to neglect their faith (2:1–4), not to fall into unbelief (3:7–4:13), to continue to grow in their faith (5:11–6:20), and to endure persecution and other temptations to give up on their faith (10:32–39). ✖

FUN BIBLE TRIVIA

Some Bible experts believe it is possible that a woman named Priscilla (who, along with her husband, Aquila, served the first-century church in Corinth and Ephesus) wrote the book of Hebrews. If that were true, Priscilla would be the only female author of a New Testament book.

POWER WORDS

Let us fix our eyes on Jesus, the author and perfecter of our faith, who for the joy set before him endured the cross, scorning its shame, and sat down at the right hand of the throne of God.

Hebrews 12:2 NIV

James

What It's About: The apostle James writes that real Christian faith is shown in a believer's actions, especially in how he or she treats others.

Important Characters/People: James, teachers, church leaders

The Writer: The writer of this letter is believed to be James (also known as James the Just), the earthly brother of Jesus (see Matthew 13:55; Mark 6:3). The Bible tells us that James was not a Christian until after Jesus' resurrection (compare John 7:3–5 with Acts 1:14; 1 Corinthians 15:7; and Galatians 1:19). Once he became a Christian, he served as one of the leaders of the church in Jerusalem (see Galatians 2:9). The book of James is believed to be the oldest book of the New Testament, written as early as AD 45.

What You'll Find in the Book of James

Have you ever heard the saying, "Don't just talk the talk—walk the walk"? That's the message behind the book of James, which encourages Christians to demonstrate their faith in a loving God by loving others through their actions. In a way, it's a more detailed explanation of these words of Jesus: " You should be a light for other people. Live so that they will see the good things you do and will praise your Father in heaven" (Matthew 5:16 NCV).

While Paul taught that Christians are saved by faith alone and not by the good things they do (see Romans 3:28), James teaches that good deeds should follow real faith. That's why he encourages all Christians to focus on living right, watching how they talk, and treating others as valuable in God's eyes—even during difficult times.

> POWER WORDS
>
> *Come near to God, and God will come near to you.*
> James 4:8 NCV

1 Peter

What It's About: When a believer suffers for Jesus, he or she should consider it a good thing.

Important Characters/People: Peter, church leaders

The Writer: The apostle Peter, with the assistance of Silvanus (5:12)

What You'll Find in the Book of 1 Peter

Peter wrote this letter to Jewish Christians living all over the Roman Empire to encourage them and challenge them. They needed the encouragement, too, because Jewish Christians faced terrible treatment from the Jews and from the Romans.

Peter not only wrote to encourage Christians to endure the bad things that happened to them, but also to rejoice and to see it as a privilege to be mistreated because of their faith in Jesus.

Peter also encouraged Christians to put others ahead of themselves—just like Jesus did. When we do that, we not only become more like Jesus, but we will also receive rewards from God. ✖

POWER WORDS

You are a chosen people. You are royal priests, a holy nation, God's very own possession. As a result, you can show others the goodness of God, for he called you out of the darkness into his wonderful light.

1 Peter 2:9

2 Peter

What It's About: Peter warns believers to watch out for people who are spreading wrong teaching in the church.

Important Characters/People: Peter, prophets, false teachers

The Writer: The apostle Peter. He wrote this letter around AD 66 or 67, near the end of his life.

What You'll Find in the Book of 2 Peter

Peter was troubled because he knew that men were coming into the churches and spreading wrong teaching about the Christian faith. He encouraged Christians to grow strong in their faith and to focus on his teaching so that they would be able to tell when someone was trying to teach them wrong things.

Peter wrote that some of these false teachers even made fun of the truth that Jesus would return again (3:3–7). Instead of listening to them, he said, hold on to the promise of Jesus' return to earth; that truth will motivate us to live the way God wants us to live (3:14).

1 John

What It's About: Jesus was a real man—just as He was really God—and He set an example for Christians to follow in the way He loved others.

Important Characters/People: John

The Writer: The letters titled 1 John, 2 John, and 3 John don't mention who wrote them, but centuries of tradition hold that it was John, one of Jesus' 12 original disciples, who wrote these three letters around AD 92. John reminds his readers that he and the other disciples knew Jesus personally: "We saw him with our own eyes and touched him with our own hands" (1 John 1:1).

What You'll Find in the Book of 1 John

One of the reasons John wrote this letter was to set believers straight about certain parts of the Christian faith. John knew that false teachers were trying to lead the Christians of that time away from the true Christian faith. The New Testament had not yet been put together into one book, so there was no single book that Christians could read in order to find out whether what they were being taught was true.

In the first two chapters of 1 John, the apostle writes about how a true Christian should live. He writes that people who claim to be Christians but don't live the way God wants them to live aren't really Christians at all (1:8). He also encourages Christians not to hide their sins but to confess them, because God is "faithful and just" to forgive those who confess their sins (1:9).

In chapters 3 and 4, John writes that God loves us so deeply, we should love Him in return and also love others the same way. John encourages his readers to love one another selflessly, even to the point of laying down their lives for one another if necessary (3:16–17).

John writes that "God is love" (4:8) and that those who really know God will love others as a result. On the other hand, those who don't love don't really know God at all. John says that when we love others, God lives within us (4:12).

In chapter 5, John writes that love and obedience to God are closely tied together and that we can approach God at any time, knowing that He hears us and will answer our prayers. ❌

POWER WORDS

See how very much our Father loves us, for he calls us his children, and that is what we are! But the people who belong to this world don't recognize that we are God's children because they don't know him.

1 John 3:1

2 John

What It's About: The apostle John warns Christians to watch out for false teachers who don't believe in Jesus' physical life and ministry here on earth.

Important Characters/People: John, "the chosen lady and her children"

The Writer: The apostle John (see page 120)

What You'll Find in the Book of 2 John

The apostle John addressed 2 John to "the chosen lady and to her children." That could have meant a woman of important position in the Ephesian church, or it could have meant the local church.

John wrote this letter to warn Christians against false teachers who taught that Jesus didn't physically rise from the dead, but rose only in a spiritual sense. John warned true believers to completely avoid people who taught that. ❌

3 John

What It's About: True Christian leaders must be humble people who are more concerned about the welfare of others than they are for their own reputation or position.

Important Characters/People: John, Gaius, Diotrephes

The Writer: The apostle John (see page 120)

What You'll Find in the Book of 3 John

John's third epistle was written to a Christian named Gaius (1:1). John wrote of Gaius as a man who demonstrated hospitality to traveling preachers who stopped off in his hometown. He also warns against the kind of leadership practiced by a man named Diotrephes, who was more interested in having power over people than he was in serving them. ⊗

Jude

What It's About: Jude warns Christians to watch out for those who try to spread wrong teaching.

Important Characters/People: Jude, Enoch

The Writer: The writer of the epistle of Jude identifies himself only as the "brother of James" (1:1). It's possible that Jude was the brother of James, who is identified as the brother of Jesus (see Matthew 13:55), but Jude does not identify himself as Jesus' brother.

What You'll Find in the Book of Jude

The book of Jude was written between AD 60 and 80, and it deals with some of the same problems Peter addresses in his second letter. Jude wanted to warn Christians not to follow the example of false teachers in the church, who were leading people away from the faith; and complainers, who weren't living right. ⊗

CHAPTER 9

THE END

What's Ahead

John's Vision of the Last Days (Revelation)

By now, you should have a pretty good idea of what the different books of the Bible are about, the key characters and events in each book, and what you can learn from reading each book.

Now we come to the last book of the Bible: Revelation. Though the Old Testament contains a lot of prophecy books, Revelation is the only New Testament book devoted to prophecy. Other New Testament books include *some* prophecy, but Revelation is the only one that is pretty much all prophecy.

Before you read on, there are some things about Revelation that you should know. First of all, this book has confused some of the most dedicated Bible scholars and Christian leaders, and it has led to some big disagreements. That's because the book uses lots of colorful imagery, and people disagree about what these symbols and pictures mean.

Revelation includes some very strange—and sometimes very scary— passages that can be taken many different ways. Some believe a lot of what we read in Revelation has already taken place and that the writer wrote the way he did in order to confuse Roman leaders who treated first-century Christians very badly. Other people believe that most of Revelation looks forward to events that haven't happened yet.

No matter what you believe about Revelation, it is a book that promises that things will turn out great for people who follow Jesus faithfully. And it also contains some practical words you can apply to your Christian life every day.

DID YOU KNOW. . . ?

The book of Revelation has also been called the Revelation of Jesus Christ, the Apocalypse of John, or simply the Apocalypse. The word *apocalypse* is sometimes used to describe worldwide destruction or a disaster, but it actually means an *unveiling* or *revealing*. That is why most people call this book Revelation.

Revelation

What It's About: Jesus will return to earth and reward those who do right and punish those who do wrong. Revelation describes the final conflict between good and evil.

Important Characters/People: John, Jesus, the dragon (Satan), two beasts, the "messenger" angels

The Writer: The book of Revelation was written by John, one of Jesus' original 12 disciples, who also wrote the Gospel of John, 1 John, 2 John, and 3 John. He received the visions he writes about in this book while living on the island of Patmos, which is off the coast of Greece. The Roman government had sent him there as punishment for preaching the Good News of Jesus (see Revelation 1:9).

POWER WORDS

"I am the Alpha and the Omega—the beginning and the end," says the Lord God. "I am the one who is, who always was, and who is still to come—the Almighty One."

Revelation 1:8

WHO, WHAT, WHERE?

Revelation 1:9 says that John received the visions he wrote in the book while living as a prisoner on Patmos, an island located in the Aegean Sea, west of Asia Minor (now Turkey). Patmos covers about 13 square miles and is thought to have been an island prison of the Roman Empire. Today, Patmos is part of Greece.

What You'll Find in the Book of Revelation

Revelation starts by telling readers what they are about to read: "The revelation of Jesus Christ, which God gave him to show his servants what must soon take place" (1:1 NIV). John then explains that he received the visions he writes about from an angel whom God had sent.

After greeting his readers, John writes that he heard a very loud voice instructing him to write down everything he was about to hear and see. Then he describes an amazing—and terrifying—vision of someone "like the Son of Man" (1:13). He was dressed in a long robe with a golden sash across his chest, and his head and hair were "white like wool, as white as snow," and his eyes were like "flames of fire" (1:14). His feet were like "polished bronze refined in a furnace" and his voice "thundered like mighty ocean waves" (1:15). He held seven stars in his hand and out of his mouth came a "sharp two-edged sword" (1:16). His face was like the shining sun (1:16).

After hearing and seeing all this, John was so frightened that he fell on his face as if he were dead. But just then, the person in John's vision laid his hand on John's shoulder and told him not to be afraid, because, "I am the First and the Last. I am the living one. I died, but look—I am alive forever and ever! And I hold the keys of death and the grave" (1:17–18).

John knew who was talking to him. It was Jesus! This was the same Jesus with whom John had spent three years when Jesus was alive on earth. But even though it was the same Jesus, He looked and sounded different, because now He had been "glorified," which means he appeared in His heavenly form.

And He had a lot for John to think and write about!

FUN BIBLE TRIVIA

The number seven appears many times in the book of Revelation (seven churches, seven horns, seven eyes, seven seals, seven trumpets, seven bowls). The number seven is important in Jewish tradition because it stands for God's perfection as He rested on the seventh day after He had finished creation. (Look it up in Genesis 2:2–3.)

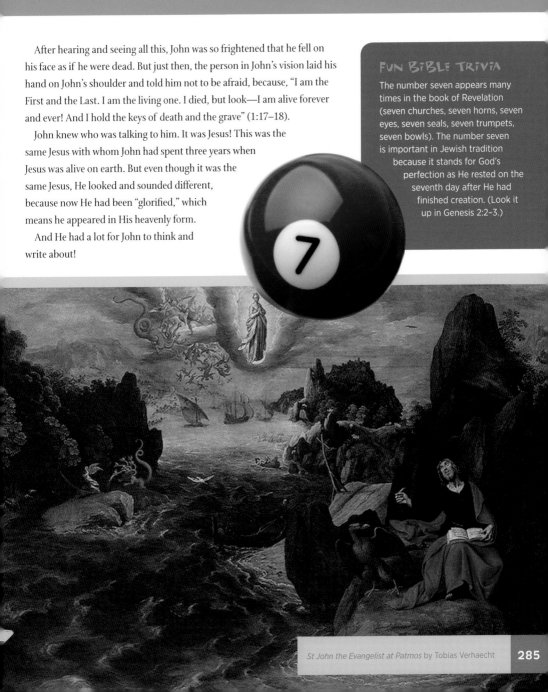

St John the Evangelist at Patmos by Tobias Verhaecht

285

Seven Messages for Seven Churches

Chapters 2 and 3 of Revelation are Jesus' own words for seven churches in Asia Minor, a place that is now part of the nation of Turkey. He encouraged some of the churches, but He challenged and criticized others.

Here is a quick look at what Jesus said to the seven churches.

1. **Ephesus (2:1–7):** Jesus praised this church for doing some good things, but He also called them to love Him and one another as they once had.
2. **Smyrna (2:8–11):** This church had little money or possessions, and they were spoken against by the outside world. But Jesus praised the church for their spiritual riches and encouraged them to "remain faithful even when facing death, [and] I will give you the crown of life" (verse 10).
3. **Pergamum (2:12–17):** Jesus gave this church high marks for remaining true to Him, even though they were treated terribly. But He also warned them to stop compromising when it came to the teaching they accepted.
4. **Thyatira (2:18–21):** Jesus noticed this church's love, faith, service, and endurance, but He warned them to get rid of the idolatry and sin that had made their way into the church.
5. **Sardis (3:1–6):** This church was spiritually asleep, and Jesus called them to wake up!
6. **Philadelphia (3:7–13):** Jesus praised this church for their faithfulness and perseverance—even though they had faced persecution from "Satan's synagogue," people who said they were Jews but were not.
7. **Laodicea (3:14–19):** Jesus reserved His toughest words for the Laodicean church because they were "'like lukewarm water, neither hot nor cold'" (3:16). Jesus called the Laodiceans to decide what they wanted to be and told them to "'be diligent and turn from your indifference'" (verse 19).

In the last four verses of Revelation 3, Jesus calls the churches to a closer relationship with Him and promises them, "Those who are victorious will sit with me on my throne, just as I was victorious and sat with my Father on his throne" (3:21).

John's Second Vision (Revelation 4–6)

After hearing the message to the seven churches, John received a second vision. This vision began with a door standing open in heaven and a voice—the same voice he had heard before—inviting him to see a throne room of God.

John saw quite a scene in the throne room. He saw a throne on which was seated a figure "as brilliant as gemstones" (4:3). This was Jesus, the Lamb of God, and His throne was surrounded by 24 more thrones, each with an "elder" sitting on it.

There were also four living creatures in the throne room, and each was covered with eyes from front to back. One looked like a lion, one like an ox, one like a human, and one like an eagle. Day after day, these creatures cried out, "Holy, holy, holy is the Lord God, the Almighty—the one who always was, who is, and who is still to come" (4:8).

In this vision, John also saw in the right hand of the one sitting on the main throne a scroll that was sealed with seven seals that no one on earth could open and read. John wept out loud because no one was worthy to open the scrolls, but one of the elders said, "Stop weeping! Look, the Lion of the tribe of Judah, the heir to David's throne, has won the victory. He is worthy to open the scroll and its seven seals" (5:5).

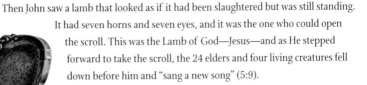

Then John saw a lamb that looked as if it had been slaughtered but was still standing. It had seven horns and seven eyes, and it was the one who could open the scroll. This was the Lamb of God—Jesus—and as He stepped forward to take the scroll, the 24 elders and four living creatures fell down before him and "sang a new song" (5:9).

The Seven Seals (6:1–8:1)

As John watched, the Lamb of God broke the seven seals one by one. When he opened the first seal, a rider on a white horse appeared and "rode out to win many battles and gain the victory" (6:2). When the second seal was broken, another horse appeared—a red one this time. On its back was a rider who was given a sword and the authority to remove peace from the earth and bring war everywhere. When the third seal was broken, a rider on a black horse appeared, holding a pair of scales in his hand. The breaking of the fourth seal brought a rider on a green horse. The rider was called Death.

When the Lamb of God opened the fifth seal, John saw the souls of Christians who had been killed on account of their faith. These souls asked God when He would punish the people who had taken their lives. Then white robes were given to each of the martyred souls, and they were told to be patient.

The sixth seal brought a huge earthquake. The sun turned black, the moon was turned as red as blood, and what looked like stars fell to the earth. All the mountains and islands of the earth disappeared. It was such a terrible scene that people hid themselves in caves and rocks and hoped the mountains would fall on them so they could escape God's judgment.

When the seventh seal was broken, John heard complete quiet in heaven for half an hour—which was just a moment of silence before the second set of God's judgments on the earth.

The Seven Trumpets (8:2–11:19)

In John's next vision, he saw seven angels with trumpets. One at a time, the angels blew their trumpets, bringing a new judgment on the earth. The first trumpet brought "hail and fire mixed with blood" on the earth that burned up a third of the trees and grass.

When the second trumpet sounded, something that looked like a huge mountain of fire was thrown into the sea, killing one-third of all the things that lived there and destroying one-third of the ships. The third trumpet brought what looked like a flaming star out of the sky. When it landed, it polluted one-third of the fresh water on the earth, leading to the deaths of many people.

When the fourth angel blew his trumpet, one-third of the sun and moon were struck, and one-third of the stars went dark. Then John looked up and saw an eagle crying, "Terror, terror, terror to all who belong to this world because of what will happen when the last three angels blow their trumpets" (8:13).

When the fifth trumpet was blown, John saw what looked like a star falling from the sky. The star "was given the key to the shaft of the bottomless pit" (9:1). When he opened it, smoke came out and darkened the sunlight and air with smoke. Then locustlike creatures with stingers came from the smoke and began attacking people who "did not have the seal of God on their foreheads" (9:4).

When the sixth trumpet sounded, an army of 200 million mounted troops wiped out one-third of humankind with "fire and smoke and burning sulfur" (9:18). Still, John wrote, "the people who did not die in these plagues still refused to repent of their evil deeds and turn to God" (9:20).

When the seventh angel blew his trumpet, John heard loud praise from heaven. The 24 elders fell on their faces and spoke praises to God, because "it is time to judge the dead and reward your servants" (11:18). There was lightning, thunder, a huge earthquake, and a hailstorm.

WHO, WHAT, WHERE?

Revelation 9:11 mentions a king who is "the angel from the bottomless pit," named Abaddon in Hebrew and Appolyon in Greek (which means "the Destroyer"). It's not certain who this king is, but some experts believe it is either the Antichrist or the devil himself.

The Arrival of the Antichrist (12–14)

Chapters 12–14 of Revelation cover the arrival of "the beast," which has also been called the Antichrist. In chapter 12, John first sees a vision of a large red dragon, with seven heads and 10 horns, who was kicked out of heaven. This was the devil himself.

Chapter 13 actually describes two beasts—one with seven heads and 10 horns that came out of the sea, and one with two horns and the voice of a dragon that came up out of the earth. This beast was allowed to do pretty much anything it wanted for 42 months (three and a half years)—including declaring war on Christians.

The second of these two beasts had all the power of the first beast and required all people to worship the first beast and to take a mark with the name of the beast or his number (666) on their right hand or forehead (see Revelation 13:16–18). Those who didn't receive this mark were not allowed to do any kind of business. This beast is later called "the false prophet."

The Seven Bowls (15:1–18:24)

John's vision of God's final judgment on the earth continues in Revelation 15. This time, seven angels carry the seven final plagues on the earth, which are called "bowls." Here are the seven "bowl judgments" listed in the book of Revelation:

1. Horrible sores break out on those who have received the "mark of the beast" (16:2).
2. The sea turns to blood (16:3).
3. Fresh water turns to blood (16:4–6).
4. People are scorched by intense heat (16:8–9).
5. Darkness and pain afflict humans (16:10–11).
6. The Euphrates River dries up, and armies gather for the Battle of Armageddon (16:12–16).
7. The earth is shaken with the worst earthquake ever—islands disappear and mountains are flattened, 75-pound hailstones fall from the sky, and a place called Babylon is divided into three sections (16:17–21).

WHO, WHAT, WHERE?

The apostle John uses the word *Armageddon* to describe the final conflict between God and the Antichrist. This word actually means "mount of Megiddo." Megiddo was an ancient city in northern Israel along the Kishon River. This is where many experts believe the final battle between good and evil will take place.

The End of Babylon, the Beast, and the Devil Himself (17–20)

After the seventh and final bowl is poured out on the earth, a loud voice declares, "It is finished!" (16:17). Babylon had been split in three pieces, and the cities of many nations had been leveled. Every island had disappeared into the oceans and seas, and the mountains had been leveled.

WHO, WHAT, WHERE?

The book of Revelation tells us that a city called Babylon will be destroyed by God near the end of time. But what is the Babylon mentioned in this book? Many experts believe "Babylon" is a code word for the Roman Empire, which oppressed Christians at the time John wrote Revelation. Whatever Babylon is in Revelation, it seems to stand for everything evil and ungodly in the world.

FUN BIBLE TRIVIA

The 1,000 years during which the devil will be tied up in chains and kept in the lake of fire while those who have served Christ will reign on earth is sometimes called the Millennium.

After this vision, one of the seven angels who poured the bowls of judgment out on the earth appeared to John and announced that Babylon would be destroyed and that the leaders of the nations would cry and grieve when they saw the city burning.

In heaven, on the other hand, there would be celebration that Babylon was finished (18:20).

Later in chapter 19, after John listened to an angel announcing the end of Babylon, he heard what sounded like a huge crowd in heaven praising God. As he continued to listen, he saw heaven open and a white horse with a rider named Faithful and True (19:11). The rider's eyes looked like blazing fire, and he had many crowns on his head and wore a robe dipped in blood. On his robe and on his thigh was the name "King of kings and Lord of lords" (19:11–16 niv).

It was Jesus!

At the same time, the beast gathered his armies for the final battle against God and the armies of heaven. But it wasn't much of a battle. "Both the beast and his false prophet were thrown alive into the fiery lake of burning sulfur" (19:20), and their armies were destroyed.

Then John saw an angel come down from heaven and tie Satan up in chains and throw him into the same lake of fire, where he would stay for 1,000 years. During those 1,000 years, those who had died because of their

faith in Christ, as well as the people who hadn't worshipped the beast or taken his mark, "reigned with Christ" (20:4).

At the end of the 1,000 years, the devil was released from the lake of fire and immediately began deceiving people. He gathered an army and surrounded God's people, but he was then thrown into the lake of fire, where he, the beast, and the false prophet would stay forever.

With the devil taken care of for good, everyone who had died before was judged before a "great white throne" (20:11). They were judged for the things they had done when they were alive, and everyone whose name was not found in the Book of Life was thrown into the lake of fire.

A Peek at Heaven (21–22)

The book of Revelation describes some pretty scary visions of judgment on the earth after the people had turned their backs on God. But we can be grateful that the story doesn't leave off there. As terrible as some of these events might seem, what you're about to read makes reading the scary stuff worth it.

The last two chapters of Revelation record John's visions of what is ahead for people who have put their faith in Jesus. Even though chapters 4–20 are very hard to understand, the remaining two chapters of Revelation spell things out so that they are easy to grasp.

These chapters cover how things will one day turn out for you and everyone else who knows Jesus. And it's something you can look forward to!

In with the New

After seeing the devil and death being done away with, John saw in his vision "a new heaven and a new earth, for the old heaven and the old earth had disappeared" (21:1). The sea was also gone, and John saw a "new Jerusalem" coming down from heaven from God, "like a bride beautifully dressed for her husband" (21:2).

John then heard a voice saying, "Now the dwelling of God is with men, and he will live with them. They will be his people, and God himself will be with them and be their God. He will wipe every tear from their eyes. There will be no more death or mourning or crying or pain, for the old order of things has passed away" (21:3–4 NIV).

POWER WORDS

"Look, I am coming soon, bringing my reward with me to repay all people according to their deeds. I am the Alpha and the Omega, the First and the Last, the Beginning and the End."
Revelation 22:12–13

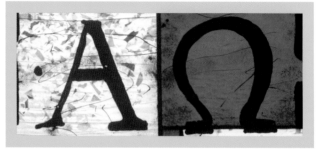

But that wasn't all. John heard that same voice saying, "I am making everything new! . . . Write this down, for what I tell you is trustworthy and true. . . . It is finished! I am the Alpha and the Omega—the Beginning and the End. To all who are thirsty I will give freely from the springs of the water of life. All who are victorious will inherit all these blessings, and I will be their God, and they will be my children" (21:5–7).

An angel then showed John the new Jerusalem, an amazing structure where there was no need for a sun or moon because God and His Son provided the light. A river flowed down the city's main street, and on each side of the street was the tree of life, which produced 12 different kinds of fruit—one for each month of the year.

It was from this place that God and His people would rule "forever and ever" (22:5). Nothing would be cursed any longer, and God's throne and Jesus' throne would be there, and His servants would worship Him.

The last 14 verses of Revelation—and of the Bible—include Jesus' promise, "I am coming soon" (22:7, 12, 20).

CHAPTER 10

Why You Should Read the Bible for Yourself... and How to Do It!

Throughout this book, you've seen little sidebars titled "What's in It for Me?" Those features were included to give you some ideas about what you can get out of certain portions of the Bible.

As you think about reading the Bible yourself, you might be wondering, *What's in it for me?* Lots of things! In fact, you should know that God wants you to desire to know the Bible more today than you did yesterday.

Here are five good reasons you should make reading the Bible a part of your life every day:

1. You can learn about God Himself. The Bible is filled to the brim with the things God has said, the things He has done, and the ways He has related to His people. When you read about those things, you get a good idea of what God is really like—what kind of person He is!

Do you want to know what makes God happy and what makes Him unhappy? Do you want to know what kinds of things people have done that make Him angry? Do you want to know what kind of love He has for you? There's no better way to learn these things than by opening up your Bible and reading what God has done and said.

2. You can learn what it takes to have a strong and growing relationship with God. When you became a Christian, God didn't just look down at you and say, "Great! Now you're the kind of person I want you to be! Now you can just wait around until it's time to go to heaven!"

No, when you became a Christian, that was just the beginning of the work God wants to do in you. That's what the apostle Paul meant when he wrote, "I am certain that God, who began the good work within you, will continue his work until it is finally finished on the day when Christ Jesus returns" (Philippians 1:6).

Growing in your relationship with God doesn't just happen on its own, any more than your body grows on its own. Just as your body requires proper nourishment and exercise to grow bigger and stronger, your relationship with God requires nourishment and exercise to grow bigger and stronger. And where do you get that nourishment? From the pages of your Bible!

3. You can learn how to be more and more like Jesus.
The Bible teaches that our goal as Christians is to become more and more like Jesus every day. That means you should be more like Him tomorrow than you were today—and a lot more like Him next year than you are right now.

Jesus is your perfect example of how to live, how to think, how to love God, and how to treat other people. And the more you're like Him in every way, the more you please God, and the more you let people around you see how amazing He really is!

Okay, so now that you know that God wants you to be more and more like Jesus every day, the question is, how can you learn what Jesus was like? By reading the Bible! You can see what Jesus was really like—how He thought, prayed, lived, and cared for others—by reading the books of the Bible called the Gospels. Remember where they are? If not, turn back in this book to chapter 6 for a quick reminder.

But you don't need to stop at just the Gospels. Remember, Jesus was God in human form, and everything God the Father says, does, and thinks, Jesus does, says, and thinks right along with Him. So you can learn to be more like Jesus by reading from the entire Bible!

4. You can learn how God wants you to live.
Someone once said that being a Christian isn't about following a bunch of rules; it's about having a real, personal relationship with God through Jesus Christ.

POWER WORDS

All Scripture is inspired by God and is useful to teach us what is true and to make us realize what is wrong in our lives. It corrects us when we are wrong and teaches us to do what is right.

2 Timothy 3:16

How true that is!

At the same time, though, the Bible includes a lot of really important commands, encouragements, promises, and guidelines for living the Christian life. So if you want to know how God wants you to live, go straight to the source for His instructions: the Bible!

You almost can't open your Bible without finding some of God's commands, encouragements, promises, and guidelines for life. So when you read your Bible, pay close attention to things God might want you to focus on. Hint: Pay *really* close attention when you're reading books like Proverbs, the Gospels, and the New Testament epistles (Romans through Jude).

5. You can learn how God wants you to treat other people. More than anything,

the Bible is about how to have a relationship with God. But it also has a lot to say about how to treat other people, especially other Christians.

If there is one statement that tells us how we are to treat others, it is Jesus' words to His disciples just before His death on the cross: "A new command I give you: Love one another" (John 13:34 NIV). The apostle John, who recorded those words from Jesus, also wrote, "Dear friends, let us love one another, for love comes from God" (1 John 4:7 NIV).

But what does it mean for us to love one another? Should we just have warm, fuzzy feelings for other people? Should we just tell people that we love them and let that be good enough? No! The Bible teaches that we show our love through our words and also through our actions.

You can find great guidelines for how to treat people with God's love in many places in the Bible. If you want a good place to start, read Jesus' teaching—and pay close attention to the Sermon on the Mount (Matthew 5–7). You can also find some great guidelines for how to treat others by reading the book of Proverbs and the New Testament epistles.

Show love for one another with your actions.

JANUARY

1

DECEMBER

31

DECEMBER

30

EMBER

Now for the "Hows" of Bible Reading and Study

Okay, now you have a pretty good idea of *why* you should read the Bible. But if you're like most Christians, you are probably wondering *how* to do it. If you're not sure about the best way to approach reading and studying the Bible, don't feel bad. Just realize that there are a lot of really good ways to read the Bible so that you can get the very most out of it.

First is the most obvious way: reading it cover to cover, starting with Genesis 1 and ending with Revelation 22. The best thing about reading the Bible from beginning to end is that you get a good idea of the order in which things happened (keeping in mind that the Old Testament prophecy books were written during different times in Israel's history).

It's a good idea for any Christian to read the Bible all the way through at least once. And it's not as hard as you might think, especially since there are so many prepared schedules you can use to get it done in one year. (See appendix A for a one-year Bible-reading schedule.) But reading through the Bible in a year—or in less time if you're a fast reader—is only the beginning. And truthfully, if you want to get the most out of your Bible reading, it's a good idea to do it in ways other than just cover to cover.

Don't Just Read. . . . Study!

Have you ever read something—part of one of your school textbooks, for example—only to forget what you read five minutes later? Some people have a talent for remembering everything they read, but most of us need to put in some extra effort to remember what we read.

That extra effort is called studying. Studying means not just to read something, but to read it over again, think about what you've read, and try to learn as much as you can from what you've read.

The Bible is a great book to study—by yourself, with your family, with your friends. And just as there are all kinds of settings to study the Bible in, there are also all kinds of ways to do it.

Here are some great ways to study your Bible:

Studying in a Certain Book

One of the things you've learned in reading this book—we hope—is that each book of the Bible has its own writer, its own story, its own background, and its own topics and ideas. Obviously, there's no better way to find out those things about a certain book of the Bible than by reading and studying it yourself.

That's where a book like this one can come in really handy. When you decide you want to read and study a book of the Bible, you can look up *that* book in *this* book to learn the basics.

For example, if you want to read and study the Gospel of Matthew, you can take a look at what this book has to tell you about that particular Gospel. You'll learn that it was written by a man named Matthew, that it was originally written to Jewish people, and that it has a lot to say about how Jesus fulfilled Old Testament prophecies about the coming Messiah.

You'll be amazed just how much knowing things like that will help you as you prepare to read and study a certain book of the Bible. Go ahead and try it!

Studying a Certain Word

Are there words from the Bible you have heard but don't know exactly what they mean—at least what they mean in the Bible? Do you know what the word *grace* means? How about *mercy* or *pardon*? You can learn what the Bible means when it uses those words when you read and study the Bible using key words that appear in the different books.

To do this kind of study, all you need is your Bible and a concordance, a reference book that lists the different words used in the Bible and tells you where you can find them. If you don't have a concordance, then you can use one of several online concordances available on the Internet.

When you study the Bible this way, try using different forms of different words—for example, when you want to study God's forgiveness, take the time to look up the words *forgive, forgiving,* and *forgiven.* You can also look up different words that mean the same thing (these words are called synonyms). That way, you'll get a better idea of what those words mean in the Bible.

Some good words to start with are *love, grace, mercy, pardon,* and *forgiveness*—simply because these words are so much a part of God's character.

WHAT'S iN iT FOR ME?

If you want to get the absolute most you can out of your Bible study, it's a good idea to have at least some of these tools to help you out:

Bible: This might seen too obvious to mention, but which Bible you choose will go a long way in determining how much you learn in your Bible study. Choose a translation that is easy for you to understand, and you'll get a lot more out of your Bible study.

Dictionary: A good dictionary is always handy to have when you're studying anything, including the Bible. When you see a word you don't know, you can look it up in your dictionary to see what it means.

Bible Dictionary: There are a lot of good Bible dictionaries out there to help you with your study. You can even find good ones on the Internet. A Bible dictionary will explain what certain words and ideas mean in the Bible.

Concordance: Remember, this is a book made up of an alphabetical list of all Bible words.

Bible Commentary: There are a lot of great Bible commentaries written by people who know the Bible cover to cover. A Bible commentary can help you gain insights when you study. You can find good Bible commentaries online, at your library, or at the local bookstore.

Bible Atlas: An atlas is a book of maps that will help you understand where the Bible stories you read took place. It can also help you to understand more about the stories and other passages you read.

Pencil and Paper: Bible study time is a good time to take some notes!

Studying a Certain Subject

If your teacher were to give you an assignment to write a report about a certain animal—let's say a giraffe—how would you research giraffes so that you could write a good report? You probably wouldn't check out a library book about animals that live in Africa and start reading it cover to cover, would you? More than likely, you'd check out that same book and go directly to the section about giraffes. That would save you a lot of time and also allow you to learn more about giraffes because you had spent some time learning all you could about them.

You can study your Bible the same way. Let's say you want to study what the Bible has to say about the subject of God's forgiveness. You'd look up verses and passages in both the Old Testament and the New Testament that had to do with God's forgiveness. Then you would focus on what those verses and passages said, how they were the same or different, and how they applied to you.

By the time you were done doing this kind of study, you'd have a pretty good idea of what God says about any subject you chose.

Studying a Certain Passage (Section)

The Bible is filled with some amazing sections—sometimes called passages—with some great lessons for you today. Another great way to read and study the Bible is to concentrate on one of those sections and see what God is saying to you through it.

As you study a passage of the Bible, pay close attention to the things people do and say, as well as what happened as a result. Don't forget to notice how God responds to the things that people do and say.

There are literally hundreds of great Bible passages to study and learn from. Here are just a few to help you get started with your own study of the Bible:

Genesis 1–2—The creation of the universe, the earth, and humans
Genesis 6:9–8:22—Noah and the flood
Joshua 1—God's instructions and encouragement for Joshua
1 Samuel 17:12–54—David's battle with the giant Goliath
Psalm 1—The blessed man
Daniel 6—The prophet Daniel in the lions' den
Luke 2:1–20—The birth of Jesus

Matthew 5–7—Jesus' Sermon on the Mount
Acts 2—The believers in Jerusalem receive the Holy Spirit
1 Corinthians 13—The "love chapter"
Hebrews 11—Great biblical examples of faith

Studying Certain People, Places, and Things

WHO, WHAT, WHERE?

Do you want a good list to start with as you study the lives of important people in the Bible?
Try these names first: Adam and Eve, Noah, Abraham, Joseph, Moses, Joshua, David, Solomon, Jesus (of course!), Peter, the apostle John, and the apostle Paul. Of course, there are hundreds of other people you can study, but this list gives you a good place to start.

The Bible has many examples of how God deals with people—with His own people as well as with people who do not know Him. Another great way to study the Bible is to focus on the people, places, and events of the Bible.

Who are some of the people from the Bible you want to know more about? Adam and Eve? Moses? Joshua? David? Jesus and His disciples? The apostle Paul? Take the time to read all you can about these people (it never hurts to use a Bible dictionary or encyclopedia to help you along), and as you read, pay close attention to their lives—the things they did right, the things they did wrong, and the way God responded to them.

When you focus your attention on a personality from the Bible and learn all you can about him or her, you will find that person's story is filled with great lessons for your own life.

One quick note: When you start a study on a certain person in the Bible, make sure you aren't reading about two or more different people who went by the same name. That's easier to do than you might think. There are 28 men in the Bible named Azariah, 27 named Zechariah, and 25 named Shemaiah. Altogether, there are 23 names connected with 10 or more people.

As for studying places and things, you can apply the same steps you would use if you were studying a person.

Other Things You Can Do with the Bible

Of course, reading and studying your Bible are things God wants you to do. But did you know you can take your reading and studying to another level—or two or three?

As this book draws to a finish, we want you to think about some of the things you can use the Bible for. Some of them might surprise you!

Memorize Bible Verses

Have you ever met someone who seemed to have the ability to quote Bible verses off the top of his or her head? Or maybe you've noticed the pastor or teachers at your church can quote verses without looking them up?

Those things don't just happen. Usually, people who can quote Bible passages have spent time memorizing some of the more important verses. It's not as hard as it sounds. All it takes is a little repetition, a little time, and some effort.

What are some of the benefits of memorizing Bible verses? Suppose you had a friend who wanted to know more about your Christian faith. Of course you can tell that person what God has done for you, but when you can remember some important passages from the Bible, you can better explain what the Bible says about becoming a Christian.

POWER WORDS

I have hidden your word in my heart, that I might not sin against you.

Psalm 119:11

THE BIBLE
AND
OLY SCRIPTVRE
CONTEYNED IN
THE OLDE AND NEWE
Teftament.

RANSLATED ACCOR
ding to the Ebrue and Greke, and conferred W
he beft tranflations in diuers langages.

TH MOSTE PROFITABLE ANNOT.
tions vpon all the hard places, and other things of gr
importance as may appeare in the Epiftle to the Reader

FEARE TE NOT STAND STIL, AND BEHOLDE
the faluation of the Lord, which he wil forte to you this day. Exod. 14.13.

THE LORD SHAL FIGHT FOR YOU; THEREFORE
holde you your peace. Exod. 14. verf.14.

AT GENEVA.
PRINTED BY ROVLAND HALL
M·D·LX.

DID YOU KNOW. . . ?

In 1560, the Geneva Bible was printed. It was the first English Bible with a feature that makes Bible memorization easier today: chapter and verse divisions. Three years before that, an Englishman named William Whittingham produced the first English-language New Testament with verse divisions.

One of the best ways to memorize Bible verses is to simply read them over and over until they are recorded in your memory. And it really helps when you follow these basic Bible memorization steps:

- Pick out a Bible version you like and can most easily understand.
- Pick out the verse or verses you want to memorize.
- Don't try to memorize too much at once.
- Write the verse or verses down. Use flash cards if that helps.
- Work with a friend or family member.

One last thing: It's good to memorize the words of different Bible verses, but it's also really helpful to memorize where they are in the Bible. That means you should also memorize the book, the chapter, and the verse where you found the words you have memorized.

Take It Personally!

Have you ever thought of the words recorded in your Bible as God's personal message to you? Well, you can, because that's exactly what they are! God made sure that every important word, thought, promise, command, and warning made it into the pages of your Bible, and He did that just for you.

One of the best ways to really personalize the Bible is to read a particular passage or verse and then write it down using words like *I* and *me* when the Bible says "you." For example, you can write down Philippians 4:19, which says, "My God shall supply all your need according to His riches in glory by Christ Jesus" (NKJV), like this:

My God shall supply all MY needs according to His riches in glory by Christ Jesus!

When you read and study the Bible that way, you'll understand more and more every day that the Bible is a book written just for you.

And you'll also see how cool a book it really is.

APPENDIX A

Through the Bible in a Year

A 365-Day Bible-Reading Schedule

Start your own Bible adventure—read through the whole Bible in a year. It'll only take you about 20 minutes a day!

Day 1	Genesis 1–2	Matthew 1	Psalm 1
Day 2	Genesis 3–4	Matthew 2	Psalm 2
Day 3	Genesis 5–7	Matthew 3	Psalm 3
Day 4	Genesis 8–10	Matthew 4	Psalm 4
Day 5	Genesis 11–13	Matthew 5:1–20	Psalm 5
Day 6	Genesis 14–16	Matthew 5:21–48	Psalm 6
Day 7	Genesis 17–18	Matthew 6:1–18	Psalm 7
Day 8	Genesis 19–20	Matthew 6:19–34	Psalm 8
Day 9	Genesis 21–23	Matthew 7:1–11	Psalm 9:1–8
Day 10	Genesis 24	Matthew 7:12–29	Psalm 9:9–20
Day 11	Genesis 25–26	Matthew 8:1–17	Psalm 10:1–11
Day 12	Genesis 27:1–28:9	Matthew 8:18–34	Psalm 10:12–18
Day 13	Genesis 28:10–29:35	Matthew 9	Psalm 11
Day 14	Genesis 30:1–31:21	Matthew 10:1–15	Psalm 12
Day 15	Genesis 31:22–32:21	Matthew 10:16–36	Psalm 13
Day 16	Genesis 32:22–34:31	Matthew 10:37–11:6	Psalm 14
Day 17	Genesis 35–36	Matthew 11:7–24	Psalm 15
Day 18	Genesis 37–38	Matthew 11:25–30	Psalm 16
Day 19	Genesis 39–40	Matthew 12:1–29	Psalm 17
Day 20	Genesis 41	Matthew 12:30–50	Psalm 18:1–15
Day 21	Genesis 42–43	Matthew 13:1–9	Psalm 18:16–29
Day 22	Genesis 44–45	Matthew 13:10–23	Psalm 18:30–50

Day 303	Jeremiah 45–47	1 Timothy 5:17–6:21	Proverbs 14:1–6
Day 304	Jeremiah 48:1–49:6	2 Timothy 1	Proverbs 14:7–22
Day 305	Jeremiah 49:7–50:16	2 Timothy 2	Proverbs 14:23–27
Day 306	Jeremiah 50:17–51:14	2 Timothy 3	Proverbs 14:28–35
Day 307	Jeremiah 51:15–64	2 Timothy 4	Proverbs 15:1–9
Day 308	Jeremiah 52–Lamentations 1	Titus 1:1–9	Proverbs 15:10–17
Day 309	Lamentations 2:1–3:38	Titus 1:10–2:15	Proverbs 15:18–26
Day 310	Lamentations 3:39–5:22	Titus 3	Proverbs 15:27–33
Day 311	Ezekiel 1:1–3:21	Philemon 1	Proverbs 16:1–9
Day 312	Ezekiel 3:22–5:17	Hebrews 1:1–2:4	Proverbs 16:10–21
Day 313	Ezekiel 6–7	Hebrews 2:5–18	Proverbs 16:22–33
Day 314	Ezekiel 8–10	Hebrews 3:1–4:3	Proverbs 17:1–5
Day 315	Ezekiel 11–12	Hebrews 4:4–5:10	Proverbs 17:6–12
Day 316	Ezekiel 13–14	Hebrews 5:11–6:20	Proverbs 17:13–22
Day 317	Ezekiel 15:1–16:43	Hebrews 7:1–28	Proverbs 17:23–28
Day 318	Ezekiel 16:44–17:24	Hebrews 8:1–9:10	Proverbs 18:1–7
Day 319	Ezekiel 18–19	Hebrews 9:11–28	Proverbs 18:8–17
Day 320	Ezekiel 20	Hebrews 10:1–25	Proverbs 18:18–24
Day 321	Ezekiel 21–22	Hebrews 10:26–39	Proverbs 19:1–8
Day 322	Ezekiel 23	Hebrews 11:1–31	Proverbs 19:9–14
Day 323	Ezekiel 24–26	Hebrews 11:32–40	Proverbs 19:15–21
Day 324	Ezekiel 27–28	Hebrews 12:1–13	Proverbs 19:22–29
Day 325	Ezekiel 29–30	Hebrews 12:14–29	Proverbs 20:1–18
Day 326	Ezekiel 31–32	Hebrews 13	Proverbs 20:19–24
Day 327	Ezekiel 33:1–34:10	James 1	Proverbs 20:25–30
Day 328	Ezekiel 34:11–36:15	James 2	Proverbs 21:1–8
Day 329	Ezekiel 36:16–37:28	James 3	Proverbs 21:9–18
Day 330	Ezekiel 38–39	James 4:1–5:6	Proverbs 21:19–24
Day 331	Ezekiel 40	James 5:7–20	Proverbs 21:25–31
Day 332	Ezekiel 41:1–43:12	1 Peter 1:1–12	Proverbs 22:1–9
Day 333	Ezekiel 43:13–44:31	1 Peter 1:13–2:3	Proverbs 22:10–23
Day 334	Ezekiel 45–46	1 Peter 2:4–17	Proverbs 22:24–29
Day 335	Ezekiel 47–48	1 Peter 2:18–3:7	Proverbs 23:1–9
Day 336	Daniel 1:1–2:23	1 Peter 3:8–4:19	Proverbs 23:10–16
Day 337	Daniel 2:24–3:30	1 Peter 5	Proverbs 23:17–25

APPENDIX B

Timeline of Important Biblical Events

About 4000 BC—The Fall

About 2350 BC—The Flood

About 2235 BC—Dispersion of the races

About 2100–1500 BC—Age of the Patriarchs

About 1950 BC—Amorites conquer Mesopotamia

About 1925 BC—Call of Abraham

About 1720 BC—Joseph becomes governor of Egypt

About 1635 BC—Joseph's death

About 1575 BC—Birth of Moses

About 1500–1200 BC—Exodus and Promised Land conquest

About 1492 BC—Exodus from Egypt

About 1452 BC—Joshua appointed leader of the people of Israel

About 1451 BC—Crossing of the Jordan

About 1451–44 BC—Conquest of Canaan

About 1394–1095 BC—Period of the Judges

About 1095–1055 BC—King Saul, Israel's first monarch

About 1055–1015 BC—King David

About 1050 BC—Philistines settle in southern Palestine

About 1015–975 BC—King Solomon

About 1005 BC—Dedication of the Temple

About 975–587—The divided kingdom (Judah and Israel)

About 721 BC—Captivity of Israel

About 587 BC—Babylonian Captivity (Judah)

About 535 BC—Return of the Jews to Jerusalem under Zerubbabel

About 515 BC—Second Temple dedicated

About 458 BC—Ezra leads second wave of Jews back to Jerusalem

About 445 BC—Nehemiah returns to Jerusalem and begins rebuilding city walls

About 37 BC–AD 4—Reign of Herod the Great, Roman-appointed king of Judea

About 4 BC–AD 6—Rule of Herod Archelaus, ethnarch (governor) of Judea, Samaria, and Idumea

About 4 BC–AD 34—Rule of Herod Philip, tetrarch of Iturea and Trachonitis

About 4 BC–AD 39—Rule of Herod Antipas, tetrarch (governor) of Galilee and Perea

About 6-4 BC—Birth of Jesus Christ

About 2 BC—Birth of Saul of Tarsus (later known as the apostle Paul)

About AD 20—Reconstruction of the Temple begins

About AD 25–27—Jesus' baptism

About AD 25–28—Ministry of John the Baptist

About AD 26–37—Pontius Pilate, prefect (official who enforces the law) of Judea

About AD 29–30—Christ's crucifixion and resurrection

About AD 31–37—Conversion of Saul of Tarsus (the apostle Paul)

About AD 31–95—Books of the New Testament written

About AD 45–58—The apostle Paul's missionary journeys

About AD 59–60—Paul's first imprisonment begins

About AD 67–68—Paul's final imprisonment and death in Rome

APPENDIX C

Important Dates (and Facts) in Bible Writing, Translation, and Publishing

About 1400 BC— The Ten Commandments delivered to Moses

About 500–400 BC—Completion of Hebrew manuscripts that would become the 39 Old Testament books

Third and second centuries BC—Completion of the Septuagint, a translation of all 39 books of the Old Testament canon and the 14 books of the Apocrypha into Greek

First century AD—Completion of all original manuscripts that make up the 27 New Testament books

About 315—Athanasius, bishop of Alexandria, identifies the 27 books of the New Testament

About 362—Council of Laodicea adopts canon of Old and New Testaments and the Apocrypha

393—Council of Hippo affirms canon of New Testament

397—Council of Carthage affirms canon of New Testament

About 400—Jerome completes the Latin Vulgate, a Greek manuscript containing the 39 books of the Old Testament, the 27 books of the New Testament, and the 14 books of the Apocrypha

995—Anglo-Saxon (early roots of English language) translations of the New Testament

About 1207–28—Archbishop of Canterbury Cardinal Stephen Langdon believed to have divided Bible into chapters and verses still used today

About 1246—Cardinal Hugo de Sancto Caro introduces system of Bible chapters

1384—Death of John Wycliffe, who had started the translation of the Bible (the 66 books in the canon of scripture as well as the Apocrypha) into English. The work was completed after his death.

About 1455—German inventor Johannes Gutenberg develops movable-type printing press, allowing for mass production of books. The first book printed is the Gutenberg Bible.

1516—Dutch theologian Desiderius Erasmus produces Greek/Latin parallel New Testament

1522—Martin Luther's German New Testament published

1526—William Tyndale's complete New Testament, the first printed in English

1534—Martin Luther's complete German translation published

1535—Myles Coverdale's Bible, the first complete Bible in English, printed

1537—Matthew-Tyndale Bible, the second complete Bible printed in English. Done by John "Thomas Matthew" Rogers

1539—The Great Bible, the first English-language Bible authorized for public use, printed

1560—The Geneva Bible, the first English-language Bible to include chapter and verse references, printed

1568—The Bishops' Bible printed; revised substantially in 1572; the revised edition was the base text for the King James Version of 1611

1609—The Douay Old Testament and the Rheims New Testament (produced in 1582) are combined to make the first complete English Catholic Bible

1611—The King James Bible, including the Apocrypha, printed; Apocrypha removed in 1885, leaving the 66 books we have today

1782—Robert Aitken's Bible (King James Version), the first English-language Bible printed in America, published

1885—The English Revised Version Bible, the first major revision of the King James Version, published

1900—American publishing company Thomas Nelson & Sons publishes the American Standard Version Old Testament; the following year, the company released the entire Bible, the first major American revision of the King James Bible

1952—The Revised Standard Version published

1965—The Amplified Bible published

1971—The New American Standard Bible and *The Living Bible* published

1978—The complete New International Version (NIV) published

1982—The complete New King James Version published

1996—The complete New Living Translation published

2002—The complete Bible paraphrase, *The Message,* published

2004—Holman Christian Standard Bible published

ART CREDITS